341.69
M219n

Miale.

The Nuremberg.mind.

March 1976

THE
NUREMBERG
MIND

THE NUREMBERG MIND

The Psychology of the Nazi Leaders

FLORENCE R. MIALE

and

MICHAEL SELZER

With an Introduction and Rorschach records by
Gustave M. Gilbert, Ph.D.
Long Island University;
formerly the prison psychologist at the
Nuremberg Trial of Major Nazi War Criminals

Quadrangle/The New York Times Book Co.

Brooklyn College of the City University of New York
Research Center for Interdisciplinary Applications of Psychoanalysis
Monograph #1

Book design: Tere LoPrete

Library of Congress Cataloging in Publication Data

Miale, Florence R
    The Nuremberg mind.

    Bibliography: p.
    1. War criminals—Germany—Psychology. 2. Ror-
schach test. 3. Nuremberg Trial of Major German
War Criminals, 1945–1946. I. Selzer, Michael,
joint author. II. Title. [DNLM: 1. Rorschach
test. 2. Criminal psychology. WM145 M619n]
DD244.M5   341.69   75-8300
    ISBN 0-8129-0581-4

To Their Victims, Living and Dead

זכור את אשר־עשה לך עמלק

—Deuteronomy, XXV: 17

Rabbi Berekiah said: "Israel spake before the Holy One, blessed be He: 'Lord of the Universe, didst Thou write for us in Thy Torah, *Remember what Amalek did unto thee*—did he do it to me and not to Thee? Did he not destroy Thy sanctuary?' "

—Midrash Rabbah: Lamentations, V:1

What you have done unto even one of the least of your brethren, that you have done unto God.

—Matthew, XXV:40

Contents

(Colored Rorschach illustrations follow page 18.)

Authors' Note

This book presents the Rorschach records, and our interpretations of them, of sixteen of the major Nazi war criminals who were tried at Nuremberg in 1945 and 1946. Records of the other six defendants —Doenitz, Frick, Jodl, Ley, Raeder, and Streicher—either were not obtained or were unavailable to us at the time of writing.

The materials in this book have important contributions to make to the historian who studies Nazi Germany and to political scientists, sociologists, and other social scientists who are interested in the theory of leadership in general and of totalitarianism in particular. To avert any misunderstanding about the scope of this book, however, it seems important to us to stress what we have *not* attempted to do here. The historical materials incorporated in the summary section of each analysis are intended as illustrative and do not fill the need for a thorough integration of the psychological data presented here with the vast accumulation of information about Nazi Germany that is available to the professional historian.

In the final chapter, by the same token, we comment on what seem to be some of the implications of our data for an understanding of political leadership. Cursory as they are, those comments are intended merely as suggestive and should not be viewed by the reader in any other vein; certainly, they are not a substitute for the full-length theoretical study of political leadership which one of the co-authors of this book hopes to publish in due course.

We owe a special debt of gratitude to Susanna Morgenthau, who introduced us to each other and who followed the progress of our work with interest and encouragement. Daniel Kahan, Frederick E. Low, and Nancy Smallens were our research assistants and lightened many of our burdens. George Miale read the entire manuscript with critical and editorial skill; while Gertrude Baltimore, Camilla Kemple, Hazel Kahan, Michael Kahan, and Walter Miale read parts of the manuscript and contributed many useful suggestions. Camilla Kemple collaborated with Florence Miale for many years on the development of most of the basic concepts of Rorschach interpretation used here. The experience and enthusiasm of our editor, Roger Jellinek, have been of inestimable value to us, as has been the help, in a variety of ways, of his assistant, Addie Sneider. We would also like to acknowledge here the initiative of Gustave M. Gilbert in making these records in the first place, and his generosity in sharing them with us; it is of course a source of gratification to us that he has contributed an introduction to this volume.

Finally, we would like to say that this book is a true collaboration; the order in which our names appear on the title page is alphabetical. We started out as two people trained in different academic disciplines —political science and psychology—and assumed that we would carry out our task on the basis of a clearcut division of labor. In fact, to an extent that neither of us could have anticipated at the outset, we learned from each other and discovered that we were both contributing to every phase of the overall work. Learning from each other (and learning from each other how to do so) has been a mutually enriching experience.

Florence R. Miale
Michael Selzer
NEW YORK, MARCH 1975

Introduction
G. M. Gilbert, Ph.D.

It was an extraordinary coincidence that a psychologist with both a knowledge of German and a familiarity with the still-new Rorschach diagnostic technique should have been assigned to the prison staff at Nuremberg. Certainly the administration of the Rorschach ink-blot method to the leading Nazi war criminals was the farthest thing from the minds of the military and civilian authorities setting up the trial. Since it may not only illuminate an early chapter in psycho-history but also explain the imperfect state of the Nazi Rorschach examination series, I shall briefly recount the circumstances that produced the records quoted and interpreted in this volume.

In 1945 the interest of many of the world's social scientists, not to mention that of millions of participants in and survivors of a disastrous world war, was at a fever pitch as the victorious Allies prepared to bring the surviving Nazi leaders to an orderly trial. (Hitler; Himmler, the SS–Gestapo chief; and Goebbels, the chief of the Propaganda Ministry, had already committed suicide.) The charges on which they were to be tried were war crimes and so-called "crimes against humanity" exceeding in scope anything yet recorded in human history, which had led to widespread speculation concerning the sanity or lack of it on the part of the whole Nazi leadership. Nevertheless, considering the undeveloped state of clinical psychology at the time, no thought had been given to having a psychologist included on the staff of the International Military Tribunal or the prison security force.

The actual impetus for my involvement in the study of the leading Nazi personalities came from a letter written by Professor Hadley Cantril, the noted social psychologist from Princeton, to a mutual colleague of ours who was active in military government in Germany at the end of the war in Europe. Cantril stressed the supreme importance of having a psychologist assigned to the prison staff in order to probe the minds of the Nazi leaders before it was too late. He realized that only an officer engaged in some aspect of military government would have any direct access to the staffing procedures of the Nuremberg Tribunal. We, on the other hand, realized that only a G–2 (military intelligence) officer with experience in interrogating German officers and some training as a clinical psychologist (still a very ill defined profession at the time) would stand a chance of being assigned to the prison and conducting an unobtrusive but meaningful study of the defendants. Having already done some probing in this direction during the climactic Battle of the Bulge and more recently at G–2 Headquarters in Berlin, I realized that Cantril's imperative pointed directly at me.

But G–2 Headquarters were concerned only with rounding up witnesses and documents to be used at the Nuremberg trial and maintaining security as they delivered prisoners to the jail. The prosecution staffs of the four nations involved were interested only in building up their immensely complicated cases against individual Nazi leaders and organizations. The tribunal itself was interested in psychiatry only insofar as any plea of insanity would require an examination by an ad hoc international psychiatric commission; even if a psychologist were to be called in, it would be as a "one-shot" arrangement for one or two cases. And the prison custodial force was interested only in keeping close guard on the prisoners, maintaining communications at the trial through an elaborate multilingual intercom system, and facilitating the logistics of the trial and of press coverage. Although many in and around the elaborate trial bureaucracy expressed interest in "what made those Nazis tick," there seemed to be no way to get a psychologist in there behind the scenes to find out what did.

Soon an opening presented itself. The post of Prison Commandant's Interpreter and Liaison Officer to the Nazi defendants became vacant several weeks before the trial was to begin. A call came to G–2 Headquarters for an officer qualified to fill the post and willing to remain in Germany for an extended period. I expressed my willingness.

Upon my arrival at the Nuremberg jail, I promptly set about establishing my role as a "participant–observer" in my official capacity as the Commandant's Liaison Officer, now expanded to include the title of "prison psychologist." To the Prison Commandant, this latter designation was undoubtedly a convenient afterthought to enhance my rapport with the prisoners and keep better tabs on their morale for reasons of security and "due process." For me it was, of course, a once-in-a-lifetime opportunity to probe the fascist mind at first hand in as favorable a setting for realistic participant observation as one could have imagined.

My duties as prison psychologist and liaison officer, which I felt obliged to exploit to the fullest without being obtrusive, gave me free access to all prisoners at all times. Indeed, this unlimited access was in practice mine alone. The chaplains, one Lutheran and one Catholic, could see their own church members. The medical officers would, of course, see prisoners briefly, but only when complaints demanded their attention. There was a psychiatrist on the medical staff, but he was unable to speak a word of German and left for home after the second month of the year-long trial. He was followed by a succession of American psychiatrists, none of whom could speak German and each of whom left after a brief period. Each German defense attorney could see his own client, but only under strict security and on a "strictly business" basis for the conduct of the defense. I, on the other hand, was able, for the entire duration of the trial, to see any or all of the defendants privately in their cells or in group situations, as in court or in the lunchroom, where I was directly in charge of them.

As for official clinical duties in connection with the trial itself; only in the case of Rudolf Hess, the Fuehrer's Party Deputy with the strange amnesia, was I requested by the tribunal to submit decisive testimony on his sanity, after the psychiatric commission had left and the issue had remained in doubt. I testified that Hess was legally sane, though suffering from recurrent amnesia.

The Rorschach records which are analyzed in this volume (the records of Karl Doenitz, Wilhelm Frick, Alfred Jodl, Robert Ley, Erich Raeder, and Julius Steicher were not available for this book) were administered by me during the pretrial period, while the defendants were in solitary confinement but not yet subject to the strains and distractions of the trial. Before administering any tests I first had three weeks of informal conversation with each defendant, to establish rapport. I then administered the Rorschach and an improvised version of the Wechsler–Bellevue IQ test to all the defendants. As an American officer with a genuine professional interest in trying to understand them, I was able to elicit good cooperation from each of these former dignitaries in taking the tests. As Albert Speer says in his memoirs:

> Who would have thought, for example, while he was still a Field Marshal, Admiral of the Fleet, or Minister of State, that he would submit to an intelligence test by an American military psychologist? And yet this test took place not only without resistance, but each one took pains to see that his abilities were confirmed (Speer, 1970, p. 511).

Similar cooperation was obtained on the Rorschach examination, though here the rationale for giving it was not quite as clear to the defendants and they had to rely on my matter-of-fact manner in presenting it as part of the prison psychologist's routine. Unfortunately, the spontaneity of some of the Rorschach records had been slightly spoiled by a premature attempt by the first prison psychiatrist, Dr. Douglas M. Kelley, to administer some of the tests through an interpreter, before he knew that a German-speaking psychologist was coming. This rendered both the completeness and the accuracy of those tests somewhat doubtful, and also interfered with the "inquiry" and "testing the limits" phases required by standard procedure in the administration of the Rorschach. This lack of continuity at least prevented suggestive carry-over to the retest I administered in those cases, and I am convinced that the retests are essentially valid. The records presented here, whether original or retest, may be regarded as fairly complete, spontaneous, and accurately translated by the tester. In some cases, depressive or inhibitory tendencies may have been accentuated by the depressive influence of the impending trial. This, I would judge, would not have been sufficient to obscure the individual differences in symptomatology that Rorschach interpreters look for. Only in the case of Albert Speer did I feel that a visual projective test was misleading and probably invalid, because of his own difficulty with visual imagery and a propensity to auditory imagery.

The daily record of my conversations with the Nazi leaders behind the scenes of the Nuremberg trial is contained in the *Nuremberg Diary* (1947). My own psychosocial analysis of the entire study, including some brief commentaries on the tests, is contained in *The Psychology of Dictatorship* (1950). The present volume serves the purpose of an independent and detailed analysis of the Rorschach examination.

I hope students of psychohistory will benefit from this microscopic examination of Nazi thought processes provided by this detailed interpretation of their responses to the Rorschach examinations I administered at Nuremberg. After all, even a little unexpected gesture like Goering's attempt to flick off the red (blood) spots on Card III with his forefinger did betray some of the underlying physical aggression and guilt whose "damned spot" had left its bloody imprint on the pages of history.

New York
April 1975

THE
NUREMBERG
MIND

1

Banality?

"We were only obeying orders . . ."

After the end of World War II, thousands of men were brought to trial for the horrendous deeds which they had committed during the twelve years of the Nazi Reich.

Almost invariably, regardless of the rank that they had held in the Nazi hierarchy or the scope of the crimes of which they were accused, these men pleaded the same case in their defense. "We were only following orders," they claimed, depicting themselves as decent and law-abiding citizens who obeyed legitimate orders from their legitimate superiors just as decent and law-abiding citizens do anywhere else in the world. If what they had done was wrong, they asserted, then not they but the individuals who had issued those orders to them should be tried and punished. From the lowliest soldier in the SS to the highest officials in Hitler's immediate entourage, and with only a few notable exceptions, the indicted pointed the finger of guilt at someone above them. Ultimately, they claimed, only one man in Nazi Germany was really responsible for all the terrible tragedies that had occurred. He was the *Fuehrer*, and the orders which they had obeyed stemmed from his authority.

This spurious and contemptible argument was consistently rejected by international tribunals, military courts, and criminal courts in countries throughout Europe. One element in it, however, raises questions which deserve close consideration.

In support of their contention that they were merely obeying orders, the Nazi criminals insisted that they were not the subhuman beasts, the insatiable sadists, of popular imagination. They claimed, rather, that they were ordinary, normal people, fundamentally similar to you and us. They had not wanted to do the terrible things of which they now stood accused—so they said—and had not enjoyed doing them. Far from being brutal and violent perverts, they were so averse to violence that they would get upset if they had so much as to punish their own children for misbehaving.

At first glance there appears to be no reason why we should pay any attention to this outrageous notion. We *know* that the Nazis were not ordinary, normal people, just as we *know* that we, as ordinary, normal people, could never do what they did. But a moment's reflection might lead us to think otherwise, or at least to recognize that the problems posed by the Nazis' claims are rather more complex than they initially appear to be.

We assume that ordinary people are basically decent, and this is one of the reasons why we find it so difficult to take seriously the assertion that the Nazis were ordinary people. But what is the evidence for this assumption? Although a belief in human decency is a necessary underpinning for our democratic institutions, it surely rests on an ideological commitment rather than on empirical fact. As such, it flies in the face of other views of human nature. Whoever first remarked that *homo hominis lupus* ("man is a wolf to man"), for example, would by no means have taken it for granted that the Nazis represented a point well beyond the furthest extremes of human normality. Of course, this view is no more capable of empirical demonstration than the one which asserts that human beings are fundamentally decent. Both are assumptions that probably tell us more about the people who hold them, and the societies which institutionalize them, than they do about human nature itself. Depending on how you choose to look at it, history provides ample justification for either view—or for neither, or for both. For our purposes here, however, it is important to establish the arbitrariness of the belief that the Nazis could not have been ordinary people because ordinary people are basically decent.

In its own bizarre way, moreover, the Nazi defense echoes some of the most basic findings of modern social science. These have pointed to the very considerable extent to which the perceptions, values, and behavior of individuals are shaped by social forces beyond our control—and often, indeed, beyond our recognition. Is it not, then, at least possible that under the extraordinary circumstances of Nazi Germany quite ordinary people could indeed have been induced to do the most revolting things? Perhaps the Nazis really were what they claimed to be: normal, ordinary people who acted as they did not because they were sadists or perverts or brutes but because they were powerless to resist the ineluctable logic of the situations in which they found themselves, victims of social forces not of their own making and whose distinctive qualities they did not necessarily endorse or even recognize. If the prime ministers of England and France could believe that Adolf Hitler was a peaceful and honorable man, are ordinary Germans to be considered base perverts for having trusted him? If a Catholic pope and an American president, each in complicitous silence, failed to hinder the destruction of European Jewry, are ordinary Germans to be considered bloodthirsty demons for not having impeded Hitler's genocidal lust? It is not a

moral question which we are asking here, but rather a phenomenologi-
cal one regarding the kind of behavior which, in a highly abnormal
context, is compatible with human normality.

In the past thirty years or so, a number of prominent scholars and
intellectuals have lent their own authority to this aspect of the Nazi
defense. They have suggested, in effect not only that ordinary, normal
people can behave like the Nazis, but also that *the Nazi leaders themselves were ordinary, normal people*. Their opinions, we suspect,
have been rather more influential than scholars' opinions usually are,
and for this reason we wish to examine them carefully. We will focus
in particular on the work of Hannah Arendt, Stanley Milgram, and
Douglas Kelley. Arendt is one of the major political philosophers of
our day; Milgram is a leading social psychologist; Kelley was for
several months the psychiatrist in charge of the prisoners in the trial
of the major Nazi war criminals at Nuremberg, and, by the time of
his death in 1958, had established a reputation as a leading criminolo-
gist.

Evil, according to Hannah Arendt, even evil on the unparalleled
order of magnitude practiced by the Nazis, does not flourish only because of the insatiable sadism of evil men. It can, rather, thrive
because of the *banality* of quite ordinary men. One of these, according to Arendt, was SS *Obersturmbannfuehrer* Adolf Eichmann.
Eichmann, who as much as any other single individual was responsible for the implementation of the "final solution of the Jewish prob
lem," is seen by Arendt as a tritely and trivially ordinary person, a
humdrum, busy little man who attended as conscientiously to his task
of administering the destruction of European Jewry as he would
have done to any other assignment his superiors gave him. This is not
to say that Eichmann did not find at least some aspects of his work
highly upsetting: he could not bear *to watch* Jews being murdered,
we are told. But that, it would appear, was a purely personal feeling
which had nothing to do in his own mind with his obligation to obey
his superiors. Certainly, it was not cause to disobey their orders.
Neither, for that matter, was the fact that Eichmann did not hate his
victims and felt no ideological malice toward them. And it was Eichmann's ability to perform any task without regard to its moral nature
and no matter how gruesome it was—acting, not out of malevolent
fantasy but in a humdrum spirit of obedience to orders, which was the
only moral obligation he could recognize—which Arendt characterizes as his banality.

In large measure, Arendt bases this remarkable assessment of
Eichmann's personality on his own statements about himself. Eichmann, she reports, "was perfectly sure that he was not what he called
an *innere Schweinhund*, a dirty bastard, in the depths of his heart.

And as for conscience, he remembered perfectly well that he would have had a bad conscience only if he had not done what he had been ordered to do" (Arendt, 1964, p. 25).

Arendt accepts this and similar testimony as self-evident. She fails to reflect on the *psychologically* aberrant nature of an adult person who defines good and evil merely as synonyms for obedience and disobedience to one's superiors. Nor does she explain at any point why it is banal for a man to behave and feel in the way that Eichmann did. Since most people would not consider the ability to organize the murder of millions of human beings commonplace, (particularly, perhaps, when one does not hate them) nor the inability to feel guilty about such a deed trivial, Arendt's characterization of Eichmann as *banal* must at the very least be considered an idosyncratic and arbitrary use of the word.

Nevertheless, Arendt insists on the ordinariness of Eichmann, on his normality. "Everybody" in the Jerusalem courtroom where Eichmann was tried, she states, "could see that this man was not a monster" (Arendt, 1964, p. 54). She adds that his was "obviously also no case of fanatical hatred of Jews, of fanatical anti-Semitism or indoctrination of any kind" (ibid., p. 26). And she accepts that Eichmann acted out of obedience to "his duty. . . . He not only obeyed orders, he also obeyed the law" (ibid., p. 135).

Eichmann, then, in Hannah Arendt's judgment, was "an average, 'normal' person, neither feeble-minded nor indoctrinated nor cynical" (Arendt, 1964, p. 26). And to dispel any doubts that Eichmann, she, and indeed "everybody" else just might be wrong on this score, she declares:

> Half a dozen psychiatrists had certified him as "normal"—
> "more normal, at any rate, than I am after having examined him,"
> one of them was said to have exclaimed, while another found that
> his whole psychological outlook toward his wife and his children,
> mother and father, brothers, sisters and friends, was "not only
> normal but most admirable"—and finally the minister who had
> paid regular visits to him in prison after the Supreme Court had
> finished hearing his appeal reassured everybody by declaring
> Eichmann to be a man "with very positive ideas" (Arendt,
> 1964, p. 26).

These rather startling psychological findings were never presented publicly. Miss Arendt reports that she was given them informally during the course of the trial, but she does not say by whom. We have no way of discovering whether the opinions were reported to her correctly, and no way of assessing the bases on which they were reached. The only published psychological evaluation of Eichmann's personality presents a very different portrait of the man. In an article published after the trial, Gideon Hausner, Eichmann's prosecutor, reported that the Szondi test had been administered to Eichmann and sent to Dr. Szondi for analysis—without any indication as to the subject's identity. In his reply, Hausner reported, Szondi "started by saying that he never analyzed tests of people who had not been identified for him but then added that when he'd glanced briefly at the results they were so extraordinary that he performed a complete analysis. The person who'd taken the test, he declared, revealed in all phases 'a man obsessed with a dangerous and insatiable urge to kill, arising out of a desire for power . . . a perverted, sadistic personality'" (Hausner, 1962).

Arendt, who read Hausner's article, implies either that she does not believe him or else that she rejects Szondi's findings. She adds that if Szondi's analysis of the results as reported was indeed correct, then Eichmann "would have belonged in an insane asylum" (Arendt, 1964, p. 26). Her discussion of these findings is confined to one parenthetical remark and in no way affects her analysis of Eichmann's personality. Inexplicably, Arendt gives far greater credence to the unpublished conclusions of six anonymous psychiatrists, reported to her at second hand and corroborated only by Eichmann's own testimony, than she does to one of the world's leading psychological testers. Under the circumstances it is surely difficult to entertain seriously her claim regarding the normality of the Nazi personality as represented by Adolf Eichmann.

At about the time that the Eichmann trial was taking place in Jerusalem, Stanley Milgram, a psychologist at Yale University, launched a study which has often been referred to since as "the Eichmann experiment."

Milgram sought to discover the extent to which human beings will obey commands which come increasingly into conflict with their consciences. The experiment was conducted along the following lines.

Volunteers were invited through an advertisement in a newspaper to participate in an experimental study of memory and learning. Assigned the role of "teacher," they were given a brief explanation of what was expected of them and assured that they could abandon the experiment at any time they chose to, and that they would receive the small fee and bus fare promised in the advertisement regardless of the point at which they did break off. They were then seated in front of an impressive-looking machine called a "shock generator." The control panel of the machine had thirty switches on it whose voltage increased in 15-volt increments from 15 to 450; verbal designations ranging from SLIGHT SHOCK to DANGER—SEVERE SHOCK identified groups of four or more switches.

The "teacher's" task was to administer an electric shock to another person— the "learner," who was strapped into a chair—every time he made a mistake in a simple memory test. The first mistake was punished by a shock of 15 volts, the second by one of 30 volts, and so on. In fact, the "learner" was an actor who in reality received no shock at all. As his "punishment" increased in severity, however, he began to indicate discomfort. At 75 volts he grunted; at 120 volts he complained verbally; at 150 volts he demanded to be released from the experiment. "At 285 volts," reports Milgram, "his response can only be described as an agonized scream." Shortly thereafter he slumped forward, apparently unconscious—or dead.

In the experiments, the teacher typically experienced intense inner conflict as he administered what he believed to be ever more painful and dangerous shocks. His behavior was carefully supervised by the experimenter himself. When the teacher asked for advice as to whether to continue increasing the punishments, or else indicated that he did not wish to continue the task, the experimenter responded with a series of verbal "prods," the mildest of which was "Please continue" and the most severe, "You have no other choice, you *must* go on."

Sweating, trembling, and in other ways indicating their extreme reluctance to continue administering the punishments, *65 percent of the teachers nevertheless obeyed orders all the way to the end of the scale on the shock generator!* Not a single teacher disobeyed the experimenter's orders before reaching 300 volts—marked INTENSE SHOCK—and only 12.5 percent of them stopped at this point (Milgram, 1974, p. 35). The mean maximum shock level administered by the teachers before refusing to go further was 405 volts, or well within the DANGER—SEVERE SHOCK range.

Using other groups of teachers, Milgram then altered the experimental design. In one version, the experimenter was called away from the laboratory and the teacher was left to continue the shocks on his own; in another, the teacher was supervised by two experimenters who, when appealed to by the teacher, would give contradictory orders, one telling him to discontinue the experiment if he felt that he should, the other insisting that he continue, regardless of his own feelings. In yet another version, the teacher was not instructed to administer the punishments in increasingly severe shocks but was left to select the voltage level by himself.

These variations produced interesting results. Obedience dropped sharply when the experimenter was physically absent from the laboratory and when two experimenters were giving the teacher contradictory instructions. The most dramatic results were obtained when the teachers were left to select the shock level by themselves; in this series of experiments the average shock administered by the teachers was about 55 volts (SLIGHT SHOCK), a level which elicited no signs of discomfort from the learner (Milgram, 1974, pp. 35, 60–61).

What do these findings indicate? Milgram's explanation of them is unequivocal. "Whatever leads to shocking the victims at the highest levels cannot be explained by autonomously generated aggression," he declares, "but needs to be explained by the transformation of behavior that comes through obedience to orders" (Milgram, 1974, p. 72). Indeed, Milgram goes on to suggest that while the teachers in his experiments may have been *upset* about having to administer the shocks, they did not consider their actions *wrong* at the time that they were performing them. And this not only because they did not regard themselves as responsible for their actions (they were merely obeying orders given to them by others), but also because they had transferred to the experimenter the *responsibility for determining whether their actions were immoral or not.* "Although the subject performs the action," Milgram declares, "he allows the authority to define its meaning" (Milgram, 1974, p. 145).

The human being's ability to obey an order and to avoid considering (or at least being deterred from obedience by) its manifest immorality is, Milgram suggests, rooted in our species' evolutionary struggle for survival. Without this capacity we would not be able to function in a hierarchical social organization. But with it we can, thereby making it possible for an individual to belong to a group whose strength and, therefore, capacity for survival is far greater than his own. Every human being possesses the capacity to function as an individual exercising his own moral judgment and equally, the capacity to relinquish his autonomy and, as a member of a social hierarchy, obey his superior's orders and accept *his* moral judgment.

When the individual in *on his own*, conscience is brought into play. But when he functions in an organizational mode, directions that come from the higher level component are not assessed against the internal standards of moral judgment. . . . The psychology of obedience does not depend on the placement within the larger hierarchy: the psychological adjustments of an obedient Wehrmacht general to Adolf Hitler parallel those of the lowest infantry man to his superior, and so forth, throughout the system. Only the psychology of the ultimate leader demands a different set of explanatory principles. . . . The social psychology of this century reveals a major lesson: often, it is not so much the kind of person a man is as the kind of situation in which he finds himself that determines how he will act (Milgram, 1974, pp. 129–130, 205. Cf. pp. 5ff.).

Eichmann and his fellows, then, were right; and so is Hannah Arendt. The most vicious act in human history is not to be explained by the viciousness of the human beings who perpetrated it. Rather, the largest slaughter of human beings in history is to be accounted for by a mechanism that has its origins in the human struggle for survival. Obedience rather than aggression is what made the ghastly tragedy possible. Moreover, under the conditions which prevailed in Nazi Germany, any of us decent, normal people could have behaved as the most bestial Nazi did.

This, at least, is what Milgram would have us believe. But are the conclusions which he draws from the results of his experiments warranted?

A close look at the way in which he reached those conclusions reveals that they rest on a surprising measure of arbitrariness and dogmatism. To begin with, let us note how Milgram accounts for the *disobedience* of some of the teachers. "Residues of selfhood," he says of them, "keep personal values alive in the subject and lead to strain which, if sufficiently powerful, can result in disobedience" (Milgram, 1974, p. 155).

Obedient subjects, then, are those who have failed to keep their personal values alive in the situation in which they found themselves, while disobedient ones have managed to do so.

Surely the results could be explained equally well along different lines. It could be argued that the disobedient subjects did not merely keep their personal values alive, as Milgram suggests, but that *they actually had different values to start with*. Milgram tacitly equates "personal values" with "not causing pain to others." But where is the evidence that these were, indeed, the personal values of *all* his subjects? Is it not possible that the disobedient subjects disobeyed because they were more moral, more averse to inflicting pain on other human beings, than the obedient subjects?

Milgram seeks to anticipate this objection by referring to the version of the experiment in which the teacher is allowed to select the shock level by himself. On these occasions, it will be recalled, very much lower voltages were chosen than were administered under the instructions of the experimenter. With reference to these results, Milgram asks: "If destructive impulses were really pressing for release, and the subject could justify his use of high shock levels in the cause of science, why did they [*sic*] not make the victim suffer?" (Milgram, 1974, p. 167).

One answer to this question is, indeed, that which Milgram offers. The difference between obedients and disobedients vanishes, to all intents and purposes, in the absence of external authority. From this, Milgram infers that the presence of that external authority is the factor which led many of the subjects to administer inordinately high shocks. Since authority demands obedience, this argument goes, the reason the subjects administered such high shocks was that they were obeying the authority of the experimenter.

But another explanation of the same facts is, at the least, equally plausible. If we assume that the obedients were more aggressive and more violent than the disobedients, it becomes reasonable to see the function of the authority of the experimenter in rather different terms from those suggested by Milgram. The authoritative command of the experimenter to administer the shocks, we may speculate, *gave sanction to and released the aggressive drives of the so-called obedient subjects.*

Those drives, controlled under other circumstances by the superego, are legitimized, as it were, by the authority of the experimenter—which weakens the superego in its task of restraining them. The manifest tension observed in the teachers as they administered the higher voltage shocks reflects a struggle, not between their "personal values" and their inclination to surrender these to the experimenter (as Milgram argues), but between their aggressive drives and their own internal (superego) restraints on them.

The function of the authority's command, then, is not to say, in effect, "be violent *despite* yourself; let me do the judging for you," but rather, "I won't punish you if you indulge your appetite for violence: indeed, I would really like you to do so." Some people, because of the amount of violence in them and the relative weakness of their superegos, are more likely to accept this invitation than others. But even in the most violent of Milgram's subjects the superego was strong enough to put up a good fight *against* that invitation; if it could not prevent the subjects from being violent, it at least made them feel extremely uneasy about what they were doing.

This hypothesis is also consistent with the fact that without external sanction all subjects administered a far lower level of shock. In this situation the potentially obedient subjects are deprived of the invitation to do great violence to another human being. Without such an overt, external stimulus, the potential obedient's aggressive drives are once again brought under the control of the superego, with the result that he behaves in much the same way as the potential disobedient.

The difference between these two groups, then, does not lie in the durability or otherwise of their "personal values" but in the nature of those values. One group is less prone to violence—more moral, more decent—than the other. And the social lesson to be learned from this is not that in a wicked world decent people will act in a wicked way but that in a wicked world people with a penchant for wickedness will freely indulge it, justifying themselves (when called upon to do so) on the grounds that they were merely obeying orders.

Here then is a radically different explanation from the one offered by Milgram. Both explanations are based on the same facts but draw different conclusions from them. More data would, perhaps, enable us to settle the debate one way or another. Unfortunately, those facts are not available, because Milgram chose not to pursue them.

The first group of subjects in his experiment—thirty-four Yale students—were subsequently examined by another psychologist, Lawrence Kohlberg, who has specialized in the study of the development of moral judgment in individuals as they mature. Kohlberg's finding was that the students who broke off were at a higher level of moral development than those who remained obedient to the end (Kohlberg). Reporting this, however, Milgram merely says that "Kohlberg's findings are suggestive, though not very strong" (Milgram, 1974, p. 205). He does not explain this judgment, and he does not incorporate even the "suggestive" aspects of Kohlberg's work into his own analysis. More important, Milgram makes no attempt to account for his failure to develop independent information on the moral caliber of all of his subjects. Without this information, his hypothesis about their behavior can be neither proven nor disproven.

It is interesting to speculate about what the results would have been if Milgram had run one series of experiments with criminals guilty of repeated crimes of violence. As confirmed disobedients, Milgram would presumably expect them to administer significantly lower levels of shocks than normal, law-abiding citizens.

As the paradigm of the Nazi world which Milgram claims that they are, his experiments suffer from at least one overwhelming defect. It is well known that the Jews were subjected to intense vilification by the Nazi propaganda machine for several years before their actual extermination began. This propaganda gave official sanction to what had always been strong anti-Semitic currents in German life and disposed Germans all the more to regard Jews as sinister, dangerous, hateful, and altogether less than human.

Of the actor–learner in his experiments, on the other hand, Milgram writes: "The victim was played by a 47-year-old accountant, trained for the role; he was of Irish–American descent and most observers found him mild-mannered and likable" (Milgram, 1974, p. 16). Milgram does not explain why he chose this individual as the learner in preference to some other personality type. The effect, if not the intention, of this selection is to weight the scales in favor of his interpretation of the results. Who would want to vent his aggressive impulses on a mild and likeable middle-aged man? *Therefore*, we have additional reason to believe that the teachers acted out of obedience rather than from aggression. Milgram does not say this, of course, but it is a bias in the implementation of the experimental design which deserves to be noted.

But the Jews whom the Nazis exterminated were not, as we have seen, viewed by their torturers as "mild-mannered and likable"— indeed, quite the opposite. For his experiments to have approximated conditions in Nazi Germany, Milgram would have had to have had members of, shall we say, the Ku Klux Klan as teachers and a black person as learner. He did not do so, of course, and we must conclude therefore, that his experiments are almost as irrelevant to an understanding of the Nazi phenomenon in Germany as his interpretation of the results of those experiments is inconclusive (Wrightsman).

Finally, we come to the assessment of Douglas Kelley, the Nuremberg prison psychiatrist. Unlike Arendt, Kelley was a professional psychiatrist; unlike Milgram, he did not have to rely on an attempted simulation of Nazi Germany, for the men under his care in the Nuremberg prison were the surviving leaders of the Third Reich. Kelley spent five months with the twenty-two prisoners, conducted interviews with them almost daily, and administered psychological tests to a number of them. Although he did not have the opportunity to probe their personalities at the deep level possible in psychoanalytic sessions, he succeeded, in his own professional judgment, in getting to know these individuals very well.

Of the prisoners as a group, Kelley wrote that "although many of them were not what we would call ideally normal, none of them were sufficiently deviate to require custodial care according to the laws of our country." They were, he adds, "a group of individuals who were essentially sane . . . although in some instances somewhat deviated from normal" (Kelley, 1946, pp. 46–47).

It is difficult, for two reasons, to make much sense of Kelley's findings. Were "many" or only "some" of the Nazis deviants? And how deviant were they? Were they "not what we would call ideally normal" or were they "somewhat deviated from normal"? There is presumably, a difference between the two descriptions, and it is surprising to discover such imprecision in a clinical report presented to a professional audience.

Still more to the point, however, is the fact that the extensive clinical tests conducted on the Nuremberg prisoners (some of them by Kelley himself), which were used by him in arriving at some of his assessments, simply do not bear out his own analysis. He describes Goering, for example, as a "brilliant, brave, ruthless, grasping, shrewd executive" (Kelley, 1947, p. 51). But Gustave Gilbert—the psychologist who administered the Rorschach to the indicted Nazis at Nuremberg, and whose records form the basis for this book—found that Goering was an "intelligent but sadistic egotist with little real ego strength . . . an aggressive psychopath" (Gilbert, 1950, pp. 109, 284).

There is not much more that can be said about Kelley's evaluation of his erstwhile wards beyond the fact that it is profoundly at variance with the conclusions reached by other qualified professionals. What we will see as the strikingly, and manifestly, erroneous nature of Kelley's findings, is particularly odd in view of his considerable ability in the field. It is possible that the nature of his own death may throw light on his idiosyncratic perception of the Nazi leaders. Goering, it will be recalled, had cheated the hangman by swallowing a cyanide capsule which had been smuggled into his cell—we still do not know by whom. A number of extra capsules were found on his body. Douglas Kelley committed suicide with one of these (*The New York Times,* Jan. 1, 1958).

Neither Arendt, nor Milgram nor Kelley, accordingly, has established a persuasive case in favor of their contentions that the Nazi leadership was composed of normal, ordinary people. At best, Arendt has demonstrated that a man may kill millions of human beings without hating them. Since Eichmann had fifteen postwar years to get over his ideological passions, however, his assertion that he did not, in fact, hate Jews is highly disputable and, in any case, would not establish that he was a normal, ordinary person. The most startling fact established by Milgram is that under the conditions prevailing in his laboratory (which are not quite as representative of Nazi Germany as he claims they are), a surprisingly large proportion of people will inflict a great deal of pain on an innocent and helpless person. Whether this indicates that most people are capable of mindless obedience even to brutal orders, as Milgram suggests, or, alternatively, that many more people than we would like to believe have a terrifyingly great capacity for violence when the restraints against it are removed is, as we have seen, open to question.

Be that as it may, these scholars have not persuaded us that the major Nazi war criminals were normal, ordinary people fundamentally similar to you and us. The claim that they were, it should be said, has by no means gone unchallenged in clinical circles. As we have seen, Szondi unequivocally identified Eichmann's personality as a highly deviant one. Gilbert, while finding "little evidence for pathological explanations" of the behavior of "the comparatively 'normal and respectable' members of Hitler's entourage" who were diplomats, businessmen and professional soldiers, found that for many of the "revolutionary nucleus" of the Nazi leadership "the fascist ideology provided outlets for pathological tendencies that had already been deeply rooted in their personality development" (Gilbert, 1950, p. 274).

Were *all* the Nazi leaders, then, "normal" people? Or were only some of them relatively normal, while others were psychotic or psychopathic? Or, finally, could it be that none of them resembled what might reasonably be considered a normal personality? The remarkable collection of materials compiled by Gilbert and published here for the first time enables us to answer the question of the Nazi leaders' normality, or lack of it, with as much certainty as modern science allows.

2

The Rorschach Method

It would be a mistake to suppose that a science consists entirely of proved theses, and it would be unjust to require this. Only a disposition with a passion for authority will raise such a demand—someone with a craving to replace his religious catechism by another, though it is a scientific one. Science has only a few apodeictic propositions in its catechism: the rest are assertions promoted by it to some particular degree of probability. It is actually a sign of a scientific mode of thought to find satisfaction in these approximations to certainty and to be able to pursue constructive work in spite of the absence of final confirmation.

—SIGMUND FREUD,
Introductory Lectures on Psychoanalysis
(Third Lecture)

Depth psychology rests on a series of assumptions—not facts, but what appear to be the most plausible explanations of them—about how the human mind functions and is structured. It assumes, first of all, that the mind comprises both unconscious and conscious components, and that in many important respects the former determine the ways in which the latter operate. Equally, psychoanalysis proceeds from the assumption that although the unconscious mind is just that—unconscious—it is possible for us to discover its contents.

A further assumption is that such commonplace and seemingly trivial phenomena as dreams, slips of the tongue, lapses of memory, and many apparent accidents are not random occurrences or—in the case of dreams—messages from supernatural powers. Rather, they are considered involuntary (because uncontrolled by the conscious mind) expressions of unconscious feelings and drives.

As long ago as 1857, a scholar noticed that it was possible to see a variety of objects in a blot of ink on a piece of paper—and that individuals differed greatly in the objects which they saw in it. As the years went by, psychologists studied the phenomenon but were unable to come up with any satisfactory explanation of it. "Why one subject should see in a blot a 'cabbage head' " wrote G. V. Dearborn, an American psychologist, in 1897, "and the next an 'animal with his mouth open,' or why a professor should be reminded by a blot of 'half a sweet pea blossom' and his wife of a 'snake coiled round a stick,' . . . no one can pretend at present to explain . . ." (quoted in Klopfer and Davidson, p. 4).

Shortly before the outbreak of World War I, a young Swiss psychiatrist named Hermann Rorschach began what would be the most exhaustive investigation yet undertaken of the psychological meaning of the responses evoked by ink blots. Nearly ten years later, after experimenting with thousands of different blots, Rorschach published his findings in a slim volume, *Psychodiagnostics*, which revolutionized the field of psychological diagnosis and evaluation. In 1922, a year after the publication of this work, Rorschach died at the age of 37.

In a manner consistent with the basic Freudian understanding of the human mind, Rorschach hypothesized that the objects which people saw in the ink blots were perceived not at random but rather on the basis of the distinctive characteristics of the individuals involved. Those characteristics, Rorschach suggested, could be identified through the careful analysis of people's responses to the blots.

Rorschach's *Psychodiagnostics* has, in several important respects, been superseded by later research, beginning with the posthumous publication in 1923 of a paper of which he was coauthor. Hardly less important than his theoretical work, however, were the ten blots —the so-called Rorschach cards—which he finally selected as the standard instruments to be used in the application of his method. After half a century, these ten blots remain unrivaled in their capacity to evoke a wide range of psychologically significant responses from individuals who look at them.

All sets of Rorschach cards are of uniform size, shape, and color. Each card is referred to by a standard designation (e.g., Card I, Card II). Reproductions of the cards in full color will be found following page 18, and reproductions in black-and-white accompany each response in the ensuing chapters. In accordance with standard practice (the object of which is not to undermine the clinical usefulness of the cards by making them too familiar to the general public), they are reproduced here at about one-sixth of their original size. Each blot is symmetrical; small asymmetries may be perceived when the cards are shown full size. Cards I, IV, V, VI, and VII are each comprised of varying shades of grey and black, while Cards II and III have, in addition, shades of red. Cards VIII, IX, and X, on the other hand, are made up of a larger number of colors, mainly pastel, each in a variety of shadings.

A standard procedure is followed in administering the cards and in recording the subject's responses to them. After a brief introduction, in which he is instructed to report what the blots look like, the subject is handed Card I in an upright position. He may give one or more responses to it, utilizing the entire blot or any portion of it. He may turn the card sideways or upside down; if he is unable to see anything in the blot, he may put the card down and wait for the next one to be handed to him. And he may take as long as he wishes to tell the examiner what he sees in the blot. All in all, then, the subject is free to respond to the card in whatever way he chooses. These options, however, are not identified for him: to the extent possible, the examiner avoids structuring the situation. After the subject has completed his responses to the first card he is handed the second, and so on until all ten have been presented to him.

After the initial "performance," as this phase of the procedure is called, the examiner puts the cards face up on the table and asks the subject a series of questions about his responses. This "inquiry" phase is aimed at ascertaining the portion of the blot used by the subject in his response, whether color and shading were utilized by the subject, and, in the case of human and animal figure responses, whether the figures were seen as alive and in motion or not. During the inquiry the subject frequently elaborates his responses in other ways as well; and it can also happen that he comes up with additional responses.

Finally, under certain circumstances (for example, with subjects who have produced few or meager responses), a procedure called "testing the limits" may be applied. Some examiners, as in these records, ask direct questions, such as "Sometimes two female figures are seen in this card. Do you see them?"—with the general aim of determining whether the subject can see specific concepts or is capable of using certain details, shadings, and colors in his responses. Other examiners use more indirect methods to see how close to or far from availability are capacities which the subject has not used spontaneously.

The examiner records, usually verbatim, the subject's responses and other details in accordance with standard procedures. Among the details recorded are general comments by the subject (e.g., "Hmmm, this is difficult"); expressive gestures and mannerisms; the length of time (in seconds) that elapses from the moment the card is handed to the subject until he makes each response in the initial, performance section; the portion of the blot that is used in each response; and whether the subject turns the card sideways or upside down. A code is used to indicate the portions of the blot used, with (W) standing for the entire blot, (S) for the use of white spaces,

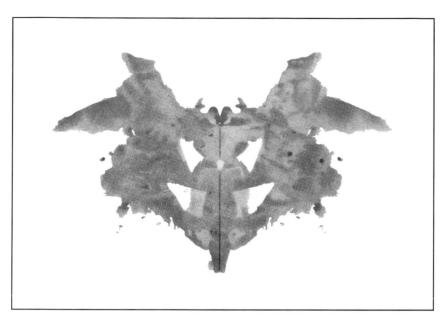

CARD I

CARD II

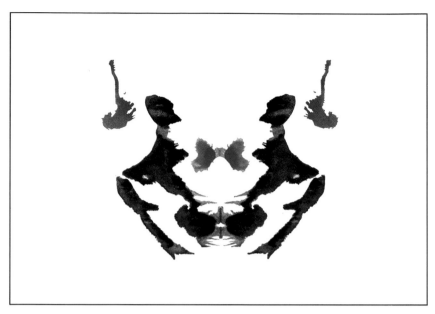

CARD III

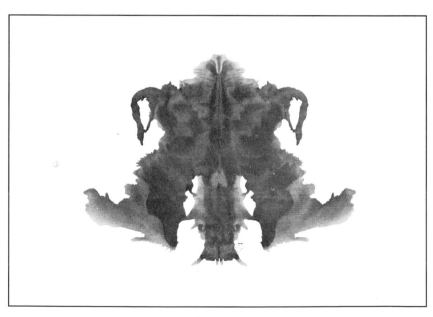

CARD IV

CARD V

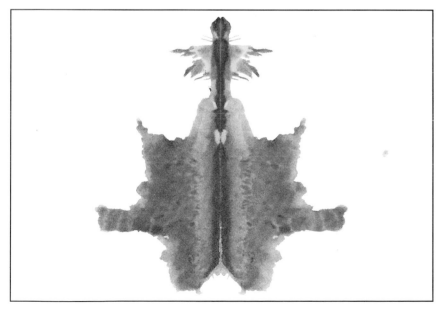

CARD VI

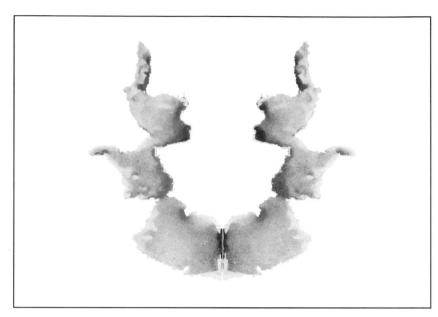

CARD VII

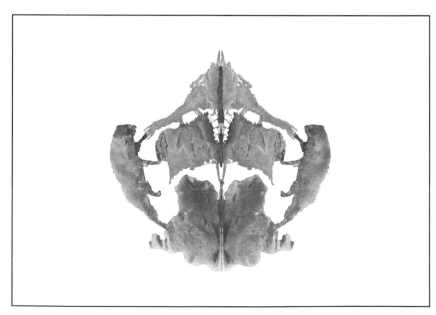

CARD VIII

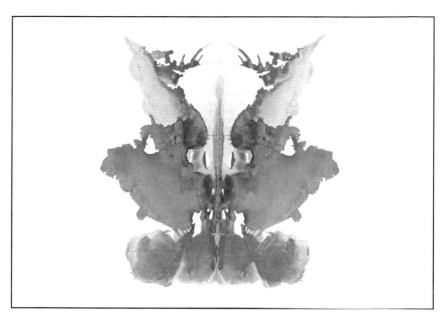

CARD IX

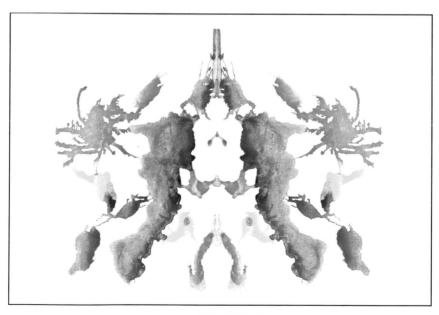

CARD X

Hans Frank

Hans Fritzsche

Walther Funk

Hermann Goering

Rudolf Hess

Ernst Kaltenbrunner

Wilhelm Keitel

Constantin von Neurath

Franz von Papen

Joachim von Ribbentrop

Alfred Rosenberg

Fritz Sauckel

Hjalmar Schacht

Baldur von Schirach

Artur Seyss-Inquart

Albert Speer

and so on. The symbols ∧, ∨, >, and <, respectively, indicate that the card is being held in the upright position, upside down, or sideways. (See list of Rorschach terms and symbols on pages 29–30). In the records in this book, if the card position is not noted, the card was held upright throughout the record.

Contrary to what is frequently assumed, the Rorschach is not a test, and there are no "right" and "wrong" responses to the cards. Every person is at once a social animal and a unique, distinct individual. We function within a socially constructed reality of meanings and values that are common to our group; but we also bring our own, personal interpretations and additions to these meanings and values. In general, our idiosyncratic responses to situations are addressed to those aspects of them which are intrinsically ambiguous or which we perceive as ambiguous—though of course it can also be that for ideological and other reasons we refuse or are unable to accept conventional definitions of reality.

To the considerable extent, then, that reality is ambiguous, each individual interprets it idiosyncratically. It is true that life situations have a more definite outline, a clearer character, than do Rorschach blots, and that the extent to which our view is clear and objective is a measure of our sanity. Nevertheless, much of life has ambiguity, too. Two sons may describe a father in such different terms that an outsider would think they must be talking about two different individuals. Two employees endow an employer with such contrasting characteristics that the listener is eager to see for himself what the employer is really like. He does, and what *he* sees is different from both descriptions. Which is the reality? One view may indeed be far more accurate and objective than the others, but all will be blends of objective and subjective components.

The relatively unstructured way in which the Rorschach method is administered is intended to enhance the ambiguity of the setting to which the subject must devise his own way of responding. By the same token, the form, color, and shading of each blot are ambiguous in the sense that they can be used to create a very large variety of concepts, and must be organized by each subject in his own way. All in all, then, there is little in the subject's prior experience as a socialized human being to guide him in his responses to the cards. Rather, the cards represent ambiguous situations which *he* must define and for which there are no conventional definitions available to him. The manner in which he does so is believed to be "a reflection, or projection, of his private world" (Rapaport).

The projective hypothesis, as this belief is called, proceeds from the assumption that personality tends to be an organized and consistent whole, and that to the extent that a person handles a situation in his own way, in the absence of conventional definitions of it, he will do so in a manner that is thoroughly consistent with his whole personality. We impose our own inner structure, according to this hypothesis, on unstructured situations that we encounter; from which it follows that it is possible to identify that inner structure—the individual's "private world"—by studying the way in which the person arranges unstructured situations.

Although some of the phenomena to which we referred at the outset of this chapter—dreams, slips of the tongue, forgetfulness, etc.— are interpreted psychoanalytically as involuntary expressions of the unconscious mind, we assume that responses to the ink blots need not involve a "breakthrough" of unconscious content for them to be diagnostically valuable. Because of the essential unity of the conscious and the unconscious, conscious material in the Rorschach responses may be interpreted in terms of the whole personality, with its unconscious as well as its conscious aspects.

The Rorschach cards, it is also assumed, provide a simulation of "real" life situations; the way in which we respond to the cards is very similar to the way in which we respond to that which is ambiguous in the environment (Miale, 1959, 1975). But if this is indeed so, why do we not analyze a person's responses to that which is ambiguous in the external environment in which he ordinarily moves, instead of eliciting responses through the simulated reality of Rorschach cards?

Although ambiguous, the Rorschach cards—like life situations— are not meaningless. Objects *can* be recognized in them. What is more, prolonged examination of the cards, along with the records of tens of thousands of subjects who have taken the Rorschach, has established that certain concepts do suggest themselves, some more and others less readily, out of the form, color, and shading of the blots. It has thus been ascertained that each card has its distinctive qualities, and these qualities are known to the expert in Rorschach analysis.

Seen in this light, the crucial difference between the Rorschach cards and the everyday life situations which individuals interpret idiosyncratically does not lie in the nature of the material presented for interpretation; rather, the difference lies in the degree to which the situation—the properties of the stimuli it contains—can be known to the interpreter. The ink blots do not change under observation and do not interact with the subject. In this sense, they are stable, and their stability makes possible the collection of the kind of comparative data that can provide a sound empirical base for interpretation.

By contrast, it is not possible empirically to establish norms or common meanings for the interpretation of ambiguous life situations, which are changing and are never exactly repeated. Their properties cannot be forseen in detail, and they are too impermanent to permit the kind of leisurely and extended study which enables us to know the characteristics of the Rorschach cards. It is for this reason that projective methods such as the Rorschach are valuable for the analysis of personality. Almost paradoxically, we can speak of the known properties of the stimuli contained in the novel situations presented by the Rorschach cards, in contrast to the unknown characteristics of even many familiar situations of everyday life.

Ambiguous, complex and full of potential as the cards are to the subject, accordingly, they are a situation with which the Rorschach analyst himself is familiar. And the difficult and subtle task which the analyst is called on to perform is to identify the ways in which the individual is being himself, to focus on the unwittingly expressed aspects of the response or expression, while the subject who is being observed is concentrating on quite other, and frequently quite different, aspects of the stimulus situation.

Handwriting analysis provides perhaps the clearest analogy. A person, while writing, is generally concerned first with content, then perhaps with aspects of handwriting like legibility and attractiveness. He is not occupied with (and could modify very little if he were) features like writing stroke, pressure, the relative size of different parts of his letters, or the type of curve he uses in connecting vertical strokes of his pen—to mention only a few of the many features of handwriting which the graphologist utilizes.

Similarly, if not as clearly, the Rorschach interpreter utilizes features of responses which are not subject to conscious selection or control by the subject, who indeed may suppress sexual associations or show off his sophisticated knowledge of art or—as with the Nazis in this collection—insist on his basic decency as a human being and his innocence of the terrible crimes in which he participated, but who cannot do much to alter what is essential about the images that, as it were, jump out at him from the ink blots. It would be virtually impossible for a subject (not only because he is familiar with the cards as a result of previous testing, but even if he has had previous training and experience in the method) to be so adept as to be able to conceal significant information about himself from a skilled Rorschach analyst.

Rorschach's initial presentation of his method emphasized almost exclusively the "formal characteristics" of the response, and proposed an essentially *quantitative* system of analysis known as scoring. In this system, each response is scored in terms of five characteristics (Klopfer and Davidson, chap. 4):

1. *Location*: Where on the card was the concept seen?
2. *Determinant*: What qualities of the blot determined the concept? (Eg., form, color, shading.)

3. *Content*: What was the subject matter of the concept?

4. *Popularity–Originality*: A response is termed "popular" when it conforms to responses that have been found to be most frequent, (e.g., a bat or a butterfly in Card I). An original response, the scoring symbol for which is "O", is one which has been found to occur in fewer than one in a hundred records. Most responses are neither original nor popular.

5. *Form Level*: How accurately is the concept seen? How closely does it fit the part of the blot for which it is used? To what extent is the concept appropriately elaborated?

In a paper published shortly after his death, Rorschach suggested that a careful analysis of the *contents* of the responses would greatly enhance the analysis of the "formal characteristics." This proposal was generally ignored. As *Psychodiagnostics* became famous in the nineteen thirties and forties, psychologists were captivated by the promise that scoring, adding up of scores, arranging them in ratios, graphing them, and developing norms for them, would provide an objective, scientific personality test uncontaminated by the clinician—and not requiring his talent or training, or experience. Psychodiagnosis would no longer be an art; it was being elevated to the status of a science.

The trouble was that Rorschach scores were not really scores at all. In mental testing, scores are based on frequency distributions, on the assumption that many traits and abilities are distributed in the population according to a normal curve. For example, intelligence tests have been constructed on the reasonable (and to an extent verifiable) assumption that certain aspects of intellectual functioning are distributed normally in the population: that there are about as many idiots as there are geniuses, about as many people above average as below it in the ability to do certain important kinds of reasoning and retain certain useful items of information.

But there is no evidence at all that Rorschach scores are normally distributed in the general population. Indeed, the term "score" is an unfortunate one. Rorschach scores are shorthand signs which note aspects of the blots to which a subject responds: as such, they are important. But to treat them as the basic Rorschach material and to play statistical games with them is about as appropriate as interpreting X-ray photographs by the use of a ruler instead of through the experienced, skilled perception of a roentgenologist.

The roentgenologist knows that he is looking at images of bones and organs. In focusing on the content of Rorschach responses, on the other hand, Rorschach analysts have been considerably less certain as to just what it is that those responses are symbols of. A survey of the field (Mindess) has shown that while one psychologist interprets the responses as statements referring to the inner state, the early memories, and even the organic condition of the respondent, another regards them as revealing the subject's attitudes about certain forces in himself, as indicating certain tendencies within himself, and as statements concerning his attempt to view, or else his view of, himself and others. Yet another psychologist finds in the Rorschach responses facts about the life history of the respondent.

C.G. Jung has pointed to two levels of dream interpretation, which he terms the "objective" and the "subjective" (Jung, 1953, p. 83). The former examines the contents of dreams in terms of the dreamer's experience of and response to life situations and the people and relationships involved in them; while the latter looks at the contents of dreams as symbolic of aspects of the dreamer's personality. The two levels are closely related in life, since the dreamer's images of the objects and people in his environment have an element of projection in them. The way one views a person in waking life as well as in dreams is to a considerable extent a function of the aspect of oneself that the other represents.

While Jung concedes that interpretation on the objective level can often be of value clinically, his emphasis is on the subjective, or self-referent, interpretation. "The dream," he says, "is the theater where the dreamer is at once scene, actor, prompter, stage manager, author, audience and critic" (Jung, 1928, p. 162).

In the same way, we are suggesting that Rorschach symbols may be viewed as self-referent, as faithful representations of the inner states of the respondent—of aspects of his own personality.

This understanding is broad enough to encompass many of the other meanings ascribed to Rorschach symbols. Where one interpreter might ask: Does this figure represent the subject's father? Is that one his mother? Is this one representative of his views of women?, we assume that the Rorschach symbol represents primarily an aspect of the subject's personality. His image of his actual mother, father, or whomever, is determined to a considerable extent by aspects of his own personality. These often have their origins in relations with parents and siblings, and are likely to be projected in a person's view of figures in his environment.

Thus, if we interpret Rorschach symbols as revealing aspects of the subject's own personality, we will also be able to make inferences about his images of important figures in his environment and his relations with these figures, as well as inferences about the genesis of those qualities. Other aspects of his attitudes toward himself and others, of how he views the world, and even of his organic condition may likewise be inferred from a self-referent interpretation of Rorschach material.

This approach also enables us to avoid certain pitfalls. Some interpret Rorschach symbols in terms of generalizations about the subject's life history. While such interpretations are not necessarily incorrect, they tell us very little about the particular individual we are studying. To explain a given person's problems in terms of sibling rivalry, castration anxiety, or an Oedipus complex, for example, is to clarify very little of the particular experiences he has had of these phenomena. Again, while inferences can sometimes be made from Rorschach material concerning significant past experiences of a person, or concerning his overt behavior, simpler methods of obtaining such information generally exist, which are likely to have the added advantage of assessing the situations in which the subject behaves as well as the behavior itself.

Thus, the most relevant use of the Rorschach is not to find out what experiences a person has had but rather to learn what his experiences mean to him, and what he has become through them. It is the role of a given experience in the present, not the fact of its occurrence in the past, which is significant for an understanding of the person.

A hypothetical example will illustrate the contrast between self-referent interpretation and other approaches to the content of Rorschach responses. A subject may see in the blots a series of images of contest, competition, and mutual hostility. The figures in the side details of Card I may be seen as trying to wrest the center from each other, those in II as arguing, in III as competing, in VII as fighting, and so on. One might infer from this that there are strong aggressive impulses in the subject (W. Klopfer, p. 381). Or one might focus on the implication that he views people as hostile. Again, one might conclude that his environment, early or current or both, contained much conflict and aggression, that his parents, for example, were ill-matched or actually quarreled a great deal. Any or all of these inferences might be correct in an individual case. If the self-referent character of Rorschach responses is borne in mind, however, the problem of interpretation is not one of arbitrarily choosing one of these possibilities over the others. It is, rather, a matter of recognizing *the essential quality within the subject's personality* which must be present if any of the above-mentioned conditions is of such central importance as to pervade his responses. Any person who responds to the ink blots in this fashion is one who experiences intense internal conflict, one in whom aspects of himself are at war with one another.

For one person such inner conflict may be symbolized in his mind by (and have its origins in) his ill-matched or quarrelsome parents; for another, it may be experienced in the form of projection onto others, who are then viewed as hostile to him. Any or all of these expressions may be present in the person. It is possible that in a particular case the conflict may be represented in none of these ways but simply experienced directly as inner struggle, as opposition within the self.

The specific images among the human figures are a specially rich source of portrayals of the self, or of aspects of the self. In images involving the opposite sex, much is explained about those aspects of the person which he least associates with his conscious role. At least in recent and contemporary Western culture, masculinity tends to be equated with strength, power, aggression, decisiveness, etc.; femininity with tenderness, creativeness, feeling, passivity. Clearly a developed, mature person of either sex has integrated both kinds of qualities. It is in this sense that within this volume frequent references are made to the "feminine" aspects of the men being studied.

What holds true of human figures also applies to the animals, plants, islands, explosions, articles of clothing, and items of food that are so frequently found in Rorschach records. These are commonly used to throw light on interests and conscious preoccupations of the subject, on his mental breadth or stereotypy. Important information may be obtained, however, by treating these responses, too as reflections of deeper aspects of the personality.

Jung's interpretation of dream symbols as "subjective" embodies this approach. He says that interpretation on this level "detaches the underlying complexes of memory from their external causes, regards them as tendencies or components of the subject. . . . All the contents of the dream are treated as symbols for subjective contents" (Jung, 1953, p. 83). He illustrates this approach in connection with the following dream of a patient:

> She is about to cross a wide river. There is no bridge, but she finds a ford where she can cross. She is on the point of doing so when a large crab that has lain hidden in the water siezes her by the foot and will not let her go. (Ibid., p. 80).

Jung comments: "The dreamer is the whole dream; she is the river, the ford, and the crab, or rather these details express conditions and tendencies in the unconscious of the subject" (ibid., p. 83). With the aid of the dreamer's associations, but *essentially on the basis of the intrinsic qualities of the images,* he interprets the river which the dreamer must cross as an inner obstacle to her development, and the crab which comes up from the bottom of the river to attack her as an aggressive instinctual aspect of her personality which threatens her from the depths of the unconscious.

A similar approach to Rorschach symbols has been proposed by Mindess who suggests investigation of their meaning not on the basis of physical appearance but rather on the basis of the intrinsic quality of the object identified in the response. The latter point, in particular, represents a real contribution. It is necessary, however, to go beyond what Mindess calls the psychological quality of the response and to consider the specific meaning of the object referred to in the concept. Animals are creatures guided by instinct and impulse. Thus an image employing animals may be interpreted as referring to this realm of psychic existence. And different qualities are attached to different animals: lions and rabbits will not be used to represent the same qualities. The crab—armored, aggressive, primitive dweller in the depths—is a different image in important respects from the snail, which, while also armored, uses defenses of passive withdrawal. *By identifying the intrinsic qualities of any image, whether human, animal, or inanimate, the interpreter can understand the language of Rorschach content. For the referents of such images possess qualities that are also psychic qualities.*

Analysis of Rorschach responses is, to an extent, facilitated by the fact that there are a number of terms—symbols, or metaphors—which recur with relative frequency, and whose meaning is by now readily recognized. References to the blackness of an object, for example, are indicative of a depressive mood in the subject, just as references to headgear point to a preoccupation with status.

The Rorschach analyst, however, must extend his knowledge and skill far beyond mere familiarity with the recurring symbols in Rorschach responses and the stimulus properties of the cards which evoke them. His insights must match the subtleties of the human mind itself, and he must refine, to an unusual degree, his ability to perceive and explicate the nuances of meaning in the language of Rorschach responses. Alert to every detail of each response, he must, like any good detective, also note what has been omitted, ponder the meaning of the sequence in which a group of responses to a particular card has been presented, and evaluate each item in the context of the overall production of responses and without automatically attributing the same meaning to it regardless of the setting in which it appears. It is impossible to overemphasize the importance of experience, skill, intelligence and the refined delicacy of perception in Rorschach analysis.

In addition to developing these qualities in himself, the Rorschach analyst must take pains to avoid two pitfalls, in particular. The first is a hazard of clinical psychology in general: the analyst may have important personal problems of which he is not conscious or with which he has not dealt adequately. He is then liable, by projecting these on to the subject, to attribute what is actually in himself to the person he is analyzing.

Secondly, projective methods of personality assessment, including the Rorschach, were originally designed as aids in psychiatric diagnosis. As such, they tend to stress the pathological aspects in the subject's personality, a tendency known as "negative bias." The specific factors which result in negative bias are known, however, and a skilled and experienced Rorschach analyst uses this knowledge to counteract the distorting effects of this tendency. (For a fuller discussion, see Miale, 1959, chap. 4).

How do we know whether the underlying assumptions of Rorschach's method are correct? Efforts have been made to validate Rorschach findings by comparing them with those based on other methods. The results have not been satisfactory, largely because of a number of methodological shortcomings which are, perhaps, too technical to be discussed here (Miale, 1959, chap. 4). In an important sense, however, projective methods, including the Rorschach, cannot be validated, for the validity of the method cannot be considered apart from the validity of the interpreter, whose skill is an integral part of the instrument. Clinical experience indicates that at least some psychologists are able to use the Rorschach effectively —that their diagnoses, based solely on a patient's responses to the ten Rorschach cards, are confirmed by findings obtained through a variety of other methods, including psychoanalysis. The problem of validation thus becomes largely one of the validation of the method which is represented by the skill of the interpreter. So far, methods for the measurement of clinical skills are very little developed.

Hermann Goering's Rorschach record (with the reference to Schacht in Card III deleted) was shown to a small group of Rorschach experts at an informal gathering. Although the identity of the subject was not revealed, the psychologists readily recognized the record as one of a dangerous, malevolent, psychopathic person. In reality, of course, clinicians do not ordinarily look at Rorschach records or at other projective material "blind." In general, a knowledge of the life history of a subject is part of the data used in clinical assessment— which is not to say that the assessment merely restates previously known facts in psychological terms. Rather, those facts are used to help the psychologist determine the salience of certain psychological characteristics in the subject that are revealed in the clinical material, to help account for the ways in which the subject deals with them at the conscious and behavioral levels, to understand their origins in the life of the subject, and so on.

With the present group of subjects—sixteen of the major Nazi war criminals tried at Nuremberg—we know something of the life history of each individual, we know the kinds of activities in which they engaged, and we are familiar with the social and political context in which they lived—and which, indeed, they played a large part in constructing. This information is part of their psychological record, though it is perhaps worth mentioning that for a variety of practical and theoretical reasons we did not do the kind of detailed biographical research reflected in the summaries appended to each record until we had completed analyzing the Rorschach material. Nevertheless, the analysis of each subject's record was done with an awareness that we were dealing with a prominent Nazi and with some knowledge of his life and career. This, as we indicated above, is ordinarily standard practice in clinical assessment. If the reader occasionally finds that our analyses of these records have a judgmental tone, then this is because we knew what kinds of things these men did and with whom they were associated. Such knowledge does not undermine the validity of our assessments, but rather is a legitimate part of them.

In conclusion, then, the Rorschach method is based on a series of hypotheses. They have not been "proven" correct, but the accuracy of the insights obtained through the skilled application of the method has repeatedly been demonstrated. Certainly, these hypotheses stand unrivaled as the most persuasive answer to date to the question which, as we saw at the outset of this chapter, a psychologist asked more than three-quarters of a century ago: "Why one subject should see in a blot a cabbage head, and the next an animal with his mouth open . . ."

SOME RORSCHACH TERMS AND SYMBOLS

PERFORMANCE: The subject's initial responses to the cards; the images, or concepts, which the blots evoke in him.

INQUIRY: The phase of the procedure after the entire performance in which various aspects of the concepts are ascertained through direct questioning—e.g., where in the blot was the image seen; were shading, color, or movement used? A subject will sometimes elaborate or modify his initial concept during this phase.

TESTING THE LIMITS: A procedure sometimes employed after the inquiry, to see how close to or far from availability are capacities which the subject has not used spontaneously.

TIMING: The length of time that elapses from the moment a card is first handed to the subject until he begins each response is indicated in seconds: thus, (50″) indicates a fifty-second lapse.

POSITION: ∧ indicates that the card is held in the upright position. ∨ indicates that the card is held upside down. > or < indicates that the card is held sideways. (The apex always indicates the top of the card.)

ADDITIONAL: New concept offered by the subject during the inquiry.

FORM LEVEL (OR FORM QUALITY): The congruence between the concept and the shape of the blot, or blot portion, for which it is used.

SOME "SCORING" SYMBOLS:

LOCATION
W: The whole blot is used. In formal scoring, a "cut-off whole" is also identified, when the clear intention is to use the entire blot, al-

though some details are not accounted for. E.g., Card III: "Two cannibals beating drums, although the red parts don't fit."

D: Frequently used large detail, e.g., center portion of Card I.

d: Frequently used small detail, e.g., upper, outer extensions of Card IV.

Dd: Rarely used detail. Sometimes divided into:

dd: tiny detail, e.g., tiny dots below bottom outer edges of Card I.

de: edge detail, in which only contour of blot, e.g., for profile or coastline, is used.

di: inside detail, whose contours are determined by differences in shading within a blot.

do: small detail, only a part of a figure (e.g., the head) is seen where others see the whole body.

dr: rarely used detail, usually part of a D or d, or a rare combination of usual details.

S: White space. Sometimes in combination with other locations, as WS, SD, dS (order depending on relative importance in concept).

DETERMINANTS are "scored." F (form), C (color), M (human movement), FM (animal movement), m (inanimate or abstract movement), K (shading as diffusion, e.g., clouds, smoke), c (shading as texture, e.g., fur, rock). Combinations of these determinants are also scored: e.g., form—color, movement plus color.

CONTENT is "scored" in general terms: animal, human, object, geography, etc.

3

Hans Frank

Like his father, Hans Frank (born 1900) was a lawyer by profession. Unlike his father, who was disbarred for swindling, Frank went on to reach the heights of the German legal profession as leader of the National Socialist Lawyers Organization, president of the German Academy of Law, and Reich Commissar for the Coordination of Justice in the States and for the Reformation of the Law. It is open to question, however, whether his professional standards were any more reputable than those of his father. In his first cases, he was counsel for the defense in various suits brought against the Nazi party. His courtroom successes led to his appointment as head of the party's legal office and, after the Nazi accession to power, as Bavarian Minister of Justice. As Minister of Justice, Frank continued his private practice—which, understandably, became the leading one in Bavaria, and enabled him to acquire a substantial fortune before pressure from Hitler forced him to close it down. Minister Frank also arranged the reinstatement of his father as a member of the bar. The latter quickly became involved in new embezzlements, however, and not even his dutiful son could prevent a second disbarment.

Shortly after the German conquest of Poland, Frank was appointed that country's Governor–General. The German occupation of Poland surpassed in brutality that of any other country during World War II—a sordid distinction for which Frank, "the butcher of Poland," was in large measure responsible. Shortly after his appointment he issued a statement concerning the policies he would pursue in office:

> Poland can only be administered by utilizing the country through means of ruthless exploitation, deportation of all supplies, raw materials, machines, factory installations, etc., which are important to the German war economy, availability of all workers for work within Germany, reducation of the entire Polish economy to absolute minimum necessary for bare existence of the population, closing of all educational institutions, especially technical schools and colleges, in order to prevent the growth of a new Polish intelligentsia. Poland shall be treated as a colony; the Poles shall be the slaves of the Greater German World Empire (NCA., Vol. II, p. 632).

The Jews of Poland were herded into ghettoes, starved, and shipped off to extermination camps; the Gentile population, too, was decimated by starvation, mass killings of hostages, and other measures. The horrifying nature of these deeds is matched by the indescribably crude language in which Frank enjoyed boasting of them. "I could not eliminate all lice and Jews in only one year," he told a gathering of his subordinates, "but in the course of time, and if you help me, this end will be attained" (quoted in Shirer, p. 876). When he heard that posters had been put up throughout Czechoslovakia announcing the execution of seven students, Frank boasted to a Nazi journalist, "If I wished to order that one should hang up posters about every seven Poles shot, there would not be enough forests in Poland with which to make the paper for these posters" (ibid., p. 875).

Having failed in a suicide attempt after his capture by Allied forces, Frank underwent a conversion to Catholicism in his Nuremberg cell. His fulsome philosophizing about his own guilt and that of Nazi Germany did not succeed in averting a death sentence. He was executed on October 16, 1946.

CARD I

1. (∧ 10″) I know just exactly what I said before—the top of a Roman staff, looking at it diagonally from above—*senatus populusque Romanus* (SPQR)
2. (50″) photo of a pelvic girdle and backbone—a cross section
3. (70″) bell hanging from a cross-bar
4. (90″) grotesque profiles looking out
5. (110″) two little birds
6. (125″) two breasts—women's breasts
7. (150″) little angels' heads, lips protruded as if blowing, cherubs
8. (180″) horn stumps of a deer—first and second stages
9. (210″) Caduceus without staff
10. (240″) two little bears, a grizzly bear looking up

INQUIRY

1. It's the top [of the staff] with the legion eagle—strong symbolism . . . Hmmm . . . also a world power . . . how they come and go . . . (W)
2. has bone-and-marrow texture (W)
3. just the shape (D)
4. outline of outer edges (D)
5. little birds or cuckoos sitting on mountaintop (top peaks) (Dr)
6. outline (de)
7. outline (de)
8. (Dr)
9. just the shape (W)
10. grizzly fur . . . very clear fur coloring (top peaks) (Dr)

The popular concept of a winged creature is seen here by Frank—but with a twist! In grandiose language and without reference to the reality of the details of the blot, he inflates the bird into a symbol of power and provides himself with an opportunity to make pontifical statements about political philosophy. The pretentiousness of his response almost conceals the fact that the winged creature of the popular concept is, in his response, merely an inanimate object. Beneath the elaborated exterior, then, there are qualities of flatness and emptiness.

Those qualities are more directly evident in the next concept. Employing his sensitivity, he uses the differentiated texture of the blot to describe "bone and marrow." But these are hard, flat, and uncomforting objects and indicate the flattened and distorted nature of his own sensitivity. The backbone here signifies a preoccupation with his own weakness. The pretension of scientific knowledge in this response is unpersuasive, since the form quality is mediocre: the blot does not resemble a pelvic girdle very much.

The bell he sees is rarely used spontaneously by Rorschach subjects. Frank's identification of it suggests good sense in recognizing and dealing appropriately with an often neglected part of the stimulus situation. That the bell is *hanging* suggests a certain experience of weakness.

If the bell is rarely seen spontaneously by Rorschach subjects, the "profiles" of the next response are extremely mundane. Anyone can find profiles in almost every edge of each Rorschach blot, and there is something rather *cheap* about a man with Frank's intelligence pointing to them here. There is also an ambiguous quality to their "looking out." Are they looking *at* something, are they live human beings? Or, alternatively, is Frank seeing them only as *facing* out, without committing them to sentient human activity and existence? The ambiguity has a possibly psychopathic connotation, and the peripheral profiles suggest very little by way of individuality, of a developed self.

These and the ensuing responses—the birds, the breasts, the angel heads, the horn stumps, and Caduceus—show an obsessive concern with rather irrelevant and unrelated detail—the fragmented productions of an obsessive but unproductive mind. It should be noted that his more lively creatures—the two birds—are placed at a great height. Initially depicting a capacity for flight, for rising above one's present self, they quickly become for Frank symbols of craziness instead. A crazy man has reached close to the top of power and is making ridiculous noises . . .

From the Caduceus symbol Frank has removed the magic wand of healing and left only the dangerous serpents. This is especially striking because his first response to this card involved a staff—of power and violent conquest, not of healing—in the same location.

The image, unique for this group, of "women's breasts," together with the unusual reference to the "bottle" in Card II, the alcoholic nose in Card V, and other responses suggest a degree of concern with what Freudians call "oral needs," that is, extreme infantile de-

pendence. These responses raise the question of dependence on al-
cohol in Frank's life.

The hanging bell in this card, the grave of Christ in Card VI, the
image of "going down the drain" in Card VII, the "magnificent"
sword symbol in Card IX, and a number of other responses suggest a
degree of preoccupation with death in Frank that goes far beyond the
fear of conviction (and of a possible death sentence) that appears in
many of the other records in this group, and indicates a profound
suicidal (and homicidal) trend in Frank which must have been basic
to his personality.

Using a minor and peripheral portion of the stimulus situation, he
responds to its textural qualities again to produce a relatively lively
concept—the bears. Again his good mind is used for the elaboration
of irrelevant detail, while the *little* bears of his concept almost immediately become a fearsome grizzly bear.

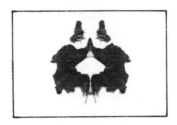

CARD II

1. (∧ 3″) Those are my darling bears [laughs]
2. (30″) beautiful prima ballerina dancing in white dress, with red
   light shining from below . . . [afterthought] black cloak spread
   out, about to wrap it around her
3. (80″) If you just glance at it quickly, it is a top spinning
4. (100″) white, luminescent glass lamp
5. (120″) The red spots could be part of a red butterfly
6. (150″) . . . or a flower
7. (160″) a lake (S) with a canal and a distant tower, moonlight
   gleaming on the water, a little bridge up here

INQUIRY

1. They're holding a bottle . . . just the top part of th
   furry texture (D)
2. She is stepping toward you on the stage, red light c
   footlights (S+D)

3. It is balanced by spinning . . . just the shape (S)
4. It is so bright (glaring) because it is in the darkness (SW)
5. two red wings (top red) (D)
6. red leaves (top red) (D)
7. perspective as from an airplane at night, with moonlight reflected in the water (WS)

He starts with the popular bears, showing (for this group of subjects) unusual vitality in his acceptance of his "animal" instincts. The activity in which the bears are engaged seems inappropriate and arbitrary, however. The reference to the "furry texture" on live animals reflects the egocentric basis on which his sensitivity to other people and other feelings rests.

In the second response, his combination of a well-seen shape, the original additions, and the appropriate use of the red, black, and white colors points to a very good mind. He retreats into the empty background for the central part of his concept, however, indicating a deeply depressed retreat into the void, a confusion of emptiness with substance, and an inability to utilize creative and artistic feminine qualities in a productive way. Finally, his strong concern with public display, and the display quality of his emotionality, becomes apparent in his use of the red as footlights. In his retreat into the void, and possibly also in connection with public display, he experiences the loss of ego control indicated by the spinning top. In the fourth response he again uses the white space, showing how very much centered he is in his emptiness and emphasizing the darkness within him by overemphasising the brightness ("It is so bright . . . because it is in the darkness"). This borderline-manic thinking not only reveals the strength of his depression but also shows that the apparent elation is caused not by any joy but rather by his flight from depression. He has the capacity for ecstatic experience, but only in a setting of headlong flight from profound depression.

His next response indicates the fragmentation of his emotional adaptive responses, as well as his lack of substance and of a center. The wings are not held together by anything live and solid—by a body. In a characteristically random and irrelevant way he now leaps to another concept, the flower. The form is only minimally good, and the color is not appropriate. While there are red leaves, he demands a degree of artistic licence that the quality of this concept, in terms of the shape and color of the blot, does not merit. We see from this that both his thinking and his emotional response can be extremely careless and pretentious.

The final response shows him drawn again to the central empty space of the card. He integrates the empty space with the rest of the blot in a rather brilliant combination of form and shading. This is a quite lovely, appropriate, detailed vista response. But note that the setting is night, the perspective is from above, and the high tower is distant. He is, evidently, engaged in an examined experiencing of the waste which his life represents, but he is doing so in a manner characterized by a flight from reality and by irrationality. The scene, as he describes it, would be very clear from a horizontal perspective; from an airplane, on the other hand, the tower and bridge could not be seen in the way he describes.

CARD III

1. (2″) ah yes, the two Negroes bowing to each other with tailcoats and top hats, a piece of white vest showing, flower in lapel
2. (30″) flying fish
3. (70″) a crab

INQUIRY

1. (usual figures) (W)
2. jumping (lower side) (D)
3. shape (lower center D)

Like so many of his colleagues, Frank responds to this card with an image of himself as a person whose inner dialogue is polite, formal —and superficial. As we might expect from a person with his intelligence, however, his concept is more elaborated than those of his colleagues, but it reflects an obsessive concern with minor detail. We see a concern with status ("hats") and an emphasis on black and white which reflects not only his depression but also his simplistic moral judgment. He wears his sentimentality in the lapel, as it were, using it for adornment and display in a setting of subtly contemptuous attitudes toward other people (he surely had derogatory associations with the "Negroes," who seem here depicted as entertainers).

The flying fish in the second response is good form. As in many of these records, however, when animals are seen in movement—indicating the expression of the person's instinctive vital forces—there is something inappropriate about their action. Here, he choses the one fish whose way of life it is to take on the characteristics of a bird before sinking rapidly back into its deep marine world—an animal which appears unable to determine which is its proper habitat and spends its life leaping from one extreme to the other.

His final response to this card is a concept of the primitive, armored, aggressive dweller in the depths—the crab.

CARD IV

1. (∧ 5″) a big fur for a North Pole traveler . . . a hunter. It lies spread out; upper appendages are not arms but straps to tie it with; the fur stands out clearly and plastically [i.e., in depth]
2. (30″) a railroad track through a dark forest and water (S) left and right, dammed up to make way for the railroad embankment
3. (70″) snakes or eels

INQUIRY

1. It's the outside, hairy, fur side of the animal hide . . . very clear (W)
2. The coloring is like dark woods; trees and grass indicated by the shading. The center line is a straight track through it (DS)
3. just the shape (upper side details)

The shading is used in the first response to produce something warm and soft, indicating Frank's capacity to experience nuances of feeling in human relationships and to derive satisfaction from them. The emphasis on the function of the animal skin, on the other hand, indicates that he is living in a very cold world and that his sensitivity is used to protect him from that world rather than as something warm and comforting. The "straps" of this fur are consistent with its function as a garment and provide an intelligent explanation of what are described in other responses as forelegs, but they emphasize Frank's fear of exposure.

The second concept has a markedly dysphoric quality. He is concerned with transportation from one place in his life to another. The natural flow of water has been interfered with so as to make that journey possible.

The third response seems to reflect his compulsive need to explain every detail in the blot. These are the only two details that he responds to in this card, however, and he has already used them as the straps of his fur garment in the first response. The strong compulsion which draws him back to these details reveals the strength of his need unwittingly to describe himself—through the "snakes or eels"—as a slithery, unpredictable, and low-living animal.

CARD V

1. (∧ 2″) a bat . . . wings, head, legs; it is mounted; could never be like that in real life
2. (40″) two ugly heads . . . one-eyed Cyclops . . . one eye in a criminal head and a beard . . . *scheusslich*! [horrible!] . . . The nose is illuminated . . . like a mask

INQUIRY

1. just the shape; it is furry, but color isn't clear . . . It is opened and mounted (W)
2. profile . . . It has an alcoholic nose . . . ugly (D)

Comment: *Scheusslich! Widerlich!* [Horrible! Revolting!] . . . like Stalin. . . . Did you know that I knew Lenin as a kid in Munich?

At first glance this seems like the most ordinary of conventional, popular responses to this card, scarcely worth commenting on except for its conventionality. A closer examination of the response, however, exposes the great irrationality that can suddenly and startlingly emerge as Frank responds, in what appears to be a conventional way, to a most ordinary situation. Why could a bat "never be like that in real life"? What makes it furry if the color is not clear? If it is the coloring that makes it furry, why is the coloring unclear? Why *is* the bat furry? The notion that this is an *opened* bat, moreover—that is to say, a bat that has been cut open—is quite irrational and not related to the form of the blot. In Frank, then, the appearance of conventionality is unsustained, and is interrupted by spasms of irrationality and violence that reflect his own experience of being opened up and unreal.

The two heads of his second concept are not infrequently seen by subjects of reasonably good intelligence. They are not just the arbitrary profiles he saw in Card I, for he points out various features such as the eye, beard, and nose. On the other hand, there is no basis in the blot for calling the profile a one-eyed Cyclops, and his high-handed attribution of criminality and alcoholism to the head and nose is in no way justified. Indeed, the unjustified projection onto these relatively neutral heads is so great that we may regard it as indicative of serious paranoid distortions in Frank's thinking. The notion of an illuminated nose is quite irrational and is not effectively justified by the explanation that it is an alcoholic nose or by the reference to the mask. Frank's exclamations of horror, moreover, seem quite disproportionate. It is noteworthy that his unwitting self-portrait resembles, in his own mind, the evil figure of Stalin; his identification with dictatorial personalities becomes almost explicit in the reference to Lenin.

CARD VI

1. (∧ 2″) two silver fox furs hanging elegantly on a turned coat-hanger pole . . . soft fur
2. (50″) The outside is a spread-out fur, cat's fur; top a feathery thing . . . whole thing makes a fur display in a show window
3. (90″) could be a grave . . . cross on top, wreaths still on grave and four stakes marking it off . . . a symbol of sorrow . . . flaming metal golden rays from Christ's body on top

4. (150″) grotesque heads
5. (190″) two big fish . . . shimmering silver bodies

INQUIRY

1. It has the texture of soft fur . . . the pole is a masterpiece; shiny black wood (D)
2. outside fur is a different texture (D)
   (1 and 2 make combination W)
3. symbol of death; pieta . . . wreaths hang from cross over grave; two weeks after burial, therefore Christ's figure not finished on cross . . . That's just how it looks [well seen] (W)
4. shape of side profile (D)
5. middle shiny areas (D)

The furs in Frank's first concept are on display in a show window, indicating that the main purpose to which he puts his sensitivity is for the manipulation of other people. A mere "cat's fur" lies underneath; above it is the valuable, and showy, silver fox, the fashionable display fur of the time. The elaborateness of the display, and the piling of layer upon layer, indicates the energy and intelligence that went into Frank's use of his contact with other people for his psychopathic, manipulative purposes. The shiny black pole which he adds to this concept in the inquiry suggests the two sides of Frank's reaction to his own sensitivity. The combination of the impressionable warmth of the fur with the resistant, hard, shiny, and depressingly black qualities of the pole suggests extremes in his reactions to this sensitivity. The hardness is an exaggerated defense against softness. He could from one moment to the next shift from a soft, differentiated understanding of people to a display of ostentatious toughness.

His third concept is a highly elaborated image of tragedy, which, in its well-seen form, again reveals his qualities of intelligence. But the experience of tragedy suggested here is not altogether plausible. Although the grave occupies a large part of the blot, it is more or less ignored in his articulation of the concept. Instead of focusing on the fact of death (including his own imminent execution) and on the colossal destruction which he has brought to the world, he turns his attention to an exploration, in loving but gaudy, sentimental, and rather vulgar detail, of the symbols of redemption. Kitschy as these symbols are, moreover, they are not even completed—as if he is unable to find them very persuasive. The entire concept shares much of the show-window-display quality of the previous response. Fittingly, it is followed by the grotesque heads of the fourth response, for the quality of grotesqueness is much closer to his experience of himself and of the world than is the showy and gaudy compensation for it suggested by the adornments on the grave. In his final response this impression is confirmed still further. He began this card with soft, warm fur and ends with a submerged animal whose texture is that of hard and shiny scales—underneath which there is a largely undifferentiated and undeveloped body.

CARD VII

1. (∧ 5″) two Negresses dressed up with eighteenth-century head-dresses or wigs; kinky hair visible under wigs
2. (40″) bottom part is clouds
3. (60″) [excited] Just look! a powder box . . . very elegant . . . wonderfully shaped, even the screwthread in the neck
4. (100″) melted snow running down the drain, dirty
5. (140″) two Mongolian heads . . . sultans with headdresses

INQUIRY

1. They are making mocking gestures to each other (upper ⅔) (D)
2. brightly illuminated, like clouds (D)
3. outline (S)
4. shading of melted snow, running down the drain, dark and dirty (lower D)
5. (middle D)

Frank is one of the small proportion of this group of subjects who are able to see female figures in Card VII. There is a not very subtle denigration of the feminine aspect, however—in himself and in others—as indicated by the fact that the women are depicted as mocking each other and are referred to, presumably derogatorily, as "Negresses." There is also a careless and unsustained pretentiousness in the elaboration of detail in this concept: why are they eighteenth-century headdresses, and where does he see the "kinky hair visible under wigs"?

Since the Negresses were seen by Frank only in the upper two-thirds of the blot, his organized mind now leads him to account for the lower third, where he sees clouds. We see that the feminine rests, for him, on amorphous and intangible foundations ("clouds") just as it is rather phony, too ("kinky hair . . . under wigs"). As with many of the subjects in this group, Frank sees the lower part of the card in amorphous and undifferentiated terms, revealing a lack of development in, and an immature relationship to, his instinctual life. The "bright illumination," an original addition to the use of this blot as clouds, seems to be a product of false elation. There is no basis in the blot for this concept; if anything, the clouds are more appropriately described as dark. His flight from depression is thus rather disorganized.

In the third response, he is able, by reversing figure and ground and retreating from the dark figures and the amorphous clouds into the empty space, to produce an elegant, beautiful, and irrelevant object. The form is good, and again we have an illustration of Frank's sharp and at times original intelligence. But that intelligence operates, as it were, in a vacuum. When he returns to the substance of the blot again, we have as striking a contrast with the elegant powder box as it is possible to imagine. The dark and dirty melted snow running down the drain, while not poor in form, is extremely dysphoric, and reflects his experience of himself as a dark, dirty person who is going down the drain. The sense of failure, depression, and loss of self expressed in this response is acute, as is the contrast it offers with the elated quality of some of his other images.

The final concept is of rather ugly figures endowed with symbols of high status—another unwitting self-portrait with arbitrary and somewhat irrational qualities (why are these Mongolians or sultans; and on what basis does one leap from Mongolians to sultans?).

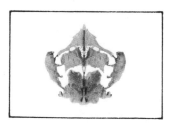

CARD VIII

1. (∧ 5″) wonderful symbols . . . blue silk banners of eighteenth-century hanging across corner of trophy room

2. (50″) [surprised] And here are two animals . . . they could be chameleons

INQUIRY

1. bottom part might be paper flowers, red and orange; banner in middle is typical eighteenth-century blue silk; a victory display (D)
2. just the shape, climbing (D)

There are remnants present—but only remnants—of a rather delicate sensitivity in the blue color and silken texture of his banner. But what they have become is, merely, the tattered relic of an outmoded symbol of masculine prowess. His victory display rests very fragilely on paper flowers.

In intellect and imagination, Frank is considerably more developed than many of his colleagues. That the same primitive symbol of ambitious opportunism found repeatedly in the other records in this collection also appears here serves to remind us of the important ways in which he does, after all, resemble them. He is so taken by the whole that when the obvious animals appear he expresses surprise. Ordinarily, the animals are seen first or, when the other portions of the blot are used as a trophy or display, are incorporated into it. Frank is unable to do that, as if his opportunism is unconnected with and in some respects even overwhelmed by the display quality of his masculinity, and its rather insubstantial nature.

CARD IX

1. (∧ 8″) [enthusiastic] a wonderful sword going up into the light . . . It comes from the fire inside the earth, through the green earth into the sunlight . . . *Herrlich*! [Wonderful!] You could write above, *pax aeterna in coelo* [eternal peace in heaven] [dramatic gesture]
2. (70″) There's the coast of Norway
3. (100″) reindeer horns

   "That sword symbol is wonderful! . . . inspiring!"

INQUIRY

1. [gasps on seeing card again] red flames . . . golden handle of sword, lost in heavenly light above . . . It is a cosmic symbol of life; we rise from the earth through life into the heavens above . . . You see, they just wanted to make an ink blot, but a symbol of life resulted! (W)
2. upper inner right outline (de)
3. just shape (D)

The image of the sword going up into the light is a reasonably appropriate one for this card; form and shading are quite well combined in this response. The overblown, overdramatic details of the image and of the comments that accompany it, however, are striking evidence of Frank's mood disturbances. The transformation of the concept to a "cosmic symbol" is not evidence of a paranoid delusional process, for the basic concept fits the form, colors, and shading of the blot quite well. But if it is not paranoidally delusional in quality, his response does once again show us Frank's escape into ecstasy, a flight from profound depression into what approaches mania.

From the grandiose, overblown concept elicited in his first response, Frank falls into a flat, empty, and mildly pretentious "coast of Norway." The form is not bad, but the contrast between the first response and this highly impoverished second response is startling.

The reindeer horns in the third response (an image once more of aggressive masculine conquest) are also not bad form and, indeed, indicate a slight recovery from his manic flight. But that recovery, such as it is, is negated by further references to the sword. These are not tempered by his direct references to cosmic symbolism and religion. We see that he does indeed find the sword wonderful and inspiring. We also see, now more clearly than before, the phoniness of his religious enthusiasm. For "the symbol of life" to which he refers is, in fact, a symbol of destruction, aggression, and death: the sword.

CARD X

1. (∧ 8″) Eiffel Tower up here, that's clear . . . and the Seine River . . . and the Ile de France . . . It's a poster, "Travel to Paris"
2. (40″) terrible-looking, crablike animals
3. (60″) poster against venereal disease, because it shows backbone and pelvic area
4. (80″) antelope head mounted on a board like a trophy
5. (100″) sun with yellow light around it
6. (115″) engine governor
7. (125″) flower with roots and earth clinging to roots
8. (140″) two ducks; wild ducks flying together carrying something in their beaks together
9. (160″) two heads

INQUIRY

1. Eiffel Tower (upper gray D,) Seine River (center S.), Ile de France (two long pink Ds) . . . just the shape, not so good (built-up WS)
2. microscopic crab shape, blue as in water or crystal (D)
3. just a colored chart (DW)
4. shape (lower green)
5. (D)
6. (usual wishbone figure) (D)
7. shape (upper gray)
8. not exactly blue, but you can see the coloring (D)
9. profile shape (edge of pink) (de)

Comment: "It's uncanny . . . They're just ink blots, but it shows that beauty and a deeper meaning can be concealed in the most unassuming forms . . . You know, it is terrifying . . . A man wants to make an ink blot . . . and the *ink itself* makes a symbol of life. It just shows that the spiritual world is greater than any man's will . . . You psychologists are ingenious in using such methods."

Although the shape of the Eiffel Tower is good in form, the rest of the image is extremely forced: the river and island are very poor form, indeed. Eventually we end up with nothing but a gray tower, with pleasure, excitement and even clarity quite absent.

The terrible-looking crablike animals of the next response reveal Frank's terrible-looking aggression. The microscopic quality of the animals reflects an inept attempt to reduce their horror and minimize his aggression; its irrationality is revealed by the reference to the animals' "microscopic *shape*." Like their fellows the chameleons, these crabs are given their color by their surroundings. Frank's aggression, then, is associated with his opportunism.

The effort at making an attractive travel poster has entirely collapsed by the third response; the Eiffel Tower has become the poorly formed backbone and pelvic area. He is unable to integrate the rest of the card into his concept. The squalor and irrationality of the notion that this is a poster warning against venereal disease are striking. The antelope head of the fourth response is more commonly seen as a rabbit's head; the good form and originality of Frank's concept show once again the operation of his intelligence, which rescues him—albeit temporarily and with the aid of his almost obsessive "horn" concept—from the irrationality and disorganization of the previous and ensuing responses. The sun with yellow light around it is an arbitrary, primitive, and rather childlike concept, reflecting an undeveloped and undifferentiated emotional reaction.

The engine governor is again a good form, and reflects Frank's concern with equilibrium and self-regulation between the extremes of euphoria and deep depression and between his fantasies and his obsessive concern with detail.

He again uses the uncolored portion of the blot to depict a flower with earth clinging to its roots. The flower is clearly dead, and the form is not good for a flower. He is drawn, inexorably, to the gray, achromatic aspect of the blot, emphasizing the recurrent theme of death that has been a part of his life for much longer than the months of his imprisonment and trial at Nuremberg.

Now, again, he shows his remarkable capacity for recovery. The flying ducks are excellent form and an original use of the inner blue portion of the card. After the pathos of the previous response this is a rather beautiful image of freedom from the earth, from the tragic reality which the earth represents to him. He cannot fit the color in, but his use of its shading ("you can see the coloring") shows a live, vital, soaring animal that is his very own, that has sensitivity and an active and possibly meaningful relationship between its two parts ("carrying something in their beaks together"). But in the very last response he retreats to the periphery with the mere outline of the head of a person that is devoid of the shadow of a substance—that is, in fact, merely the perimeter of a shadow.

His final comment involves a resurgence, characterized by an even more forced quality than some of his most euphoric responses, of his efforts to escape from earthly reality and into the "spiritual" world. There is a most incongruous relationship between the magnificent image of spiritual greatness and the toadying to the examiner represented by the final remark.

SUMMARY

"It is as though I am two people," Hans Frank, interviewed in his prison cell at Nuremberg, told Gustave Gilbert. "Me, myself, Frank here—and the other Frank, the Nazi leader. And sometimes I wonder how that man Frank could have done those things. This Frank looks at the other Frank and says, 'Hmmm, what a louse you are, Frank! How could you do such things? You certainly let your emotions run away with you, didn't you?'" (Gilbert, 1950, p. 148).

The instability of Frank's personality has been commented on by numerous writers (e.g., Fest, pp. 209ff.; Davidson, pp. 429ff., etc.), and is amply documented by the historical record. We see him on the one hand as the almost unbelievably brutal Nazi murderer, the butcher of Poland, and the fanatically enthusiastic follower of Adolf Hitler. His hostility to the law is reflected not only in the abominable deeds for which he was executed but also in innumerable statements he is on record as having made during the course of his career. Writing in an SS publication, he referred to judges as "little cloaca animals"; in a not-uncharacteristic decision which he announced during his governor-generalship he warned, "Any attempt on the part of the legal authorities to intervene . . . should be considered as treason to the State" (Davidson, pp. 443–44). And yet it was this same man who, in a series of addresses to German universities in 1942, warned that "no empire has ever been conceivable without justice—or contrary to justice":

> One cannot debase law to an article of merchandise; one cannot sell it; it exists or it does not exist. Law is not an exchange commodity. If justice is not supported, the State loses its moral foundation; it sinks into the abyss of darkness and horror. . . . I shall continue to repeat with all the strength of my conviction that it would be an evil thing if ideals advocating a police state were to be presented as distinct National Socialist ideals. . . . (Fest, p. 210; cf. Gilbert, 1950, p. 141).

Frank's outspoken statements condemning totalitarian illegality cost him his many legal positions in the Nazi party, but not his job as Governor–General. Mindless of his own exhortations, he returned to Poland and to the barbarity of his regime.

Frank's behavior at Nuremberg provides another notable instance of the extreme instability of his personality. We have already seen that after his unsuccessful suicide attempt he turned to religion and was baptized into the Catholic Church. His fulsome pieties, his expressions of guilt, remorse, and horror at what he had done during the years of the Nazi Reich have often been quoted. Particularly famous, perhaps, is his statement that "a thousand years will pass and will not take this guilt away from Germany" (quoted in Fest, p. 219). And yet, despite his repeated acknowledgments of guilt, we find him also writing, in the moments before his execution:

> I am seized now, as I prepare to say farewell to this earth, in order to follow the Fuehrer [!], by the most profound melancholy when I recall this tremendous setting out of a whole great self-confident nation that followed a strong voice as though to a celebration of the eternal Godhead himself. Why, why was it all lost, why did it all fade away, why is it all gone, destroyed? I am seized by uncomprehending horror at the senselessness of destiny (Fest, p. 219).

It is well known that Frank's grandiosity and irrationality expressed themselves in other ways, too. An SS report on his administration of Poland speaks in rather admiring, but highly resentful, detail of the magnificence of his establishment there. With only some exaggeration, it reports that "his day consists of running around from castle to castle in a magnificent carriage with guards of honor, books, music, plays, and banquets. . . . There is nothing natural, no simplicity, all is pose and playacting and serves to satisfy his intoxication, brought about by ambition and lust for power, and at the same time his likeness to Mussolini, of which he is convinced by his flatterers, is interpreted as fate and destiny . . ." (NCA, vol. VI, pp. 749ff.). Frank himself acknowledged to Dr. Gilbert his enjoyment of the perquisites of power: "Ambition," he declared, "had a lot to do with it. Just imagine—I was a minister of state at thirty; rode round in a limousine, had servants . . ." (Gilbert, 1950, p. 147). The SS report quoted above also points to Frank's irrationality and superstition, disclosing that he would spend much time consulting astrologers, palm-readers, card-readers, and other specialists in the occult in planning his future (NCA, vol. VI, p. 749).

The instability of Frank's personality, and its sources and consequences, emerges with great vividness from his Rorschach record. In the first card we see him ranging in rapid succession from the grandiosity of the Roman eagle to the flatness and emptiness of the photograph of a pelvic girdle and backbone, to a bell, to angels' heads, to the horn stumps of a deer, and so on. Rather more specific insights into the nature of these shifts are obtained in later cards. Thus in Card II we see him retreating from a conventional (if ego-centric) perception of reality into a void masked by a strong element of display and followed by the experience of loss of ego control ("a top spinning"). In Card V, we see him responding to a conventional situation with sudden and unpredictable spasms of irrationality and violence; just as in Card VI we see him shifting between (albeit manipulative) sensitivity and "shiny black" hardness. The contrast between the elegant and wonderfully shaped powder box in his third response to Card VII and his "melted snow running down the drain, dirty" of the following response is striking, and the variability of his mood states in Cards IX and X is also remarkable: we see him going from the "wonderful" sword symbolism of the first response to the coast of Norway and reindeer horns and then back to the "inspiring" sword, and from the happy prospect of a holiday in Paris to terrible-looking crablike animals and a poster warning against venereal disease. And more than any other man in this group he shifts constantly in emphasis between black and white, revealing his swings not only in mood but also in ethical judgment.

At one extreme we find him pretentious and grandiose. Without justification, and deadeningly, the popular winged animal of Card I becomes a symbol of Roman power and provides an opportunity to make banal remarks about the transitory nature of world domination. We see the strong display quality of his emotionality in Card II ("foot-lights"); and the impression of pretentiousness is particularly apparent in the turgid symbolism of Card IX and in his comment after Card X. If his condition of profound instability is reflected in the flying fish of Card III—the animal that seems always to be going from one extreme environment to another—then his ostentatiousness (and the lack of development that lies underneath it) is apparent in the shimmering silver bodies of the fish in Card VI. We see in him, too, a concern with status (Card III) and an ego-inflated identifica-tion with one of the two most brutal dictators of modern times (Card V). Images of aggression figure prominently in his record: on a low level we see crabs (Cards II, X), snakes (Card IV), and a "revolting" criminal head (Card V); violence on a more pretentious level is ex-pressed in the sword of Card IX and, to some extent, in the osten-tatious shiny black hardness of Card VI.

Here, then, is one aspect of Frank's personality—overblown, dis-torted, highly irrational at times (and yet with an extremely well-functioning mind at others), egotistical (Cards I and II), extremely manipulative (Card VI), superficial (Cards I, II, III, IX, and X), and opportunistic (Cards VIII and X).

At the other extreme, however, Frank was a weak person (Card I; "And then I am such a weak man," quoted in Fest, p. 211) highly needful of protection from the ice-cold world in which he found himself (Card IV). We see the fragmentation of his mind (Card I) and being (Card II: "part of a red butterfly"); and we see that much of his pretentiousness is really an attempt to fill the void within himself (Cards II, IX, and X). Most strikingly, we see that his flights of euphoria, bordering as they do on mania, are rooted in an attempt to escape from depression (Cards II, IX). He is a dark, dirty person going down the drain (Card VII), and he suffers from a profound sense of failure, depression, and loss of self.

Gilbert has explored in some detail the evidence for a homosexual basis for Frank's strong identification with Hitler (Gilbert, 1950, pp. 149ff.). His need for "submission to the virile authoritarian figure" (ibid., p. 149) that Hitler represented for him was a need for the protection, integration, identity, and importance that Frank lacked, and his lack of which is attributable at least in part to the unadapted and ineffective personality of his own father. But we are surely not going far wrong if we speculate that Frank also sought to meet his needs for protection, integration, identity, and importance through his legal career. Very nearly from the outset of his association with Hitler, however, an obvious conflict began to surface between the penchant for legality of one part of Frank's personality and the utter contempt for legality shown by Hitler. This conflict became more acute as the years went by. Frank's ambitiousness, opportunism, greed, and violence attracted him to Hitler, but other factors (upon which we can only speculate) made him unable to renounce his identification with the law. The conflict intensified. It took the form of a dangerous opposition to precisely those police state methods of which he was one of the foremost practitioners; and it was expressed, too, in the acute guilt which he expressed at Nuremberg while nevertheless being unable to let go of his devotion to his Fuehrer.

In the face of this conflict and the impossible tensions which it engendered in him, we see Frank leaving the field (Cards II, VII, and IX), escaping into euphoria, and experiencing an extreme loss of ego control in the process. The particular dilemma which this response represented for him lay in the fact that the resultant personality disorganization greatly exacerbated precisely those needs for protection, integration, identity, and importance with which he had started out.

4

Hans Fritzsche

The Nazi regime controlled the German population through a combination of terror and "enlightenment," the former being administered by Himmler's "security" apparatus and the latter by Goebbels's Ministry for Public Enlightenment and Propaganda. A particularly important aspect of the propaganda effort was radio broadcasting:

> The crucial role of radio in the Nazi scheme of things was reflected in Hitler's dictum, "Without motor-cars, sound films and wireless, no victory of National Socialism." . . . The extreme radio consciousness of the regime manifested itself in many . . . ways; during his first year in office, Hitler made no fewer than fifty broadcasts, and to obviate the problems posed by the relative dearth of sets, communal listening was instituted. Collective listening to important transmissions became a typical feature of public life in Nazi Germany; many broadcasts were arranged during working hours, and factories and offices had to suspend work for the occasion so that the country's entire labor force could be reached. All restaurants and cafes had to be equipped with wireless sets for such public occasions, and loudspeaker pillars were erected in the streets. . . . There can be no doubt that the Third Reich achieved a denser radio coverage than any other country in the world (Grunberger, pp. 401–2).

A leading official in this effort was August Franz Anton Hans Fritzsche. Born in 1900, the son of a minor post-office official, Fritzsche fought briefly at the end of World War I as a private soldier. Later he studied intermittently at various universities, but never earned a degree. His considerable journalistic talents brought him rapid promotion in his work, however, and by 1932 he held an important position in the Hugenberg empire, a complex of newspapers, news services, and movie studios with a decidedly right-wing bent. After the war Fritzsche had toyed briefly with the idea of joining the Communist Party, but chance encounters with anti-Semitic writers led him in the opposite direction instead. Yet it was not until May, 1933—some months after Hitler's accession to power—that he joined the Nazi Party. From then until the end of the Third Reich his career was within Goebbels's ministry. By 1939 he was in charge of news broadcasting and head of the Home Press division, through which the contents of Germany's 2,300 newspapers were carefully controlled. In 1942 he also became head of the ministry's Radio Division. In addition to his many bureaucratic functions, Fritzsche was also a leading news commentator.

The Nuremberg tribunal found that Fritzsche's broadcasts and other activities were not intended to incite atrocities, and dismissed all charges against him. He was, however, arrested by the German police in 1947 and placed on trial before a German court. With the full text of his broadcasts before it, the court found that Fritzsche had indeed incited his audiences to atrocities, as for instance in his repeated claims that the Jews had started the war and would now have to pay for it; and that he had urged Germans to continue fighting long after the war was lost (Davidson, pp. 550–51). He was sentenced to nine years in jail but pardoned and released in the fall of 1950; he died three years later of cancer.

CARD I

1. (∧ 5″) butterfly
2. (15″) dancing girl with hands in the air
3. (30″) parachute jumper

4. (60″) a priest standing before an altar, hands raised in prayer, head bowed
5. (100″) I also saw a bird without a head, but that's the same as the butterfly

INQUIRY

1. just the shape—mounted, not alive, somewhat torn (W)
2. outline of dancer in the middle with half-transparent veil around her and other veils flying, all in motion (W)
3. fleeting impression as he jumps; body in middle, head bent under, parachute just opening (W)
4. priest is praying; stained glass window behind is only partly represented, with varying shades of light coming through (W)

To the novel situation represented by the first card, Fritzsche responds conventionally and promptly. Upon inquiry, however, he describes the butterfly as "mounted . . . somewhat torn," thereby reflecting his own disintegration and a strongly depressive quality. Next he sees a female figure, an unusual response in this group of subjects, who characteristically negate their own feminine qualities. He reveals a good mind in his ability to organize the rest of the blot in a way appropriate to the dancer in the center. That the girl is described as dancing indicates an attempt to compensate for a depressive mood. In general, the response suggests some originality and some sense of an individual self and of substance as a person—though these qualities are to an extent vitiated by the feeling of exposure suggested by the half-transparent veils that surround the dancer. That these veils are *flying*—in other words, that inanimate objects are depicted in movement—indicates a sense of loss of control over the subject's internal experience, as though there are forces within him that he cannot restrain and which are in danger of taking him over.

The same quality is found in his comment, in the inquiry to the next response, that the parachute is "just opening." The parachute jumper, in contrast to the dancing girl of the previous response, is a figure of extreme masculinity, with intrepid, danger-courting qualities. The next image, of a priest standing in prayer before an altar, suggests an avoidance of the two extremes of masculinity and femininity through a measure of self-abnegation and retreat from sexual identification, as well as of submission to authority.

Fritzsche starts off by trying to make a splash, as it were, to show that he is capable of variability and versatility. But he cannot sustain this effort, and the three human figure responses are essentially minor variations on a single theme. In the last response he retreats to a more conventional concept, as if finding in conventionality refuge from his own inability to be truly versatile. He becomes rather illogical at this point, however, for a bird without a head is *not* the same as a butterfly. He has, as it were, removed the head: his intellect has become exhausted by the flights of imagination attempted in responses 2 through 4.

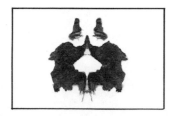

CARD II

1. (∧ 10″) two dancing bears—very clear; or gnomes or dwarfs. Makes a revolting impression; not at all friendly.

INQUIRY

1. The bloody color made me uncomfortable—it doesn't fit the picture at all. The black shape and shading of fur give the impression of dancing bears (W)

Testing the Limits [when told to include red]: Yes, I can finally include the red. Two clowns with red caps and red painted faces or masks, dancing

The bears are seen as both black and dancing, indicating a strong depressive mood and a fight against it. The bears represent the instinctual, animal side of the subject, which is shown as "revolting . . . not at all friendly"; it is also stunted and distorted, as gnomes and dwarfs are. In answer to the inquiry, he declares that the red spots make him "uncomfortable" and that they do not "fit the picture at all." The red, moreover, is described as "bloody." As such, it indicates strong aggressive emotions in the subject which are split off from the rest of his being, unintegrated and uncontrolled. Faced with emotional challenges (as represented by the red), he responds with violent outbursts which are unrelated to the situation and which make him uncomfortable, among other reasons because they are experienced as autonomous and do not seem to him to be a part of himself.

In response to a direct suggestion by the examiner during the inquiry he is able to integrate color with form to produce a relatively adaptive and quite positive image. He could, as it were, "obey orders" to respond in an adaptive way. Even so, however, there is not much real self in such a response and it is superficial and somewhat ludicrous, marked by a strong element of public display and performance ("clowns . . . painted faces . . . masks").

CARD III

1. (∧ 10″) two waiters fighting over a wine cooler
2. (60″) The red just doesn't belong

INQUIRY

1. just the shape of the black part
2. [asked about the red] Well, they could be fighting over a torn heart

The self here is represented by subservient figures ("waiters"), who are in violent competition over something very trivial. This is an arbitrary and inappropriate image and suggests internal conflict in Fritzsche over trivial matters. The intensity of his internal conflict is quite inappropriate to its shallow substance.

In the comment which follows he dismisses the emotional stimulus of the red and, on inquiry, inadvertently reveals why he has done so, by producing an image of considerable violence and brutality. The heart is poor form for this blot, and the image of waiters fighting over a torn heart is still more inappropriate, even irrational. The indications are that when he is pushed to attend to the emotional aspects of a situation Fritzsche is likely to become violent, and, in addition, to fall quite badly in the quality of his intellectual judgment.

CARD IV

1. (∧ 15″) two animal furs, one lying on top of the other

INQUIRY

1. a long fox fur in the middle on top of a broad bear fur; both hairy and distinguishable by their shape (W)

His ability to perceive the shadings of this card as furry indicates a measure of sensitivity to nuances of feeling in himself and in relationships with others. However, the view of this card as comprising *two* furs, with one lying on top of the other, is extraordinary. There is no meaning or substance in this relationship: the furs are not there for warmth or even for display; they are just lying there. Thus Fritzsche's sensitivity serves very little consistent function for him. He is the recipient of many different impressions, but there is no consistency to what he does with them.

CARD V

1. (∧ 5″) a bat, just taking off, because his legs are still down

INQUIRY

1. just the shape (W)

There is still some desire to fly in him, a liveliness and ambition indicated in the remark that the bat is just taking off. But there is also something arbitrary about his reasoning in this response. Why is the bat "just taking off"? Could it not equally well be about to land?

CARD VI

1. (∧ 15″) animal fur—so clear that it eclipses anything else
2. (45″) also makes a musical impression; there's a certain harmony

INQUIRY

1. somewhat similar to cat's fur texture, aside from the obvious cat's whiskers above (W)
2. not only the violin shape of the central portion, but the harmoniously matched texture of the wood in the lower back part; symbolic of music, not realistic (W)

He is delighted by the clarity of an easy and conventional image, and proud of the fact that the image was well made. This aspect of the response ("so clear . . .") indicates an egocentric delight where a conventional or ordinary situation fits his perception of it. The remark that this is similar to a cat's fur reflects characteristics similar to the ones on which we commented in the discussion of Card IV: a cat's fur is not a useful object and in fact is also a rather unpleasant one. Limited as the function of his human sensitivity is, there is also something rather nasty about it.

Having—much to his own delight—established the clarity of this image, Fritzsche now moves on in a compensatory effort to make it subtle and fancy ("a musical impression; there's a certain harmony"). His attempt at elaborate abstraction fails, however, to be persuasive. The violin form is somewhat arbitrary. No doubt he had a tendency to focus arbitrarily on what he chose, whether it was an intrinsically appropriate aspect of the situation or not—and then to insist on his view of it. Of course, he is not really responsible for that view in the last resort ("not realistic"), and if the going gets rough he will back away from it. But until such time as he is forced to do so he can blithely continue to talk nonsense—and with apparent conviction. (There is of course no "lower back part" on a two-dimensional inkblot!)

Like many of his fellow defendants, Fritzsche focuses on the whole blot in his responses. He is a compulsive generalizer, intellectually ambitious and with a need to make everything fit—even if it does not do so in reality.

CARD VII

1. (∧ 15″) a torn map

INQUIRY

1. just the rough outline—nothing definite (W)

Additional: Could also be white silhouette of head and shoulders of soldier in steel helmet (S)

Testing the limits: recognizes dancing figures

The map indicates impersonality, and a desire to impress as an academic or intellectual type. *But what is it a map of?* He specifies that it is a torn map—his world is indeed torn—but he does not say what the map represents; indeed, he says in response to the inquiry that there is "nothing definite" about it. This lack of specificity about something which is ordinarily capable of a great deal of specificity reveals a marked commitment to unreality, and has a psychopathic quality.

From the blank and torn map he moves to what is for him its counterbalance—a steel-helmeted figure of brutality. The blank, torn psychopath here integrates himself by identification with anonymous ("silhouette"), organized violence. This is a highly unusual response, and the reversal of figure and ground here is uncommon. Silhouettes, of course, are not white against a black background.

Fritzsche, we can see from this, not only identifies situations in black-and-white terms—showing a loss of judgmental subtlety, particularly in ethical matters—but is actually capable of a direct reversal of good and evil. He does identify with organized brutality but does not accept it as a part of himself—he denies that it is black—and in effect is identifying with the white while denying its nature.

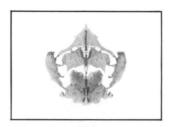

CARD VIII

1. (∧ 10″) combination of two chameleons and delicately colored blossoms and
2. (40″) withered leaves above [tries to combine it with 1, but decides they are separate]
3. (60″) could be the breastbone of a chicken

INQUIRY

1. chameleons are red at the moment, very lively; blossoms are red and brown (D)
2. color and texture; outline isn't very good (gray and blue D)
3. shape of ribs and white spaces (DS)

Additional: could also be colored top (W)

The chameleon, changing color to suit its surroundings, is, of course, an image of opportunism frequently found in these records. These chameleons, however, are "red at the moment." But chameleons do not turn red, and this response brings us back to the kinds of features discussed in Card VII. Fritzsche can, chameleonlike, adapt himself to any situation; but he can also remake a situation to fit his own very easily changeable convictions, even if this entails poor judgment on his part ("*red* chameleons"), and the lowering of his intellect in the setting of his opportunistic roleplaying. If a chameleon can be red, then white can also be black.

As so often in these records, we see the subject expressing his immature, undifferentiated, and sentimental femininity in the perception of "delicately colored blossoms." "Very lively," he goes on to say, without making it quite clear whether it is the color or the chameleons which are lively. This ambiguity suggests a constriction in his instinctual drives and an evasiveness in his emotional response. A considerable effort goes in to making things lively—even to the point of distorting reality, for blossoms are never brown—until in the next response he gives up the effort and finally acknowledges that the lively blossoms are really "withered leaves" instead.

The tenuousness of this light and lively quality, particularly when viewed in conjunction with the "torn map" of Card VII, reflects a basically depressive personality almost completely dependent for any sense of liveliness on external circumstances and structures. When these are destroyed—as they have been for Fritzsche with the collapse of the Third Reich and his own incarceration—he suffers a profound collapse. He becomes, as the withered leaves are, deprived of nourishment and warmth, and his liveliness is quite dried up.

In the failure of his effort to combine the first and second responses he shows his inability to maintain an attitude of overall generalization in the face of the strong emotional challenge of the colors.

What Fritzsche sees as the breastbone of a chicken is frequently described as human ribs. The undeveloped and unindividual nature of the chicken suggests strong regressive qualities in Fritzsche. The further remark that this "could also be a colored top" is an original and creative response. But the color is arbitrary (tops can be any color), which again suggests that he takes emotional relationships into account only in a rather superficial way. Emotional challenges are relegated to the category of playthings rather as, in Goering, human sensitivity is relegated to the bedroom.

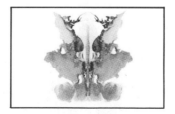

CARD IX

1. (∧ 50″) oil or gasoline lamp blowing out bright light under pressure

2. (∨ 150″) burning oil well or volcano with fiery smoke, lava, and ashes

INQUIRY

1. curved glass lampshade, center glowing flame gives light above red base of lamp (WS)
2. eruption of Vesuvius—brown lava running down mountain, dark ashes and smoke (green), red burning gas or reflection of fire on cloud above (W)

He has now moved a long way from the relatively easy surface adaptation indicated in earlier cards. In the face of the persistent emotional stimulation of Card IX, the contrast between powerful internal pressures and the effort to contain them ("lampshade") becomes extremely striking, and in the second response all containment is abandoned in an overwhelming explosion of violent emotions. The qualities of the second response, moreover, combining color, diffuse shading, and inanimate movement in an image of eruption, convey a sense of loss of control accompanied by a frightened and almost conscious recognition that this is happening. This is *not* a psychotic break, but an experience of ego loss without the actuality of that loss. In the face of persistent emotional stimuli, then, Fritzsche would react with a violent and uncontrolled outburst, which, with great anxiety, he would recognize as such without feeling able to do anything about it. This is a very pronounced version of a fairly common experience in which a person says to himself, "Am I really doing this?" even as he is doing so.

In this card there are long delays before and between responses. He needs to generalize but is having increasing difficulty, because of the strength and violence of his emotional reactions.

CARD X

1. (∧ ∨ 50″) torn flower—stem and calyx are there and colored pieces are scattered around . . . just a little botanical study

INQUIRY

1. color and form give impression of botanical charts with enlargement of cross section of a flower and various flower parts scattered around (W)

Testing the limits: see rabbit's head I saw two sea horses at first but paid no attention because I was looking for an organized picture of the whole thing (lower green D)

The reactions here are indicative of the disintegration of his emotional life. Initially, they convey a sad and pathetic quality, too. Soon, however, he makes an attempt to pull himself together and announces that this is merely a little botanical study. Thus he is able to intellectualize his experience of disintegration in an effort to cope with it.

The additional response in the inquiry is of great interest. We have already commented on this subject's recurrent tendency to respond to the whole blot rather than to parts of it as well. When drawn into commenting on details in the blot he can see the conventional rabbit's head and then adds two sea horses—primitive, undifferentiated animals which in some superficial respects resemble the much more developed animal after which they are named.

Here, then, we see the triteness, triviality, and dullness of the inner individual—characteristics amply evident in his earlier responses—and the depressingly mundane quality of the components of his personality. No wonder that he habitually "pays no attention" to the parts and is "looking for an organized picture of the whole thing." With such a marked degree of inner drabness, who can blame him?

SUMMARY

"Hier spricht Hans Fritzsche"—"This is Hans Fritzsche speaking." Every German knew the voice and was familiar with the name; many and possibly most Germans also believed the substance of his broadcast remarks, some samples of which were culled by the prosecution at Nuremberg and presented as part of the case against him:

But the crown of all wrongly-applied Rooseveltian logics is the sentence "There never was a race and there never will be a race which can serve the rest of mankind as a master." Here, too, we can only applaud Mr. Roosevelt. Precisely because there exists no race which can be the master of the rest of mankind we Germans have taken the liberty to break the domination of Jewry and of its capital in Germany; of Jewry, which believed itself to have inherited the crown of secret world domination.

It is revealed clearly once more that not a system of government, not a young nationalism, not a new and well-applied socialism brought about this war. The guilty ones are exclusively the Jews and the plutocrats. If discussion on the postwar problems brings this to light so clearly, we welcome it as a contribution for later discussions and also as a contribution to the fight that we are waging now, for we refuse to believe that world history will confide its future development to those powers which have brought about this war. This clique of Jews and plutocrats have invested their money in armaments and they had to see to it that they would get their interests and their sinking funds; hence they unleashed this war.

The evidence of letters reaching us from the front . . . demonstrates that, in this struggle in the East [i.e., the war against the Soviet Union], it is not that one political system is pitted against another, not that one view of life is fighting another, but that culture, civilization, and human decency are making a stand against the diabolical principle of a subhuman world.

Today we can only say: blitzkrieg or no, this German thunderstorm has cleansed the atmosphere of Europe. It is quite true that the dangers threatening us were eliminated one after the other with lightning speed; but in these lightning blows which shattered England's allies on the Continent we saw not a proof of their weakness, but a proof of the strength and superiority of the Fuehrer's gift as a statesman and military leader; a proof of the German peoples' force. . . . (NCA, vol. II, pp. 1047–49)

Fritzsche not only broadcast these perversions, these grotesquely deceitful substitutes for the truth; he also, apparently, believed them, swearing solemnly at his trial "that he had never lied or committed a single falsification in the case of any serious questions of policy or of the conduct of the war" (Davidson, pp. 543ff.). Ordinarily one might suspect that a claim of this sort was merely (and transparently) self-serving. But the extent to which Fritzsche instinctively functioned as a propagandist is pointed out by Davidson. Referring to the onset of the German invasion of Russia, Fritzsche recounted that "the Russian divisions had been massed on the German frontier, but General Niedermaier knew that Molotov had made no unfriendly demands" (Davidson, p. 549)! Clearly, this was a man completely at ease with any juxtaposition of truths and half-truths, even where these were mutually contradictory.

His Rorschach record is, most vividly, that of a propagandist—and of a Nazi propagandist at that. We find in him several of the qualities common to this group of subjects. He shares their propensity for violence (Cards II, III, IX), their manipulative use of such sensitivity as they possessed with regard to nuances in human relationships (Cards IV, V); their atrophied feminine attributes, which they are at best able to express in undifferentiated and sentimental form (Cards IX, X); their self-image as comical, ludicrous persons with a strong element of display (Card II); and their psychopathic denial of responsibility for their own concepts. But there are also certain qualities in Fritzsche which, if they are not entirely absent in many of his colleagues, are to be found in a particularly marked form in his personality.

In our analysis of his response to Card X, we commented on the triteness, triviality, and dullness of Fritzsche's inner self. We suggested that his strong need to generalize, to look "for an organized picture of the whole thing," was a compensation for the meagerness of the parts of which he was made up. But that meagerness was, at least to some extent, associated with and caused by a singularly evanescent quality in him. Despite some evidence of individuality (Cards I, III), he appears to find it very difficult indeed to hold on to himself, to remain, even minimally, a consistent and integrated person. In Card II we noticed that his outbursts of violence make him uncomfortable because they are experienced as autonomous and do not seem to be a part of himself—but also that he could, when guided to do so, respond in a healthy, adaptive way to emotional stimuli. Another aspect of this same basic evanescent quality became apparent in his response to Card IV, where we observed that his sensitivity serves very little consistent function for him. In Card VIII we saw that his emotional responses tend to be evasive and inconsistent.

Here then, it would appear, is the first set of ingredients in the making of Hans Fritzsche, the Nazi propagandist. Given the evanescence of his personality and the sense of a loss of control (Cards II and IX) which he experiences in situations of emotional challenge, a need for clarity and precision as he looks at the world—in this sense, for stability—is understandable enough. And indeed we find that need expressed in his enthusiasm at discovering that Card VI is an animal fur—"so clear that it eclipses anything else." The wording of this response, as well as its substance, serves to illustrate our point here, for why should Fritzsche be so delighted at the fact that "it eclipses anything else" if the constant intrusion of new possibilities, each as ephemeral as the one it supplanted, was not a familiar source of anxiety to him?

Having once managed to pin down the obvious, however, Fritzsche's pretentiousness and ambition (e.g., Card I) and, no less important, his own psychopathic inability to remain consistent force him to elaborate his concept into something grandiose—the miserable cat's fur becomes a violin with harmoniously matched texture, a symbol of music. We have arrived, accordingly, at the second group of Fritzsche's characteristics as a Nazi propagandist. Just as his psychopathic evanescence of being led to the drab and trivial nature of the parts of which his personality was composed, so, too, was his attempt at holding on to what is clear and obvious vitiated by that psychopathy. He clutches at the obvious only to have it slip beyond his grasp as, inflating it into grandiose form, he makes it unreal and implausible. In this respect he is, indeed, caught in a bind. He needs clarity but distorts it the moment he perceives it for the very same reasons which led him to need that clarity in the first place.

But that evanescence now is less problematic for him, for it has brought him up to a level of grandeur that he finds gratifying. If one cannot hold on to reality (or for that matter to unreality), it is preferable to act out the tenuousness of one's being on an inflated and pretentious scale rather than on a merely mundane one. And Fritzsche sustains himself on this high level by the conviction that his focus on things is the correct one, no matter how distorted others might consider it to be. Should the pressure of reality become too immediate, however, he can always change his perception, since he was never in any case really responsible for it (Card VI: "not realistic"; Card VIII: "chameleons are red at the moment").

All this does not yet quite add up to the distinctly *Nazi* propagandist. It is not that Fritzsche is a profoundly committed Nazi. He is, after all, a psychopathically opportunistic chameleon—"red at the moment"—who joined the Nazi party only after Hitler had seized power. The added ingredient that will make him into a Nazi propagandist is found in Card VII. Here we see him identifying with violence, but in a way that is quite distinctive. It is not just that he escapes from his blank, torn, impersonal, and pretentious map into an identification with violence. Precisely because of the nature of that map, because of his nature as described in the preceding paragraphs, he identifies with violence while denying its nature as violence.

Here, then, is Fritzsche, the Nazi propagandist. His psychopathic evanescence of being is at least in part responsible for the trivial and mundane quality of that being. His restless and perpetually tentative efforts toward achieving a grander self are also dedicated to a denial of the great violence which is also a part of his self (and which, in part, also serves to compensate for his drabness). He is the Sisyphus of the lower world; the boulder he pushes is not that of redemption but that of the most squalid, grandiose, and brutal falsity.

5

Walther Funk

Walther Funk was born in 1890 into a prosperous East Prussian family. Educated at the universities of Leipzig and Berlin, he earned a doctorate in economics and then began a career as a financial journalist. In 1916 he joined the editorial staff of the Berlin *Boersenzeitung*, a leading stock-exchange paper, and rapidly became an advocate of the interests of the major German industrialists. In 1926 he was appointed editor of the newspaper and, along with his friend Schacht, was considered among the most influential economists in postwar Germany. A homosexual scandal, however, cost him his job on the *Boersenzeitung* (Dutch, p. 176). Having already played an important role in obtaining financial support for the Nazis from Krupp, Thyssen, and other major industrialists, Funk now joined the Nazi party and was quickly appointed Hitler's personal economic advisor and the chairman of the Committee of the Nazi Party on Economic Policy.

When Schacht "came on board" the Nazi boat, Funk was moved to Goebbels's Ministry for Public Enlightenment and Propaganda as Undersecretary and head of the Press Bureau. After Schacht's resignation from the Ministry of Economics in 1938, Funk was appointed to succeed him, and he remained in that position, and as president of the Reichsbank, until the end of the war.

In these positions, Funk played an important role in the financing of Hitler's preparations for war and of the war itself. As president of the Reichsbank, moreover, Funk entered into an agreement with Himmler under which the gold, jewels, and currency stolen from the victims of the SS, including those exterminated in the concentration camps, were stored in the Reichsbank.

The Nuremberg tribunal found Funk guilty on three counts of the indictment and sentenced him to life imprisonment.

CARD I

1. (∧ 25″) [laughs] two men are grabbing a woman and she's protesting with hands in the air—or maybe they're dancing

INQUIRY

1. They're probably dancing around her (W)

The human-movement response offered by Funk differs from the winged creatures which a large proportion of Rorschach subjects usually see in this card. This is an introversive response, and shows the subject dealing with a new challenge by withdrawing into himself, into his concern for his own being and self-image. The concept he offers is not bad in form, but it is striking in its immediate image of aggression, violence, conflict, and protest. This is then quickly covered by an innocuous public performance ("they're dancing"). The aggression in the response reflects his aggression toward others and, no less, conflict within himself. Clearly, the masculine side of his personality is aggressing against the feminine and impeding its freedom. The dancing indicates efforts to counter depression, which has at least some of its roots in the collision of his masculine and feminine aspects, and for which he compensates by superficial display.

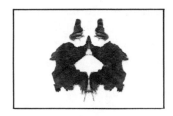

CARD II

1. (∧ 25″) could be two men dancing, an ecstatic dance, but I don't know why the head and feet are red—maybe from exertion; they're sweating

INQUIRY

1. They are harlequins clapping hands together; the little specks around their heads show they're sweating; head and feet are flushed (red) from exertion (W)

Two men are frequently seen in this card, but it is more common to find them depicted as clapping hands—as Funk describes them in the inquiry—than as in an ecstatic dance. That he initially comes up with that response indicates the intensity of his counterdepressive efforts; he is working off anxiety and depression through exertion to the point of sweat. His sudden shift to a consideration of minute and ordinarily irrelevant detail here—"the little specks"— suggests that this must have been a nit-picking sort of person.

The harlequins—masquerading clowns—are a frequent self-portrait among this group of subjects. Presumably if he had been asked why they were harlequins he would have pointed to their red hats. He then goes on to describe the harlequins' heads as flushed (red) from their exertions. In doing so he is making an effort at appropriateness, and finds good reason for it ("maybe from exertion"). But this makes the clowns' faces, and indeed their entire heads, the same color as their hats, which is surely going too far: in the end, and most implausibly, even their feet are flushed red by the exertion.

He begins, then, with a very good idea, but, carried along as he is by the strong emotional stimulus of the red, his effort at rationalizing founders. The result of his attempt to rescue himself from depression, fear, and anxiety is almost as grievous as are those feelings themselves: the attempt causes him to lose control, in terms of both emotional response and logical appropriateness. In effect, he becomes panicky and irrational. If his depression, fear, and anxiety are a Scylla, his attempts to counter them prove a Charybdis.

His deep depression is in part surely a consequence of the denouement of his dreams for himself and for the Nazi movement. With the notable exception of Speer, all the subjects in these records express profound depression. But there are distinctive ways in which each does so, and these in turn are keys to central parts of their personalities. Funk's profound depression, his attempts at rescuing himself from it, and the loss of control to which these attempts lead, tell us not only of his present quandary but of how, in general, he deals with depressing situations and moods.

CARD III

1. (∧ 5″) two apes greeting each other and taking their hats off—half-monkey, half-man
2. (40″) two monkeys hanging by their tails
3. (80″) hip bone, I suppose

INQUIRY

1. just the shape of the black part (W)
2. just the shape—there are no red monkeys—although there was a famous whorehouse in Leipzig called "the blue monkey" (outer red D)
3. just the shape (center red D)

The superficial courtesy of two apes greeting each other in this response is, of course, a self-portrait of the man who produced it. He is, then, a crude, unevolved person who, under the prompting of courtesy, can become something more than merely an ape—he can become half a man.

The red monkeys he describes in the second response are quite good form, but underline the primitive qualities of the man. There is evidently somewhat more vitality in Funk than in most of his colleagues (i.e., he sees live animals in a live position), but this is vitiated to an extent by the fact that the monkeys are merely "hanging." His stress on the fact that there are no red monkeys is an example of concrete thinking. The reference to the Leipzig whorehouse is a rather unattractive effort to be funny, worldly, and chummy with the examiner, and also suggests that his vitality is associated with a crude and impersonal sexuality.

In the third response to this card he is drawn by the exciting color of the red but is able to use the outline only, and in a withdrawn fashion. His concept is bare and isolated, suggesting a flat, lifeless, and hard quality that is devoid of emotion ("just the shape"). His attempt to show off his scientific knowledge is quite unsuccessful, as the hip bone concept is poor form.

CARD IV

1. (∧ 6″) dancing bear, but the head doesn't belong
2. (40″) head of a grotesque animal

INQUIRY

1. shape and movement of a dancing bear, and the hairy hide (W)
2. shape of jackal's head (lower D)

The intense shading and rather menacing form of this card frequently evoke concepts such as an animal skin or a large, strong masculine figure (although the latter is rarely seen in this group). The card brings out a person's capacity to give and receive emotional nourishment, his sensitivity to nuances of feeling, or the nature of his masculine qualities. In his response, Funk reveals undeveloped and distorted versions of these attributes. He does not commit himself to either an animal skin or a strong, aggressive male, but to a bear. Finally, instead of genuinely vital movement, the bear is doing something unnatural to him, which also happens to be rather comical as well (only trained bears dance). The subject might once have developed a strong, sensitive, vital masculinity, but he has been arrested in these areas. Instead, he has become rather unreal, with a mind and instincts that don't go together ("the head doesn't belong"), with a strong depressive quality, and with an immature and egocentric nature.

In the second response he does manage to deal with a head, which did not belong, as he put it, in the previous concept. The lower part of each card is habitually avoided by the subjects in the present collection, who thereby reveal their difficulty in integrating their instincts with the other parts of their personalities. The nature of at least one of our subjects' drives becomes apparent here: Funk sees a grotesque animal's head which, on inquiry, turns out to be that of a jackal. A jackal is one of the least attractive members of the animal kingdom, for he attaches himself to bands of more powerful animals and feeds on the leftovers of their victims: he is, in other words, a carrion eater.

CARD V

1. (∧ 3″) a bat, very clear

INQUIRY

1. shape of a flying bat and the dark night color (W)

This is a common response, and Funk appears delighted with the clarity of the obvious. The description of the bat as flying, and suggests a slightly closer contact with the instinctual side of his nature than is to be found in many of his colleagues. The "dark night color," with its sense of an endlessly deep and gloomy void, points to intense depression.

CARD VI

Comment: "Oy-oy-oy, they're getting crazier."
1. (∧ 30″) a sword that's been thrust in somewhere
2. (60″) animal hide stretched out

INQUIRY

1. dark shape of sword above, thrust into this center line (D)
2. valuable *dachs* (badger) fur has black–gray texture like this (W)

His mock lamentation and the comment that "they're getting crazier" is an entirely uninsightful report of his experience when confronted by the stimuli represented by this card. *He* is getting crazier in the face of these situations, and with considerable ease he projects his craziness onto the external situation, taking no responsibility whatsoever for his own irrationality. What is affecting him in this manner is the shading of this blot, with its implication of sensitivity, and, to an even greater extent, the masculine and feminine attributes of this card.

He uses the phallic projection as an instrument of pure and meaningless violence: the sword is thrust in "somewhere" and it hardly seems to matter where, so undifferentiated and purposeless is his violence. The *thrust* of the sword seems to carry some implication of a loss of control over his feelings of violence. It would seem that the violence in this man is particularly elicited in situations which call for an appropriate display of his masculinity and for some differentiated response to his own feelings and to those of others. In such situations, he will lash out blindly and with great brutality, attacking the sensitive parts of his own nature and their projected representations in the environment. "We must destroy any vestiges of softness," this man might say in response to appeals to kindliness or understanding.

The emphasis on the *stretched* hide in the second response is frequent in this group of subjects, and reveals an experience of harshness and violence where what can be evoked is softness and delicacy. The inquiry elicits an unusual concept. The fact that the badger fur is "valuable" shows his utilization of sensitivity to nuances of feeling for gain and for manipulative purposes; while the "black-gray" colour of the fur is yet another indicator of depression.

The badger, intermediate between a weasel and the bear which appears in two of Funk's responses, is a nocturnal, hibernating animal that digs itself into burrows, which it defends against attack with its powerful jaws. This self-portrait of Funk, then, is of a subterranean night animal who is frequently hunted but who has powerful and violent resources with which to protect himself.

CARD VII

1. (∧ 20″) two children or cherubs dancing on a cloud
2. (40″) monument with two figures

INQUIRY

1. shape of children's chubby cheeks and texture of clouds (W)
2. outline (lower gray inside black) (dr)

The feminine qualities of this blot are viewed by him first in childish and immediately thereafter in angelic terms. This is to say that the feminine aspects of his personality are undeveloped and have a certain unreal but cloying and sentimental quality to them. Insubstantial as such, they are made all the more so by the fact that they are dancing on clouds rather than on *terra firma*. The dancing is indicative of counterdepressive efforts; here those efforts are shown as drawing on his feminine aspects, though they are able to do so only in an ineffective and insubstantial manner.

The second concept is unusual. It presents an image of human beings dwarfed by a monolithic monument and indicates Funk's subjugation of his own person to an empty (for he makes no attempt to say what it is a monument to or of) and impersonal idea.

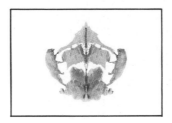

CARD VIII

1. (∧ 10″) two bears
2. (25″) fruit blossom, stalk and leaves

INQUIRY

1. just the shape of climbing bears (D)
2. red and brown blossoms below, center stalk, green leaves (D)

In the general population of Rorschach subjects, "bears" is among the most common responses to the two pink images at the side of this blot. Ordinarily, one would not comment on Funk's response except to say that he is capable of appropriate responses in conventional situations. In view of the frequency with which chameleons, in particular, occur among *this* group of subjects, however, we may speculate that Funk was perhaps less ambitious and opportunistic than his fellows.

It is also common to see the central parts of the blot as some kind of plant. However, his identification of the blue details as green leaves is arbitrary and unexplained; he inaccurately refers to the pink and orange as "red and brown"; and it is, of course, inappropriate to describe blossoms as brown. These are features which are encountered in other responses to this card among the present subjects. That Funk sees fruit blossoms rather than the fantastic marine plants seen by several of his colleagues suggests that he is rather more down-to-earth than they. In due course fruit blossoms give rise to fruit, and here are suggestive of a capacity for the development of real feeling and for creativity. In Funk, however, this capacity is unused and distorted; the brown blossoms are withered and will never produce any fruit.

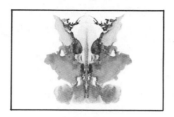

CARD IX

1. (∧10″) two deer
2. (25″) woods with tree in middle
3. (60″) man holding grotesque animals by his hand and foot, a pole projecting out of his stomach; maybe giving birth to these animals —oxen, dragons, deer

INQUIRY

1. shape of their faces and horns (di)
2. green woods and tree in middle (D)
3. shape of a man (pink D) and oxen (green D), deer (di inside green), dragons (orange D), but the colors don't apply (built-up W)

Funk's rapid response to this difficult card shows a good, quick intelligence; he responds with good, if not original, form to a detail. In a situation that is too complex for him to generalize, he can act within limitations and pick out certain aspects with which he is capable of dealing effectively. The deer—a timid and hunted animal—is a concept which represents him as both the hunter and the hunted.

To see the deer, the card must ordinarily be turned sideways. Neither in this or in any other card does Funk do so, however, and we must assume that instead of turning the card he turns his head. He is thus outwardly conforming to what he assumes is authority—the examiner has told him neither that he can turn the card nor that he can not do so—while at the same time finding, perhaps rather sneakily, his own way of circumventing authority.

His second response is an extremely primitive version of the vista response—i.e., an examination and contemplation of his life. Here again we discover in him an undeveloped and destroyed capacity. The undifferentiated and sparsely stated response indicates the poverty of mind and imagination with which he examines his life and suggests a preoccupation with status rather than with any real philosophical concern. Some capacity for spontaneous emotional reaction, albeit at an undifferentiated level, is suggested by the direct and unpretentious way in which he refers to the green woods using the color appropriately.

In his first two responses to this card, Funk behaves in a restrained and intelligent way. On further exposure to the stimuli of this card, however, he loses his good judgment, not only offering inappropriate responses but failing to recognize that he has reached the limits of his capacity and would be well advised to put this card down and wait for the next one. What seemed like a modest and realistic acceptance of his limitations, as reflected in the way in which he confined his responses to details of the blot, now gives way to a confused, elaborate, arbitrary mixture of irrelevant details held together by an irrational generalization.

The forms in this response are a striking combination of good and bad. The unpredictable but rapid movement from good to bad responses and then back to good ones, is, in the Rorschach, often an expression of schizophrenic thinking. The use of the entire pink area for the man and the green for oxen is extremely poor form, though the deer and possibly the dragon (we do not know quite how he used the orange for the dragon) are good form, and *part* of the pink would be reasonably good form for a man. Even if this response does not indicate a complete psychotic breakdown, it reveals a very considerable capacity to combine reality with the irrational, and points up an underlying schizophrenic component.

It is notable that Funk developed this entire complex and distorted concept without turning the card on its side. Funk, it is apparent from this response, has an awful lot on his hands. He is hanging on to qualities of grotesqueness and distortion, castrated bestiality, timidity, and mythically horrendous danger. Indeed, he not only has all this on his hands, but his irrationality has become so great in the face of these brutal qualities that he is even holding them by the foot. And he is also, as he suggests somewhat later, giving birth to them. As such, he is revealing the horrible distortion of his feminine side while at the same time taking credit for an increasingly vile assemblage of qualities that he is, in fact, incapable of producing, for men do not give birth. There is the most appalling ego inflation apparent here, as he identifies with the creation of bestialities that in fact surpass his own capacity to create.

The pole projecting out of the man's stomach would have been appropriate form merely as a pole; here, however, it is an example of concrete thinking and a further expression of Funk's irrationality. It is a long projection which he has not otherwise explained, so it seems obvious to him that it must be a pole projecting out of the man's stomach.

In this elaborate buildup of brutal ambition and irrationality he cannot take emotional qualities into account and must deny them; the colors, as he says, "don't apply."

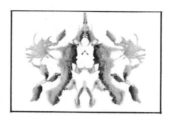

CARD X

1. (∧ 10″) again the hip bone or pelvic girdle
2. (30″) two gremlins busy with human vertebrae
3. (60″) A lot of gremlins and witch animals have torn a man's body apart—the red is the two halves of a man's body and there are pelvic bones top and middle—a representation of the witches' kitchen in Faust, the *Walpurgisnacht*

INQUIRY

1. shape (center blue D)
2. animal figures gnawing at the base of the spine (upper gray D)
3. The red is flesh color, but the colors don't apply to the other figures—it's all confused (W)

EXAMINER: That last picture might be in a concentration camp.
FUNK: I can't stand reading about those things—I get sick to my stomach. I've been occupied with art and beautiful things all my life. . . .

His initial, and speedy, response to the unrelenting emotional stimulus of this card is one which expresses his bare, hard, flat, and isolated attributes. From this he moves on to a concept of gremlins gnawing at human vertebrae. His strength and courage—his backbone—are being eaten away by two nasty, subhuman creatures.

As in Card IX, he cannot remain content with a relatively rational and unambitious response to details, but must ambitiously attempt to respond to the entire blot. As with that card, in doing so he reveals the most frightful aspects of his personality. His compulsion to include and explain everything in a grandiose way comes out as a full expression of the sadism and brutality of which he is capable. Even some of his emotions are involved in this horrible concept of a man's body being torn apart; for the most part, however, he is quite unemotional about this ghastly violence—violence of which he is both perpetrator and victim. Presently, he places this scene in a mythological context: he participates in about as evil a deed as any human being, or for that matter any gremlin or witch, can, but then denies responsibility for it with the suggestion that it is a scene from Goethe's *Faust*. The pretentiousness of this reference reminds one of the pretentious rationales which the Nazis adopted to justify their own violence. We must also note that it is only in this context of extreme violence that Funk's repressed and distorted feminine aspects—as represented by the witches and the reference to the kitchen—are able to express themselves at last.

The examiner's impressive inspiration of suggesting that the last concept might be a scene from a concentration camp reveals not only Funk's brazen dishonesty but also his unabashed egocentricity. He cannot stand reading about concentration camps, not because he is upset about the fate of the people who suffered and died in them but because it interferes with what he preposterously claims to have been a lifelong preoccupation with art and beauty.

SUMMARY

Walther Funk appears to have regarded himself as one of nature's more perfect accomplishments. His life had been devoted to the pursuit of beauty, we have seen him tell Dr. Gilbert; and in a letter—presumably to his wife—which he wrote from his cell in Spandau, he added to our view of him with these words: "I belong to those happy and yet unhappy beings born to love. I cannot hate. I cannot hate a single human being. Hate is nothing but an inferiority complex. I looked always for the beautiful, the goodness in men" (Fishman, p. 54).

Funk did indeed have a strong interest in "culture." To an extent, this was expressed by a certain talent in playing classical compositions on the piano. Much more characteristically, however, his proclivities for "art and beauty" revealed themselves in his tenure as vice-president of both the Reich Chamber of Culture and the Reich Senate for Culture from 1933 to 1945. Through these bodies, the Nazis pursued their policies of utilizing culture for their propaganda of racism and violence. As apt an evocation as any of the nature of official "culture" in the Third Reich, and of Funk's own appreciation of art and beauty, can be found in the grotesque but nevertheless "cultural" image of violence produced by Funk in his response to Card X. But even such a perversion of high culture in the service of a totalitarian state, the state's use of some of humanity's loftiest capacities to rationalize and indeed encourage some of its basest propensities, does not reveal Funk's true "lifelong preoccupation with art and beauty." His was, as we have seen, of a vulgar, flat, immature, and uninsightful nature; his sensitivity was used for gain and manipulation; the feminine aspects of his personality were undeveloped, cloying, and destructive. These qualities, surely, preclude any real ability to involve oneself in art and beauty.

The crudity of Funk's personality as revealed in the Rorschach was matched by that of his physical appearance, described by Kelley as "short, waddling, fat and paunchy-heavy, coarse-featured" (Kelley, 1947, p. 181). In his own unwitting self-portrait, Funk emerges as a "half-monkey, half-man" (Card II). As such, his aesthetic inclinations are much more accurately revealed by the "extraordinary and inexhaustible repertoire" of obscene songs for which he was known, and by the ever-more imaginative orgies that he would hold at the magnificent country estate which the grateful captains of German industry had presented to him (Fishman, pp. 40–41; cf. Card III ["the blue monkey"]).

Even more appalling in its lack of self-understanding is Funk's claim that he was a man free of hatred, one of "those happy and yet unhappy beings born to love." He was, far from this, a man of great violence and brutality. In Card IX we see his ego inflation at work as he identifies with qualities of sadistic grotesqueness that surpass his own capacities.

In the unwitting self-portrait he presented in response to Card IV, Funk was a jackal, exploiting and feeding off others' violence to an even greater extent than he was directly engaged in violent activities himself. And what could be more jackallike than his agreement with Himmler that the Reichsbank would store in its vaults the plunder torn from the murdered corpses of the concentration camp gas chambers—their gold teeth, jewels, etc?

Funk's personality was an extremely labile one. He could react even to quite ordinary situations with an undue discharge of emotional energy in which his reason would be quite overwhelmed (Card II). His volatility could also bring forth sudden explosions of great violence. We get an insight into this aspect of his personality from an incident at Spandau recorded by Fishman (p. 42). Prison regulations required that a light be shone in each convict's face three or four times an hour as he slept. This measure, designed to frustrate a suicide attempt, would sometimes drive Funk into a great rage. The guards had been instructed not to enter his cell to quiet him down on such occasions. One night, however, a guard unwisely unlocked Funk's cell, intending to go in and get him to stop creating a disturbance:

> The fat body of Funk hurled itself at the rash visitor, knocking him to the floor. A raging, screaming animal, so it appeared, then grasped the guard's neck, striving to choke the life out of him. Gasping for breath, the Frenchman somehow managed to unlock the grip on his throat, but pint-sized Funk, with the strength of madness, lifted him up and threw him bodily out of the cell.

We have seen that this thoroughly unattractive man would use his sensitivity to nuances in relationships for purposes of manipulation (Card VI). Another anecdote recounted by Fishman illustrates this aspect of his personality. Funk had suffered from a variety of chronic infirmities since early adolescence—a circumstance which he attributed to the venereal disease he had contracted at the age of 13 (Fishman, p. 40). He learned, however, to use his illnesses manipulatively to his own advantage. "If, for instance, he was visited by his crony Dr. Ley, the Labor Front leader, and realized that Ley wanted some finance or signatures from him, he would sit moaning and groaning behind his desk, giving Ley a long report on the state of his health until his visitor would finally say, 'Walther, it breaks my heart to trouble a sick man like you,' and go away without obtaining what he had come for" (Fishman, p. 40).

6

Hermann Goering

Hermann Goering was undoubtedly the most important defendant at the Nuremberg trial. Hitler's chosen successor until the last days of the Third Reich (when Hitler tried to have him assassinated), his power for a long time equalled, if it did not actually surpass, that of Goebbels and Himmler.

Goering distinguished himself as a fighter pilot during the First World War. Awarded the Pour le Mérite, Germany's highest decoration for valor, he became Von Richtofen's successor as commander of the famous "Flying Circus" squadron in 1918.

His friend Ernst Roehm introduced him to the Nazi party, which he joined in 1922. In December of that year he was appointed commander of the S.A., the Nazi vanguard of storm troopers, whom he led in the abortive beer-hall *putsch*. Injured in that uprising, Goering fled Germany and returned only in 1926 under the cover of a general amnesty. He reorganized the S.A. and in 1927 was one of the first Nazis elected to the Reichstag. Three years later he was elected president of that assembly, and in January 1933 he was one of the three Nazis in Hitler's first cabinet.

Immediately after the Nazi accession to power, Goering was appointed to a number of key positions in Prussia. In rapid succession he became Prime Minister, Minister of the Interior, and Chief of the Gestapo in Prussia. At the same time he was also made Reichsminister for Air. In that capacity, he set about rebuilding the *Luft-waffe,* the German air force, of which, in 1935, he was appointed commander in chief. In 1936 he was also appointed plenipotentiary for Hitler's Four-Year Plan.

This list of appointments, which represents only the more important ones held by Goering, will indicate the scope of his contribution to the Nazi dream. He played a leading role in the development of the police-state machinery of terror; he supervised the economic and industrial preparations for the conquest of Europe by Nazi forces; he built up the German air force as a principal tool of that conquest. It was he who created the first concentration camps, and he who was a, and possibly the, mastermind behind the Roehm purge, the Reichstag fire, and the *Kyrstallnacht.* It was he, too, who supervised the maneuvers connected with the annexation of Austria and who, by openly threatening to bomb Prague, forced the capitulation of Czechoslovakia's President Hacha to the German annexation of the Sudetenland.

The increasing ineffectiveness of the *Luftwaffe* cost Goering much of his standing with Hitler. By 1944 "he was finally out of the game; he was left his rank and position solely as an act of charity" (Fest, p. 80). So appalling was his record of crimes up to that point, however, that the judges at Nuremberg declared that "his guilt is unique in its enormity. The record discloses no excuses for this man." He was found guilty on all four counts of the indictment against him and sentenced to death by hanging. An hour or so before he was to be executed, however, Goering swallowed one of several cyanide capsules that had been smuggled into his cell—we still do not know by whom—and thus cheated the hangman.

Comment: "Oh those crazy cards again* . . . [laughs] . . . you know, one of the old gents said you showed him a lot of vulgar pictures."

CARD I

1. (∧ 10″) funny beetle
2. (30″) a bat

---

* This is a retest. Goering's original Rorschach record is not available.

INQUIRY

1. just the shape (W)
2. It is the shape of a bat, but really not so good; the gray–black color gives an involuntary impression of a night animal (W)

In the initial comment we see something of Goering's well-known humor and playfulness. The comment also reflects, however, an instinct for identifying himself with authority—regardless of the nature of that authority and regardless, too, of his former associations. Elevating himself above "the old gents"—i.e., his fellow defendants—he places himself on a par with the authority of the young, strong, professional examiner to whom he is himself now subject.

At the very outset we get an impression of a man who has very negative feelings about himself and about his situation, and who accepts responsibility for neither. It is common to find this card viewed as a winged creature, frequently a butterfly or a bat. Goering, however, first sees a beetle—an insect, possibly verminous, that is far removed from the beautiful and soaring qualities of the butterfly and from the evolved nature of the bat. In the second response he rises to the level of the conventional and sees the bat. In both concepts, however, his psychopathic dissociation of responsibility for himself is evident: the beetle is *funny*, and the bat is *really not so good* and, moreover, gives *an involuntary impression* of . . .

Ordinarily, the color of the bat is not noted. That it is described here, as in many other records in this collection, as "gray–black" points to Goering's depressive mood quality. The further description of the bat as "a night animal" has more general connotations, and indicates that his depression is not only related to his present situation; rather, the crisis in which he now finds himself has opened up, perhaps for the first time in his life, the blackness that has always been within Goering, a deep, dark, formless void.

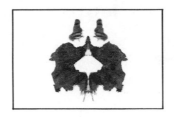

CARD II

1. (∧ 5″) [laughs] Those are the two dancing figures, very clear, shoulder here and face here, clapping hands [cuts off bottom part with hand, including red]

INQUIRY

1. Top red is head and hat; face is partly white (W)

Goering laughs with delight both at his sense of recognition of the card and at the playful image he sees in it. Dancing figures in Rorschach responses frequently represent an attempt to cover depression, however, rather than real lightheartedness, and, in view of Goering's previous and subsequent responses, this is presumably the case here. "The" dancing figures are "very clear," he remarks, as if to say, "the way I see them is the way they are." He is as gratified by clarity as he is critical of unclarity; but both are regarded by him as something in the external situation rather than in his perception of them. Where he was critical of that situation in Card I, here he is, as it were, commending the producer of the ink blot and saying, in effect, "Well done, this time it has come out very clearly."

The face is that part of our bodies which we do not cover up but show to the world, and by which we are recognized by others. Card II permits the subject rather easily to see a face in the blot itself. Goering, however, sees it partly in the white space, and partly in the blot, which rather strongly suggests the emptiness of his being: a lack of individuality and the absence of a distinctive, developed self.

But it is not only the intrinsic qualities of the face, as seen partly in the white space, that calls for comment. For if the face is partly in that space it must also merge into the red, which he uses for the hat. The use of the red for only the hat indicates an emotional preoccupation with status and a display of emotion in the context of status. In Goering's response, the distinction between the blank face and the red hat is unclear, and the elaboration of emotion in the context of status is what he substitutes for his lack of individuality and of a distinctive, developed self. In the superficialities of his status positions he can be capable of adaptive emotional response. But the gregarious, convivial, and volatile display masks a largely empty being.

The emptiness of his being also manifests itself in his response to the red at the bottom of the card. He is unable to deal with its intense emotional stimulation and cannot integrate it into his perceptions. What he does with it is arbitrarily to *cut it out* of the situation. He does not, in other words, repress the emotion or block expression of it; he eliminates it and at the same time eliminates what has aroused. It is, then, only on a superficial level that he is capable of adaptive emotional response; he deals with more intense emotional challenge by aggressively negating it.

CARD III

1. (∧ 5″) two caricature figures, with high collar like Schacht
   . . . but the red spots . . . I can't figure that out . . . can't figure
   out . . . [gets impatient, snaps forefinger at three red spots as though
   to brush them off] . . . what these thing are . . . damned if I know
2. (90″) . . . You might also say that it is an opened figure of one
   man . . . opened up, with two identical halves and the insides in
   the middle [points to lower D and center red . . . offers the idea as
   though not to be taken seriously]

INQUIRY

1. They are debating heatedly over something . . . maybe two doctors
   arguing over the inner organs of a man [laughs] (W)
2. Yes, of course, the opened man . . . [brushes it off . . . turns card
   down, ready for the next one] (W)

[N.B. Goering always puts card down when he is satisfied that he has said enough; indicates that he is ready for the next one.]

The high-collared caricatures which Goering initially sees in this card reflect the formal, unreal, and superficial aspects of himself—the facade which he uses to substitute for real substance. Like many of the Nazi leadership, he has contempt for Schacht, long Hitler's finance minister and known for the high collars he habitually wore. Here, however, the collar also represents authority—which, however, Goering sees merely as a caricature. But he does not recognize the extent to which he is describing *that part of himself* which identifies with that same image of authority, and which is not only impressed by it but also resents and mistrusts it. His own authority, then, while real and imposing, is also unreal, somewhat ludicrous and untrustworthy. In some respects he is indeed impressive in his high-collared authority; yet he is at the same time merely a caricature of authority, nothing more (as indicated in Card I) than a mere beetle. While Goering's concern with outward appearance is reflected in this response, he would also have felt contempt for people, and for that part of himself, who took seriously his fancy-dress uniforms, with their fantastic and childish quality. In part, however, those uniforms were probably a way of mocking himself as an authority figure and of caricaturing himself as well as his colleagues.

At first, Goering admits his inability to deal with the red spots on the card—to integrate into his experience the emotions which they represent. But he becomes increasingly angry at his inability to cope with the emotional situation and resolves the problem in his own way by aggressively and arbitrarily eliminating the emotions altogether, in a fashion similar to his behavior in Card II.

From the formal and superficial sense of self indicated by the caricatures in the first response, Goering now moves to the stark image of an opened man with two identical halves. The emphasis on symmetry in this image indicates an inability to tolerate conflict and ambiguity within himself and in others. This inability is further expressed by his attempt to dismiss the response as an idea that is not to be taken seriously.

The image of an opened man is a vivid and painful one. "I feel opened up, split open; I'm tortured," Goering is, in effect, saying. But there is much sadism and brutality as well in this response; Goering's ability to inflict great pain on others has its roots in his own pain.

Goering's opened man is bifurcated, split into two parts which reflect a pervasive duality in his own being. One part of this duality is the external and the other the internal. The external is convivial and jovial—and in some respects contains, and in others denies, his violence. The external is represented by the two doctors, who are the intellectual justification of, and scientific detachment from, his violence toward others; and it masks his primitive, brutal, cruel inner self. The external is also reflected in another function of his intellectually justified violence, namely that of masking his own inner emptiness, his fear of exposure, and the awareness of his own pain.

The extremely stark and unequivocal nature of these polarities makes it all the more difficult for Goering to tolerate conflict within himself. And so he brushes off the opened man.

His behavior when he has satisfied himself that he has said all that he has to say about a particular card reveals Goering in action. He dominates the psychologist—who may, after all, have further questions to put to him—and in general puts himself very much in command of the situation.

CARD IV

1. (∧ ∨ ∧ ∨ 15″) funny animal, sea animal, the kind you make smoked fish out of, has eyes

INQUIRY

1. just the structure

The outstanding feature of this card is its strong shading, which tends to evoke a subject's response to nuances of experience and particularly to subtleties in interpersonal relationships. A person who is able to establish adaptive, close, and differentiated relationships with others may see in this card a soft, furry animal skin.

An animal skin represents the sacrifice of a live animal for the sake of something warm, comfortable, and relating—the sacrifice of a primitive, instinctual part of oneself for the ability to establish (as both donor and recipient) warm, sensitive, and nourishing relationships.

Young children, who lack this capacity, generally see live animals rather than animal skins in this card. The capacity to sacrifice some of one's animal impulses is developed to varying degrees in different people. Some can respond to the shading of a live animal's fur, e.g., by seeing a soft, fuzzy dog—indicating thereby that they can offer warmth to others but only if they can be sure of receiving warmth in return. Others are deprived so early of the experience of softness and warmth that they do not see the fur at all. So intense has been their deprivation of nourishment that they are incapable of more than a narcissistic pursuit of it.

Goering was such a person. He lacked the capacity to receive emotional nourishment from others and probably never had the experience of receiving it. All he could give himself, and others, were cold, harsh, flattened, dried-out, smoked, and indeed dead sentiments masked (as we have seen in earlier cards) by a veneer of joviality.

In this complex and variegated blot, moreover, the only physical detail on which he focuses are the eyes. This suggests a large measure of suspiciousness and fear of exposure, though not enough to call for a diagnosis of paranoia.

A certain loss of judgment at the cognitive level should also be noted in his response: smoked *fish* are not made from sea *animals*.

CARD V

1. (∧ 10″) night animal . . . a flying animal, not exactly a bat . . .
    (∨ ∧) It is very symmetrical; if you fold it together it's the same

INQUIRY

1. It is more like a bat . . . the dark color is important(W)

As in some previous responses, Goering here expresses his depressive mood quality ("the dark color"), his need to deny inner conflict by stressing the fact that both sides are identical, and his psychopathic attribution of defects to external situations rather than to himself ("not exactly a bat"). The response he gives in the inquiry ("it is more like a bat") presumably refers to the image he saw in Card I.

Of particular interest in this response is his statement that what he sees is a "flying animal." Now a flying animal is either an animal which *is* flying—an animal in flight, or merely an animal that possesses the capacity to fly. The ambiguity here is highly significant. To see an animal in motion is to give some free play to the instinctual realm, to allow some spontaneity, and to have some trust in the life of the impulse. To choose a word that is merely a descriptive adjective *which sounds as if* it involves freedom of flight is a characteristic psychopathic reaction. For the ambiguity bespeaks a tendency not to commit oneself to the action that one is undertaking, to be detached from the risk of spontaneous being while giving a good imitation of being authentically involved in the action.

CARD VI

1. (∧ ∨ 10″) hide of an animal . . . Here are the legs and the backbone line . . . a bedroom rug . . .
    (∧) . . . This way, I don't know . . . This thing here [top] I can't figure out . . . [puts card away]

INQUIRY

1. It is the shading and the shape of the thing without the top piece . . . I can see it lying on the floor right before me. . . very clear . . . short-haired fur (W)

It will be recalled that in Card IV Goering was unable to respond to the furry texture that is commonly seen there. In this card, however, the fur is easier to see than in the earlier one, and the blot does not have the ominous and depressive quality of Card IV. Goering's response indicates that within certain limits he is capable of a sensitive understanding of what goes on in himself and in other people. However, being sensitive to and understanding others can be used for conning people as well as comforting them, and the fact that Goering relegates this rug to the bedroom suggests that his capacity for warmth and understanding is used by him for obtaining sensuous pleasure rather than for developing real human relationships.

Some of the dynamics of Goering's sensuality emerge in the second response. The object at the top of the card which he "can't figure out" is, in fact, a fairly simple phallic form that is in striking contrast both in texture and in form to the rest of the blot. Goering cannot see anything in this form, however, and cannot incorporate it in the rest of the blot. He does, however, of his own volition, *attempt to* identify it. That is to say, he is drawn to this portion of the blot out of concern with his helplessness in relation to male sexuality; and he attempts to deal with his impotence by denial.

CARD VII

1.   (∧ 20″) a face . . . grotesque . . . half-man, half-animal

INQUIRY

1.   [upper ⅔ heads and shoulders] [does not indicate M] (D)

Testing the limits: can see usual female figures (∧) and (∨) when suggested

This is a card whose shading is light, soft, fluffy, and generally feminine in its symbolic quality, and which readily offers the image of female figures. Goering, like many of his associates, does not see anything substantially feminine in this card; instead, he finds a bizarre, bestial, and grotesque face.

Goering's response indicates the extent to which the feminine aspects of his being—that is to say, the qualities of tenderness, nurturance, delicacy, etc.—are unacceptable to him. He rejects them as a part of himself, and distorts and even fears them as grotesque and inhuman.

The response provides further evidence that Goering was unable to relate to others in a warm, sensitive, and nurturing manner, just as he was incapable of accepting such a response from other people. He would, indeed, have been frightened of evoking such responses, seeing in others' preferred closeness and warmth only grotesque, gargoylelike qualities. He must have been a very lonely and isolated person, unable to participate in anything more than a machismolike *camaraderie*.

In this and other cards, Goering reveals his difficulty in dealing with the lower parts of the blots. This difficulty is indicative of an inability to do much with the vital, instinctive, sexual parts of himself; he characteristically deals with them by ignoring them or denying their existence.

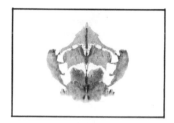

CARD VIII

1. (∧ ∨ 8″) only two things clear here . . . two animals climbing up, very clear
2. (∧ 20″) fantastic sea plants in the middle

INQUIRY

1. It is very clear no matter how you hold it [usual A] (D)
2. Of course, it's the color . . . could also be exotic flowers (D)

Perception of two animals is almost universal in this card and indicates here merely that Goering was capable of adequate conventional thinking. On the other hand, he does not identify the animals, while nevertheless insisting that they are "very clear." This ambiguity has something of the same psychopathic quality of his "flying animal" response in Card V; he is evasive and obscure and at the same time hides these qualities by insisting that he is, in fact, very clear.

In the "fantastic sea plants" he suddenly responds to the color stimuli. He does so in a way which utilizes almost nothing of the form, boundaries, control elements, and structure of the card. This is nothing but the vaguest of concepts, a shape which looks like nothing in the real world and for which once again he refuses to accept responsibility—his perception is, as he says, "fantastic."

The vague, structureless sea plants represent his repressed, undeveloped feeling. He is unable to associate this with himself as a person. Instead, it comes gushing out at the most primitive and undifferentiated level as mushy sentimentality. This aspect of his personality is one which he shares with many of his colleagues in this group.

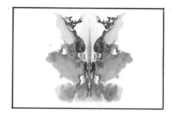

CARD IX

1. (∧ 15″) very fantastic plant
2. (30″) There are the trolls from Peer Gynt

INQUIRY

1. chiefly the color; also form (D)
2. the grotesque shape (usual orange details) (D)

Here again the plant he sees is "fantastic." He does not even identify it—specifying, for example, that it is a tropical plant that is very colorful, with large, green leaves—for such a degree of commitment would indicate a responsibility for his own perceptions that is far beyond Goering's capacity. The feminine side of his personality, we see here again, can be expressed only in this primitive and undifferentiated flowery sentimentality, split off from the rest of his being.

Nor, it would appear, can it be expressed for very long even in this form. Rather, the subhuman sadism of Peer Gynt's trolls—little, malevolent gnomes who live deep underground and attack Peer with sharp weapons—asserts itself. These are the same grotesque, half-man, half-animal creatures whom we first met in Card VII.

CARD X

1. (∧ 8″) two crablike animals
2. (15″) two troll figures, or parrots
3. (30″) little dogs
4. (50″) fantastic profiles . . . I don't know what that blue stuff is that they are blowing out

INQUIRY

1. just the shape; it's alive [blue] (D)
2. just the shape; alive [side gray] (D)
3. They are sitting on their haunches; it is independent of color [yellow] (D)
4. grotesque caricatures . . . not really alive [inner edge of pink details] (D)

Once more, in this final card, Goering does not commit himself to his perceptions. He does not see crabs, but only crab*like* animals. Nevertheless, the content of the response is apparent despite his evasiveness, for even crablike animals share the primitive, unevolved, and aggressive nature of crabs themselves—and like them, no doubt, can move in any direction without turning around. The two trolls which he sees again (cf. Card IX) are also sadistic and brutal images, consistent with the crab-like quality of his initial response. The additional remark that the same figures are also parrots possibly suggests a willingness either to be directly involved in brutality or to be the representative, the parrotlike mouthpiece, of someone else's brutality. Goering then goes on to see little dogs. Although they are merely sitting on their haunches, i.e., not moving about, they nevertheless indicate that Goering was not wholly without lively and spontaneous characteristics. Finally, he comments that he sees fantastic profiles, grotesque caricatures, that are blowing out some kind of "blue stuff." The figures are in profile, which is to say turned away from other human beings, and they are also depicted as unreal and rather horrendous. The only action in which they are engaged is a vacuous one, that of blowing out a substance without form, content, or meaning.

The examiner, evidently in an attempt to determine whether the figures are seen in any kind of action, seems routinely to have asked whether they are alive or not. Goering's reply to this question should not be given much significance. It is evident that there really is very little life in any of his responses (with the exception, perhaps, of the little dogs), and that such life as there is, is largely sadistic, brutal, and purposeless.

SUMMARY

Hermann Goering's father was a man of some importance. In 1885 he had been appointed Minister–Resident for South-West Africa, which was a German colony. It was largely due to his tact and diplomacy that the territory was made safe for German traders, and it is interesting to note that during his service in Africa he established a friendship with Cecil Rhodes. Some years later he was appointed Consul–General in Haiti. In 1892 his wife, pregnant with their fourth child, traveled home to Germany so that the child might be born there. The child was born on January 12, 1893, and was christened Hermann Wilhelm Goering. A few weeks after his birth, his mother left Germany to return to her husband in Haiti. The infant Hermann was left in the hands of a family friend, one Frau Graf of Fuerth. He did not see his mother again until he was three years old. Goering's earliest recollection was of meeting her after her return from Haiti. As she bent down to embrace him he hit her in the face with both fists.

In Africa, the elder Goering had become the close friend of one Dr. von Epenstein, a wealthy Jewish apostate. When Hermann was eight years old, his father was retired, on a relatively modest civil-service pension. His good friend Epenstein, who lived in a magnificent castle at Mauterndorf in Austria, now bought a somewhat smaller but still splendid one called Veldenstein, some fifteen miles from Nuremberg. He offered this to the Goerings as a home. The offer was eagerly accepted, at least by Frau Goering.

For that lady, considerably younger than her husband, was Epenstein's mistress. At Veldenstein, the elder Goering was not allowed to enter the suite of rooms reserved for his wife and her lover, and had to sleep in a modest bedroom on the ground floor. When the Goerings visited Epenstein's own home, he was lodged in a small house that stood apart from the castle. "In his old age," Manvell and Fraenkel report, "he found some remaining comfort in drinking and skittles, and he exercised little or no control over . . . his young children" (pp. 3–4).

These arrangements had a marked effect on young Hermann Goering's behavior. Even if we discount some of the propagandistic flights of fancy on the part of his official biographers (who, for example, attempted to demonstrate Goering's innate racial integrity by reporting that he would set his dog on local Jews), a striking picture of the boy emerges as a restless, reckless, daring bully, fascinated by military uniforms and by tales of martial exploits (Gilbert, 1950, pp. 85ff.)

The Rorschach record points up the more profound and lasting effects of Goering's childhood experience. The maternal deprivation he suffered as a small child engendered sufficient anger, as we have seen, to cause him to hit his mother in the face when he was reunited with her: significantly, this was Goering's earliest memory. Some of the violence and depression in his Rorschach record surely has its origins in this experience of deprivation and so too, we may be sure, does some of the great depression within him. One of the most striking aspects of his Rorschach is the evidence of his extreme inability to respond to nuances of feeling in human relationships— to give and receive warmth, sensitivity, and nourishment to and from others. At best, he could respond sensitively in a context of sensual enjoyment; but even this capacity was vitiated by the weakness of his male sexuality (Card VI).

This inability, too, surely has its origins in his experience of maternal deprivation as a small child. It is interesting to note that it was widely rumored that Goering was both a homosexual and impotent (Kelley, 1947, pp. 60ff.). Whether or not this was the case—and Kelley (ibid., p. 61,) discounts these reports—it is highly unlikely that Goering was able to establish other than superficial relationships with women. Significantly, when his first wife— whose jewels he had pawned to finance the early expenses of the Nazi party—lay dying in Sweden in 1931, Goering was too busy with politics in Germany to be at her bedside. No less significantly, however, three years later he brought her body to be interred, with almost pharaonic pomp, in the vast mausoleum he had built for her in his country home—the San Simeon–like Carinhall, which he had named after her. This spectacularly ostentatious display of superficial emotion, (Manvell and Frankel, pp. 105–6), masking his exploitation of Carin and his coldness toward her at the time of her death (and no doubt during most if not all of their married life together as well) is entirely consistent with the primitive and undifferentiated sentimentality which we noted in Goering's responses to Cards VIII and IX and with the superficial, adaptive responses, set in a context of status, which (as we suggested in our analysis of

Card II) he used to mask his lack of individuality and of a distinctive, developed self.

We also noted (Card III) Goering's rather unexpected attitude toward authority—and toward himself as an authority figure. Authority is experienced by Goering as somewhat ludicrous ("caricature"), untrustworthy (which is how the Nazi leadership, and indeed almost everyone else, regarded Schacht), sadistic, and characterized by an undue separation between thinking and the vital, instinctual processes (cf. the emphasis on the collar). Goering's experience of authority (in himself, it must be emphasized, as well as in others) also has its earliest and possibly decisive roots in his childhood history. His father, an important official in Bismarck's government and the descendant (as Goering loved to point out) of an even more important one in that of Frederick the Great (Manvell and Fraenkel, p. 5), proved to be nothing more than a helpless and humiliated cuckold.

The ludicrousness and impotence of this, the earliest authority figure in Goering's life, combined with the fact of his father's imposing official status, profoundly affected Goering's experience of his own authority, and help to account for the comic-opera qualities (including the Ruritanian uniforms covering his corpulence) by which he was known. But another part of his attitude toward and experience of authority was determined by the real, even if illegitimate, authority of his mother's lover, Epenstein.

It will be observed that the "caricature figures" of the initial response to Card III become, in the inquiry, "two doctors." Without perhaps making too much of this, we should note that Epenstein himself was a doctor. We may speculate that there may indeed have been many occasions on which young Goering felt that he was being cut open—torn apart—by the covert conflict between Epenstein and his own father; moreover, we may also assume that there were many occasions on which Goering felt immeasurably violent feelings toward Epenstein. Projecting this violence onto Epenstein, he would then have incorporated it into his experience of authority as violent, untrustworthy, and, no doubt, illegitimate. It hardly requires saying that Goering's anti-Semitism must have been rooted, in large part, in the knowledge that Epenstein was a Jew. But Epenstein's pretentiousness (he had bought himself his title) and his high living were among the qualities that Goering himself emulated. So, too, was Epenstein's blatant violation of propriety and, in a sense, of legality. These too were qualities which Goering emulated in his exercise of authority. "My measures will not be enfeebled by any legalistic hesitations," he announced shortly after assuming power. Here I have not to exercise justice, here I have only to destroy and exterminate, nothing else!" (quoted in Fest, p. 77).

In the end, though, Goering's fate was that of his father rather than that of Epenstein. As the ineffectiveness of his *Luftwaffe* against the Allied air forces became all too evident, Hitler's denunciations of Goering became more and more unbridled, and Goering's humiliation and anxiety such that he was forced into the most extreme efforts at appeasement. Frequently, he would send one of his own officials to Hitler's headquarters with orders to bring back detailed accounts of what the Fuehrer had said, so that at his next meeting with him Goering could present Hitler's ideas as his own (Fest, p. 75). But there were many terrible scenes, nonetheless. "Often I couldn't eat anything again until after midnight, because before then I should have vomited in my agitation," Goering would recall in prison. "When I returned to Carinhall at about nine o'clock I actually had to sit down in a chair for some hours in order to calm down. This relationship turned into downright mental prostitution to me" (quoted in Fest, p. 75).

7

Rudolf Hess

Rudolf Hess was born in 1896 in Alexandria, Egypt, where his father was a wholesale merchant. He was sent to a high school in Switzerland at the age of 15 and, a year later, to Hamburg, where he began an apprenticeship in business. He joined the German army as soon as the war broke out and served without distinction as an infantryman for several years. In 1918 he was commissioned a lieutenant in the air corps, but saw only a few weeks' active service as a fighter pilot before the Armistice.

After the war he moved to Munich and registered as a student in the university there. He met Hitler shortly thereafter, and at once fell under his influence. He participated in the unsuccessful Nazi uprising known as the Munich beer-hall *putsch*, and for this was imprisoned in Landsberg prison for about two years. There he helped his fellow prisoner Hitler write *Mein Kampf*. Released in 1924, the Nazi leadership set about rebuilding its fortunes. Hess, fanatically and without any reservation loyal to Hitler, played an important part in this effort. Following Hitler's accession to power, he was placed in charge of the extension of Nazi influence into wide areas of German life, including education, religion, and labor. No doubt utilizing his experiences as a foreign-born German, he also established an international network of pro-Nazi German bunds. During all this period he remained extremely close to Hitler, and it is said that he was the only one of the Nazi leaders to address him with the intimate "Du" (Leasor, p. 13). His devotion was rewarded with an appointment as Hitler's Deputy Fuehrer.

Hess was involved in the so-called Roehm purge, in which the S.A. ("Brownshirts") leader and a large number of his followers were murdered. He was also involved in the preparations for the invasions of Austria and Czechoslovakia and in the planning for the wider war on which Hitler had determined as early as 1937.

On May 10, 1941, Hess flew to Scotland on an unauthorized and completely harebrained mission to persuade Britain to sue for peace. The story of this bizarre episode has often been told, and the paranoia and lapses of memory which marked Hess's captivity have been studied in detail by the specialists who attended him in various prisons (Rees; Douglas–Hamilton). He was judged legally sane at Nuremberg and placed on trial with the other major war criminals. Indicted for planning and participating in a conspiracy to wage a war of aggression, he was found guilty and sentenced to life imprisonment. Now nearly eighty years old, he is the last remaining prisoner in Spandau jail.

CARD I

1. (∧ 15″) microscopic picture of something; cross section of a stem
2. (40″) an insect

INQUIRY

1. outline of a stem cross section, with spaces for the sap, like a fern; enlarged from microscopic picture (WS)
2. just the shape of the head and horns, body and wings (W)

If other subjects in this group seem impoverished, dried-out, and withered, Hess has gone a strange step beyond them: his record here has the eerie appearance of that of a dead man. His very first response is a self-image so minute that it needs to be enlarged under a microscope in order to be seen. The enlargement suggests a compensatory grandiosity. It is, moreover, a primitive, dead, and cut-open form of plant life, an empty and unspecified display in cross section. Even the sap through which the plant received its nourishment is now lacking; only the empty channels through which it once flowed are to be seen.

For this subject, the second response, dismal as it is, represents a definite improvement over the first. The insect, it will be noted, has *horns* on its head, a concept which has a sloppy, aphasic quality to it, as though he substituted a similar word for the one which he could not retrieve from his memory. Pathetically, his horns, organs which are both protective and offensive, are placed on an insect. The self reflected in these two responses is at a level of regression that is extreme even among this group of records.

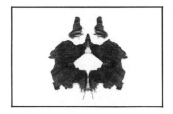

CARD II

1. (∧ 25″) also microscopic cross section; parts of an insect with blood spots
2. (50″) a mask

INQUIRY

1. the shape of the cross section of the leg of a fly with red blood spots; space in middle is the marrow, although I don't know if the leg of an insect has marrow (WS)
2. mask of an island savage, like Fiji Islanders, though I don't know them; the opening is for the mouth; it is devilish, that is why the eyes and beard are red (W)

The minuteness of his self becomes even more marked in the face of the emotional challenge posed by the color in this card: it is now represented as the cross section of the leg of a fly. The only life in him is the red color seen as blood spots, the remnants of a violent, excitable, unrelated emotionality which is still intense but is split off from contact with anything real.

He is unable to see the two decorative clown figures that are usual for this group of subjects—a concept which entails more of a sense of self, and of his own two-sidedness, than he is capable of. Instead, he comes up with the image of a mask. There is no person here at all, not even a dressed-up clown; and the mask is that of a savage, exotic, uncivilized, and (in his frame of reference) probably cannibalistic person. In a manner that occurs frequently in these records, he psychopathically rejects responsibility "I don't know them" for this concept—here that of the mask of evil incarnate.

CARD III

1. (∧ 15″) two gentlemen greeting each other
2. (30″) a red bow tie between them
3. (45″) two blood spots

INQUIRY

1. They are holding hats in their hands; it is very ornamental because it is very symmetrical; you might say the whole thing represents an expressionistic illustration for a crime novel, with the blood spots; the red tie plays some part, I suppose (built-up W)

Here Hess produces the two obvious human figures, indicating some remnant of human identity in him. His self-image here is one that suggests a concern with status ("hats") on the part of a subservient, superficial, and formal person. The reference to the symmetry of the blot indicates a need to insist, as it were, that the two sides are the same—that is to say, a need to deny internal conflict. The red bow tie is a conventional, ornamental, adaptive response. The blood spots, on the other hand, are unadaptive, and, through the exercise of a not too bad but not well-functioning mind, are made to seem part of a rather artificial and ambitious whole.

That whole is a "crime novel," indicating the effects of and his proclivity for criminal violence, which is accompanied by both adaptive and unadaptive emotional responses. That this is all merely an expressionistic illustration means that he is not really responsible for the concept—a further mark of his psychopathy.

CARD IV

1. (∧ 25″) an animal fur . . . stretched and hung on the wall

INQUIRY

1. The head is down here; the whole thing gives the impression of long-haired fur (W)

There is little if any genuine response to the subtleties of the shading in the blot. In Card VI he says that it is more the shape than the texture which makes that blot look like fur, adding that it "would still look like it if the coloring was different." It seems reasonable, therefore, to conclude that the long hair to which he refers in Card IV is probably a rationalization from the unevenness of the edges rather than a response to the shading. His is more a show of sensitivity in human relationships than a real experience of it. The fur is, moreover, decoratively on the wall, and has no real function. His reference to the head—the only part identified—suggests an emphasis on control functions rather than an integration of these with his instinctual side.

CARD V

1. (∧ 10″) skin of a bat

INQUIRY

1. the shape of a stretched-out skin, from the head and tail . . . night gray like a bat; hooked ends for grasping prey (W)

There is nothing left of this creature save for its skin, and that is stretched out and has the color of the dark void of night. The response indicates the profound failure with which Hess has had to live for several years since his grandiose flight to England—and shows how little of him is now left. But even in the remnant of him that remains, even in this moribund man, a predatory violence is still alive. His "hooked ends for grasping prey" is a most unusual response. Even in a situation that is devoid of the stimulus of bright colors, in other words even in conventional and emotionally uncharged situations, his capacity for violence can be aroused. The fact that it still exists in the "skin of a bat" suggests how powerful it must have been in the living animal.

CARD VI

[N.B.: When asked if he remembers seeing these before, he says, "Yes."]
1. (∧ 10″) a stretched fur

INQUIRY

1. also long-haired, but more the shape; would still look like it if coloring was different (W)

Testing the limits: can barely see sex symbols

See discussion of Card IV above. And compare discussion of "stretched" fur in relation to response of Funk in Card VI.

CARD VII

1. (∧ ∨ 20″) old-fashioned cravat, kind of moth-eaten . . . the sort of cravat men used to wear

INQUIRY

1. It should be silk, but this doesn't look like silk; just the shape of a cravat they used to drape round their necks (W)

Testing the limits: can see female figures ∧ and ∨

The image is of something which should be delicate in form and texture but is not; it is a moth-eaten, old-fashioned, outworn item of adornment that is no longer decorative. This response, moreover, is to a card that is full of evocations of femininity. The feminine aspects of his being—as we are calling them in this volume, his capacities for tenderness, lightness, delicacy, creativity, and warmth—never anything more than decorative, have now become moth-eaten tatters. The response also reflects an attitude toward women as nonfunctional decorations for men.

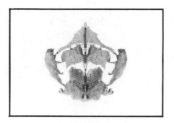

CARD VIII

1. (∧ 15″) a decoration with two animals at the edge . . . that is all

INQUIRY

1. design on Indian tapestry; the color just supports the design; the animals just look like animals, but they are not alive; the colors are immaterial . . . . could be other colors just as well (W)

The quality of deadness continues to be the outstanding feature of this record. The animals are not identified, and for that matter are not even alive; they are merely part of a decoration. The emotional element in the situation, too, has become a part of the decoration. There is no integral connection between thinking and feeling, and the colors are "immaterial." There is a striking lack of energy, interest, or conviction in this response. He does not even attempt to say what it is a decoration of, and the concept of an Indian tapestry is neither elaborated nor justified.

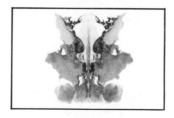

CARD IX

1. (∧ 10″) a technical representation of the cross section of either a carburetor or a fountain

INQUIRY

1. The idea comes mainly from the vaporized stream of gas or water in the middle and a receptacle underneath; the color has nothing to do with it, unless it represents different metals in a mechanical drawing (W)

He is now so far away from the world of life that there is no cross section of the leg of a fly or even the stem of a fern but rather a mechanical drawing, and that again in cross section. Color has nothing to do with the concept except to the slight extent to which it was used for the vaporized stream of gas or water. Even in this situation of extreme lifelessness there are indications of a loss of control, of being directed by ego-alien forces, as suggested by the inanimate movement of the amorphous, vaporous representations of his impulse life that is the stream of gas or water.

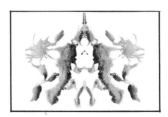

CARD X

1. ($\wedge$ $\vee$ 20″) decoration with sea animals . . . crabs, etc.
2. ($\vee$ 50″) seeds here

INQUIRY

1. just the general shapes, like the crabs; the color doesn't have anything to do with it (W)
2. yellow and shaped like acorn seeds that float in the air (D)

Additional: could also be the cross section of an orchid with red leaves; there the color plays a greater part (Pink and gray details)

There are also sea horses here by the shape of it (lower green D)

[N.B. This test administered during a period of recovery from amnesia]

Again, Hess comes up with the pale shadow of a frequently evoked response. The colors on this card, the lively emotional quality that ordinarily gives rise to the concept of underwater life, is explicitly omitted from his concept. So all is quite dead; and only the aggressive, primitive crab is identified.

The acorn seeds are either an inept, aphasic attempt to refer to maple seed pods or else a mistranslation. In any event, this response shows him leaving the animal world once again for something which is merely floating in air.

The ostentatious orchid represents the emergence, in sentimental and undifferentiated form, of the residual femininity in his personality. It is only the cross section of an orchid, however; the form is poor; and there is not much justification for the concept. Even his sentimentality lacks the coherence and scope of that of the large number of his colleagues in this group who see orchids and similar plants in Cards IX and X.

The ostentatiousness and sentimentality of the orchid response now apparently enable him to return to a form of animal life; he sees sea horses. These little animals are a primitive and undifferentiated form of life that bears a superficial resemblance to more advanced beings.

SUMMARY

"It would be erroneous to assume that an aggressive and sadistic dictatorship required personalities who were essentially aggressive and sadistic at the top executive level", Gilbert declares, ". . . a great deal of passive fanatic devotion and even mediocre ability was essential, the better to reflect the authority and omnipotence of the dictator himself. An ideal supporter from this viewpoint was Rudolf Hess, the Fuehrer's Deputy in the party, and ultimately the most celebrated psychiatric case of this half-century" (Gilbert, 1950, pp. 119–120).

In fact, Hess's Rorschach is notable for its indications of aggression and violence. The red spots of Card II are, perhaps somewhat hysterically, seen as blood, and in a distinctly savage and devilish context; in Card III the red again appears as blood and, in a setting of superficiality, formality, and display, the occasion for violent crime. The predatory "hooked ends" of the skinned bat in Card V represent a startlingly sudden and unpredictable resurgence of violence. The only animal he identifies in his initial response to Card X is the armored, aggressive crab.

Hess had lived for over four and a half years with a sense of complete personal failure, in isolation from his comrades, helplessly witnessing the collapse of the Nazi dream. The *extreme* flatness of his responses and the microscopic and inanimate qualities of his concepts are surely attributable, in part, to these experiences. Yet it is impossible to believe that the lack of sensitivity, the lifelessness, the poorly functioning intellect, the experience of loss of control, and the vitiated instinctual life which are to be observed in his record are exclusively the product of his incarceration. Rather, we must assume that the events of the preceding years had precipitated the degeneration of what had always been a low-level psychopathic and violent personality.

8

Ernst Kaltenbrunner

Ernst Kaltenbrunner was remembered by one of Hitler's servants as "a tough, callous ox, . . . looks like a big grizzly. Small brown eyes that move like a viper, all glittering. Bad teeth, some missing, so he hisses." (Stevenson, p. 88). He was almost seven feet tall and had a heavily scarred face.

Unlike many of his colleagues—his boss Himmler, for instance, who frequently struck people as an intellectual type—Kaltenbrunner looked like what he was, head of the Security Police (SIPO), the Security Service (SD) and the Reich Security Head Office (RSHA). The Gestapo, the *Einsatzgruppen*—extermination squads that murdered over two million Jews before the gas chamber was invented—and the concentration camps themselves were under his authority.

An Austrian, Kaltenbrunner was born in 1903 in Ried-on-Inn, where a grammar school classmate was his future subordinate, Adolf Eichmann. He qualified as a lawyer in 1926 and was appointed legal counselor to the 8th SS Division when he joined the Nazi Party in 1932. Briefly jailed for subversion by the Dollfuss government, he became the head of the Austrian SS and, after the annexation of Austria in 1938, State Secretary of Security. He continued to rise rapidly in the ranks of the SS and, after the assassination of "hangman" Heydrich in 1942, was appointed head of the SIPO, the SD, and the RSHA. As such, he played a major role in implementing Nazi genocidal policies and in the reign of terror that characterized Nazi rule in the occupied countries of Europe.

After the abortive attempt on Hitler's life in July, 1944, his power increased greatly—he now gained direct access to Hitler—and it is said that Himmler himself grew to fear him.

The Nuremberg tribunal, holding Kaltenbrunner responsible in part for the terrible crimes committed by the agencies of the RSHA, of which he was the chief, found him guilty of war crimes and crimes against humanity, and sentenced him to death by hanging. Kaltenbrunner was executed on October 16, 1946.

CARD I

[Approaches problem very cagily: "Of course, the first impression is a folded ink blot"]
1. (25″) Upper half is mothlike figure or bat—but all thoughts are disturbed by the symmetry of the symmetrical ink blot. After a while the possibility of an animal is excluded by this [examines card for 90″]
   (120″) [more comments on symmetry]

INQUIRY

1. Upper center part has feelers and claws—just the shape (D)

At least eight times in this record Kaltenbrunner refers to the symmetry of the blots. It is clear that his thoughts are, indeed, as he says, "disturbed by the symmetry of the symmetrical ink blot." By these comments he reveals a powerful need constantly to reassure himself that he knows the difference between fantasy and reality. In fact, he is close to or actually beyond the point at which a person is unable to make that distinction. Fighting against being enveloped by the delusional, he clings to the most concrete externals of reality. Two parts do *not* exist within me, he is saying unwittingly in his references to the symmetry; I am *not* in conflict; the distinction between fantasy and reality is perfectly clear to me. The record shows how tenaciously and frantically Kaltenbrunner examines every idea and feeling for its concrete, surface reality. By the same token, the inner content of his ideas and feelings must be identical to the external; the internal and the external *have to be symmetrical*. Devoting all his conscious effort to remaining rational, however, he constantly falls into the abyss of unreality. For emotions and thoughts that are confined to their manifest content—as outsides without insides, so to speak,—*must be* highly distorted.

We see these processes at work in his comments on and responses to the first card. "Of course, the first impression is a folded ink blot," he declares, clinging to the concrete while at the same time making sure that he has a way out which he can use if necessary: he does not, it will be noted, say that it *is* an ink blot. It merely gives the *impression* that it is one! The same process is apparent in his next remark. After a considerable while he manages to see "a mothlike figure or bat." But he has, as it were, overcommitted himself by this response. It is not, after all, a moth or a bat; it is not even an ink blot; it is merely something which gives the impression of being an ink blot. And so his thoughts—i.e., his thoughts as to what the ink blot might be, his ability to produce responses—are disturbed by the symmetry of the symmetrical ink blot. This excludes the possibility of an animal. Here, indeed, is an extreme instance of avoiding substance for the sake of the escape which emphasis on surface appearance gives. The symmetry, moreover, precludes the possibility of this being *an animal*. This remark, in an extraordinarily vivid way, illustrates the extent to which the denial of inner conflicts and differences is used by him to avoid any impulse life and instinctual experience, as represented by the animal. He denies that there is a living animal within him; all that exists within him is the exterior surface of his self and even this is fragmented. Where others use the whole blot for the moth or bat, he sees it only in the upper half, and later it shrinks even further to only the upper center.

In the inquiry he identifies only two parts of the moth/bat figure—its feelers and its claws. These, he is indicating, are the chief characteristics of his being. Surely this is a most remarkable self-portrait of the "search (feelers) and destroy (claws)" man—of the man who, as head of the *Sicherheitsdienst* (SD), did indeed devote himself to searching out and destroying those whom he considered to be his enemies! It is also noteworthy that in reply to the inquiry he does not identify the most obvious and salient aspect of the moth or bat in this card—its wings. While his failure to mention them may be attributable to the collapse of his ambition with the destruction of the Third Reich, it is probably also a statement about his basic self, about his inability to rise above where he is.

CARD II

Comment after 60″: "Here, too, there is symmetry, but no middle line."
1. (120″) The red spots are big crabs
2. (150″) Bottom red spots are crabs' claws
[N.B. responses very slow, unsure, and painful—"I can't make a final decision about this." Studies card very carefully]
3. (240″) Two people holding hands—but it requires a lot of imagination

INQUIRY

1. It has the appendages and head of a crab [center red], but the claws make it impossible because they are out of place [confabulated D]
3. They are carnival figures with red caps—I don't think it is, but a child might think so. The red socks are blotted out at the bottom. It's all fantastic

Again he is being very cagey and unspontaneous and trying hard to maintain his detachment. After a full sixty seconds he produces only the remark, "Here, too, there is symmetry, but no middle line." He is apparently disturbed by the fact that the division between the two sides is not clear enough. Then, after another minute has elapsed, he is very strongly drawn to the red spots and the affective stimuli which they represent. But he uses only their shape to produce rough, tough, primitive animals whose claws are seen as separate and "out of place."

It is important to note how confused and distorted his concept really is, and yet how cunningly effective he is in masking this. His responses are very definite—"The red spots are big crabs; the bottom red spots are crabs' claws"—but the fact is that these details do *not* look like crabs, and his perception is (as we might have been led to expect from Card I) inconsistent with reality. Yet, although his concept is confused and distorted, he presents it with such flat assertiveness, so unlike the hesitancy with which he offers quite clear concepts, that only a careful study of the response reveals its irrationality. This is probably indicative of the effectiveness with which Kaltenbrunner was able, in general, to conceal his weak grasp of reality from others.

The statement that "the claws . . . are out of place" indicates that in this person violence and rationality do not go together; his aggression operates autonomously. He also does not accept responsibility for it (*"they* are out of place"), and his evasiveness on the subject ("I can't make a final decision") indicates an arrangement in which one part of him does not want to know what the other, violent, side is up to. The fact that he assumes that in a situation fraught with complexity—and in which, of course, no "final decision" is possible, there being no "correct" answer—he must resolve his perceptions into a clear and unequivocal image, is also indicative of his need to operate in a framework of concrete (and thus flat and distorted) reality.

In his next response ("two people holding hands—but it requires a lot of imagination . . . carnival figures"), the little bit of self in him intrudes. In the context of public display he is able to integrate form and color in an adaptive fashion, though the fact that these are carnival figures suggests that the context has to be, for him, one of whipped-up celebration. This is, nevertheless, quite a lively and good response, but he then completely renounces responsibility for it. "A child might think so," he says. Even in Kaltenbrunner, then, there is, as in each of us, "a child that cannot live and cannot die." He repudiates his childlike aspect, that part of himself which has some capacity for humor, playfulness, and growth. He denies the only part of himself that is human, limited as it is.

The red socks to which he next refers also deserve comment. If he had said, for example, that children were wearing red socks, he would be revealing a capacity to sacrifice rationality and clarity for the sake of a very spontaneous emotional reaction. He cannot do this, however, for that very limited part of him which is capable of childlike spontaneity frightens him too much. And so he blots out the red socks, so that they become merely a messy, excited, unadaptive emotional reaction for which, once again, he is not responsible—for they are "fantastic."

CARD III

1. (40″) caricature of two waiters taking something away from a table [comments on symmetry]
2. (100″) perhaps two hats there which they are holding
   (150″) red spots blotted when paper was folded together
3. (200″) red bow tie in the middle

INQUIRY

1. has the shape of waiters wearing tailcoats (W)
2. (DW)
3. the shape, but it's red and pink (D)

Here Kaltenbrunner depicts himself as a servile ("waiter"), pretentious ("tailcoats") caricature of a human being. The two waiters are indeed cooperating with one another, but they are doing so in a very slack way. The idea that they are removing something from the table rather than placing something on it is altogether arbitrary; while the notion that they are holding hats is altogether illogical; waiters don't hold hats when clearing a table. These aspects of his response indicate some cognitive confusion in Kaltenbrunner. The hats the waiters hold also reflect, once again, a concern with status and a need for importance—or at least the appearance of it.

The red bow tie is a common response. But on inquiry Kaltenbrunner turns out to have seen something other than a red bow tie. He has called it a red bow tie, *but* "it's red and pink." It is almost as if he had said, "It's the shape that makes it a bow tie, but it's shown as red and pink and therefore I said red bow tie." This response shows a split between his control functions and his feelings. He can, in other words, recognize the affective nature of this situation and come up with what appears to be an appropriate response to it. In fact, however, the response is superficial and has a large measure of phoniness about it. He can *see* but not *feel* the emotional charge of a situation.

CARD IV

1. (30″) dried skin of an unknown marine animal—mounted specimen
   (80″) [more comments on symmetry]

INQUIRY

1. It has the head and eyes of an animal and the shading looks like fur. I must emphasize that it's only fantasy—there is no furry underwater animal

In certain important respects, Kaltenbrunner's response to this card resembles that of Goering, our discussion of which should be consulted at this point. The image he offers provides a vivid portrayal of deadness, unconsciousness, and lack of development.

He sees, indeed, the skin of an animal and on inquiry responds to the furlike shading of the blot. Just as the child in Kaltenbrunner is still somehow present in Card II, albeit in a highly residual and distorted form, so too is there some capacity in him for an awareness of nuances of feeling. But what a vitiated form it takes—dried-out, mounted, unknown, and fantastic as it is! His capacity for awareness of nuances of feeling in his relationships with others, and of theirs with him is, accordingly, minimal, and has a remote and unreal quality. He uses it, moreover, for manipulative and adaptive purposes rather than for affective relationships with other people. The very great stress which he places on the implausibility of his own concept—it is an unknown animal, it is only fantasy, there is no such animal—is a pronounced version of the rejection of responsibility for one's self-concept so common in these records, and as such a marked indication of psychopathic trends.

His response also indicates what Piotrowski calls "impotence": namely, the recognition of the poverty and inappropriateness of a response coupled with an inability, nonetheless, to withhold that response. As such, it may be indicative of a disturbance—whether organic or functional—in the central nervous system.

It should also be noted that while he claims that his perception is "only fantasy," there is really not very much of fantasy in it. It is, rather, an *illogical* response, and is indicative of his efforts to keep himself detached and uninvolved, and of the ineffectiveness of those efforts.

The only features of the animal which he identifies are its eyes and head. The eyes indicate feelings of suspiciousness and exposure. He holds himself together with his head, as it were; but actually the head is not functioning very well, for all the assurance it gives him. Indeed, it has brought him to the point of delusion and leads him to see things in an irrational way.

CARD V

[inspects carefully, comments on symmetrically folded ink blot]
1. (160″) could be a bat, but such a fantastic one I have never seen

INQUIRY

1. two big wings, big head and ears—just the shape (W)

A banal, popular bat, whose "fantastic" quality is not elaborated on, once again shows the subject's habit of disclaiming responsibility for his own perceptions, and indeed for what he himself is; and also reflects an empty pretentiousness.

CARD VI

1. (120″) opened flounder

INQUIRY

1. The tail is above—the shape. But understand, I don't really believe
    it's a flounder (W)

Unable to respond to the shading on this card, and the sensitivity
to nuances of feeling which it usually evokes, Kaltenbrunner sees
instead a low form of submarine life. He is, to be sure, less defended
than Goering's "smoked fish," but he is nevertheless cut open and
exposed. The flounder, it should be observed, is a flat fish which
inhabits the very bottom of the sea bed and is often camouflaged
by sand. It lives so much on its side that, although born with a
normal, fishlike shape, it flattens out as it matures and its eyes move
until they came together on its uppermost side. Here, then, is a vivid
portrait of Kaltenbrunner—a flattened, primitive being camouflaged
in its natural habitat and adapted only to the very bottom; it is,
moreover, devoid of life, having been cut open.

He takes pains to assure the examiner that "I don't really believe
it's a flounder." The remark comes close to pathologically concrete
thinking, a feature associated with certain kinds of brain damage
and schizophrenia, which leads a person to be insistently logical but
in a way devoid of relationship to the intrinsic nature of the
phenomenon he is examining. This defect in capacity for abstract
thinking could, for example, lead a person to say that people in
cattle cars are cattle!

The remark also suggests "impotence" that borders on the pathological. "I know that's not what it is, but I can't help seeing it in this
way," he seems to be saying, reflecting once more his helpless inability to modify or control behavior which he knows is inappropriate and even irrational.

CARD VII

[rejected]
("Same process—ink blot—can't imagine what . . . ")

Testing the limits: When old women are suggested he barely sees two cherub heads (Do)

His initial comment reflects a need once again to reassure himself that he knows what is going on, that he is not being fooled by mere ink blots, and that the blot is indeed just that, i.e., symmetrical.

His inability to respond to this card indicates once again the extraordinary and chilling emptiness of the man. In the face of the feminine qualities of this card, other Nazis discussed in this book frequently respond by describing grotesque and abhorrent figures, thereby indicating that they are at least troubled by these feminine qualities in themselves and need to deal with them in some way— if only to denigrate them. Kaltenbrunner, on the other hand, fails to see the stimuli represented by this card, in even this fashion: they simply do not exist in his life. Thus, a Goering, for example, when confronted by a man pleading for his life or for an end to torture, might fight against his unconscious softness by kicking him in the face; Kaltenbrunner would not even need to do that, so completely repressed are the "feminine," feeling, qualities of his inner being. It should be recognized that the absence of these qualities affects his perception not only of others but of himself as well.

When asked explicitly whether he can see female figures in this card, Kaltenbrunner barely manages to discern two cherubs' heads. He sees them not only as unreal, infantile beings, but also merely in terms of their heads, devoid of instinctual and vital qualities.

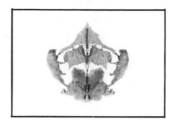

CARD VIII

[keeps commenting on folded blot with every card]
1. (60″) two chameleons
2. (120″) impossible for leaves, because they're four-cornered
3. (220″) prepared specimen of a marine animal with two eyes and two feelers

[all answers very slow, unsure, and cautious]

INQUIRY

1. just the shape [usual side animal] (D)
2. The color is for leaves, but not the shape—I thought of that because chameleons live on trees (blue D)
3. crablike shape (upper D)

Again he comments on the folded blot, seeking to reassure himself that he is able to hold himself together and that he experiences no inner conflict in the face of the emotional stimuli suggested by the colors in this card.

He perceives the common (for this group of subjects) opportunistic chameleons, and then goes on to say that the blue parts are "impossible for leaves, because they're four-cornered." Once again he gives a response despite his recognition of its inadequacy, and takes an arbitrary and inappropriate position without accepting responsibility for it. Who said that they had to be leaves? What is more, and despite his comment that "the color is for leaves," the fact is that blue is *not* a color found on leaves. There is a very tortuous and tortured logic at work here. He has invented a reality that bears no resemblance to the form or color of leaves in order to justify his perception of the chameleons. A mass of irrationality is suggested here, then, a thoroughgoing distortion of both the objective situation and its feeling tone (i.e., form and color) in the service of his manipulative and opportunistic purposes (as represented by the chameleons). Note that in his concept the chameleons are not in fact camouflaged, that they are not the same color as the "leaves".

All vitality and instinctual life is dried up, and his capacity for experiencing pain and joy extinguished, in the third response. The chameleon has given way to a primitive, lifeless, but nevertheless aggressive animal whose sole identified features—the feelers and eyes—reflect a cautious and suspicious searching out of the environment and a paranoid fear of exposure.

Here and in some other responses examined in this book, there is the implication that the subjects had or experienced themselves as having had brutalized childhoods. A "prepared" marine animal or a mounted and dissected flower has been handled—or mishandled—by someone else. This response, then, is not just a statement about the respondent as he now is, and about how he perceives, and behaves toward, himself and others; it may well also be an historical statement about his childhood, as he experienced it.

CARD IX

1. (20″) general impression is of a cuttlefish
[holds hand down center line: "It was certainly not the purpose of the folded blot to make a cuttlefish, but that's what came out. Of course it's not a cuttlefish at all"]

INQUIRY

1. It's an awful-looking animal that can pour out inklike fluid to hide itself. The colors are not right—it's the contours and general impression (W)

Here again we have a remarkably vivid self-portrait of a mass murderer. He is an awful-looking animal who hides in the fluid he emits. That fluid has some very distinctive connotations, *kuttel* being "dirt from the guts" or, in German, bowels and entrails. The cuttlefish, moreover, is distinguished by the calcareous shell, which was formerly used for making knives, that is found *inside* its body.

His comments dissociating himself from this remark no less vividly reveal another side of the Nazi leader. They are strongly paranoid and psychopathic. The former tendency is indicated by the remark that it was certainly not the purpose of the folded blot to make a cuttlefish. He "knows" that the blot *has* a purpose; perhaps he was initially fooled by it, but he's really pretty smart and knows how to watch out for himself—so he is telling the examiner. He won't be taken in by a purposeful ink blot. At the same time, he dissociates himself from responsibility for his remark ("that's what came out"). Circumstances were such, in other words, that all I could do was go along with reality. Here, too, there is a paranoid quality. Although the violence and ugliness of the awful-looking animal are projections of his own, he attributes them to external circumstances. His behavior in making a choice for which he then rejects responsibility, and his feeling that he does not possess any choice when in fact it is he who is making it, is psychopathic. This repudiation of responsibility for one's own violent and brutal behavior is nothing less than a psychological analog of the Nuremberg defense: "I had no choice but to obey orders."

CARD X

[rejected]
("the most colorful of all the representations. It tells me nothing besides the colored impression")

INQUIRY

nothing there. If you ignore the color, you might see a Chinese garden with bridges, islands, and ponds, etc.—but the colors spoil everything

He is so overpowered by the affective nature of the stimuli in this card that he is unable to function. He acknowledges the emotions present, but only intellectually, and makes it clear that emotions spoil everything. There could be a lot of beauty in life ("a Chinese garden") were it not for real feeling. *Feelings must be ignored if one is to create something satisfying.* As soon as feelings intrude, his mind goes blank—"nothing there"—except insofar as he is capable of imagining what might have been. The garden, moreover, is a "vista response," reflecting concern for one's place in the world, both philosophically and in terms of one's status, position, etc. Any perspective that this man might have on life or on himself is negated by the intrusion of emotions.

SUMMARY

The gashes that disfigured Kaltenbrunner's face were not, as was often assumed, the fencing scars that German students acquire as a boastful display of their masculinity. They were, instead, the result of an automobile accident (Kelley, 1947, p. 135).

Distasteful and even savage as we may consider the dueling tradition of German student fraternities, the scars which the young men inflict on each other do at least possess certain relatively positive qualities and associations. They are, in their own, unattractive way, purposeful. In a setting of intellectual and academic endeavor, they establish a youth's physical courage and gain for him lifelong membership in a society committed to mutual support and comradeship. A car accident, on the other hand, is not only utterly purposeless, but occurs when human beings have lost control of their machines, with senseless and calamitous consequences for man and machine alike—and often, too, for innocent people who just happened to be in the vicinity when the accident occurred. Kaltenbrunner's scars were acquired in just such circumstances, which symbolize not only his journey through life but also the dominant aspects of his personality.

The debased and repulsive self-portraits of this man become increasingly explicit in their violence and revealing in their wealth of connotations as his Rorschach record proceeds. We see first the feelers and claws of a bat; then the violently red claws of crabs; the opened flounder, and a "prepared specimen" of a marine animal; until finally he arrives at the "awful-looking" cuttlefish. There is no purpose or justification for this violence; Kaltenbrunner does not even offer something akin to the phony scientific rationale for sadism found in Goering's concept of "two doctors arguing over the inner organs of a man" (Card III). His violence just *is*; and the best he can do is hide himself behind the inky fluid he emits from his bowels or entrails (Card IX), or camouflage himself like a flounder in the very lowest environments.

He is, indeed, a creature adapted to the bottom. His perceptions are distorted by a suspiciousness that is quite paranoid. He is quite unable to experience or respond to feelings of gentleness or sensitivity; and even residual elements of childish spontaneity and receptivity to nuances of feeling in relationships exist, at best, in vitiated form. In certain situations he recognizes but cannot feel emotions; in general, he must ignore feelings if he is to create something remotely satisfying. Such emotion as he has becomes distorted in the service of his manipulative opportunism.

The same can be said of his rational faculties. He is unable to integrate his violence with his rational judgment. He can recognize but not restrain inappropriate responses. His ability to separate fantasy from reality is so tenuous that, clinging desperately to concrete reality, he lapses into concrete thinking instead. Nor can his intellect tolerate ambiguity or uncertainty in any respect: the more complex or amorphous a situation, the more definitively must he characterize it. A decision is either a final decision or it is not a decision at all; a solution, too, is either a final solution or not a solution. To the extent that his brutality had purpose, it was probably to overcome the obstacles, in reality, to his need for a concrete and wholly unambiguous world. Conceivably, too, his need in this regard was so great that he was able to settle for the mere *administration* of brutality rather than the direct experience of it as a guard in a concentration camp or a torturer in one of the cellars of the Gestapo.

Kaltenbrunner's behavior in the Nuremberg prison reflected the same primitivity of being that characterized him at other points in his life. Before the trial began he went through a period of great depression, in which he would frequently break down and cry. "He was frightened and wanted to be comforted," Kelley reports (Kelley, 1947, p. 134). This reaction, regressive in the extreme, was significantly different in its infantile simplicity from the attempts of most of the other defendants to rationalize their plight in one way or another. Those attempts may not have been persuasive, but they do indicate, at least by comparison with those of Kaltenbrunner, a relatively advanced level of ego functioning. Kaltenbrunner, undeveloped creature that he was, could respond only like a baby.

A different expression of the same crude primitivity appeared after the trial began, and following the imposition of his death sentence. "This macrocephalic giant," Gilbert observes, "had little to say, and it was hard to establish rapport. His sensitivity was so blunted that he shocked the Nazis themselves with his clumsy lying and denials. After being sentenced to death, he appeared too bored by the whole thing to bother with an appeal, but he casually wrote an essay condemning Himmler when we offered him a piece of chocolate for his opinion" (Gilbert, 1950, p. 253).

9

Wilhelm Keitel

Wilhelm Keitel's bearing, appearance, and military career gave rise to the widespread assumption that he was a Prussian Junker. In fact, he was neither a Prussian nor an aristocrat but came from a middle-class landowning Hanoverian family which, as it happens, had a strongly anti-Prussian tradition (Keitel, p. 11). He entered the army in 1901 at the age of 18—rather reluctantly, for he would much have preferred to follow his father as a gentleman farmer; but his father was still alive and had no intention of relinquishing the family estates to him. Keitel's military career during the First World War and in the years of the Weimar Republic was undistinguished, and at best merely promising. After Hitler's accession to power, however, and the rearmament of Germany, Keitel began a rapid ascent in the ranks. He had been only a colonel in 1931; four years later, he was appointed Chief of Staff of the Supreme Command of the German Armed Forces. In 1938, when Hitler took over direct command of the armed forces, he appointed Keitel Chief of the High Command of the Armed Forces (OKW), with the rank of lieutenant–general as well as that of Reich Minister.

Keitel played important roles in connection with the annexation of Austria, the invasion of Czechoslovakia and Poland, and the assaults against Norway, Denmark, France, and the Low Countries. It was he, in fact, who read the terms of surrender to France in the historic railroad car at Compiegne, after which ceremony he was promoted to the rank of field–marshal by his jubilant Fuehrer. Keitel, indeed, played a major role in virtually every German military undertaking of the war.

He also played a notable role in a great many of the atrocities carried out by the German military. It was he who issued directives ordering the execution of captured commando troops and of escaped prisoners of war on their recapture and who tacitly sanctioned the lynching of downed Allied airmen. It was he, too, who issued orders for the execution of hostages (approximately 70,000 of whom were killed in the Western countries alone) and for the implementation of the infamous *Nacht und Nebel* decree, ordering that opponents of Nazi occupation were to be shipped off to Germany and murdered there without trial and without any information provided to their families. It was he, too, who in Poland and elsewhere instructed the German army to cooperate with the SS extermination squads in their gruesome endeavors.

"There is nothing in mitigation," the Nuremberg tribunal said of him, convicting him on all four counts of the indictment and sentencing him to death by hanging.

CARD I

1. (10″) clearly a butterfly with wings and feelers

INQUIRY

1. just the shape of the whole thing. The body is transparent here like X-ray picture (W)

By stressing that the butterfly—an easy and conventional response to this card—is *clearly* one, Keitel reveals a tendency to emphasize the clarity of the obvious. The reference to the butterfly's "feelers" indicates a suspicious searching out of the environment that is found in many of the records in this collection. Highly unusual, however, is the concept of an X-rayed butterfly, which reveals his feelings of exposure. The notion of an X-rayed butterfly is quite irrational—there is surely no point in X-raying a butterfly, after all—and suggests not only a loss of judgment connected with these feelings of exposure, but a striking *emptiness* as well.

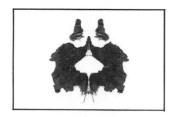

CARD II

Comment: "Hmmm . . . remarkable—rather similar to the one before. The red repulses me—it irritates me."

1. (50″) could be two dogs' heads with eyes, nose, and neck. But the red doesn't belong—and the white space, I don't know.

INQUIRY

1. Could be bears' heads putting their snouts together, playing, not the whole animal; it's just the shape and normal color (W)

Testing the limits: cannot recognize clowns

Keitel's comments show how impressed he is ("remarkable") by the intense, excitable emotional qualities of the red color on this card—and how he deals with such stimuli. In the face of these emotions he experiences, for one, a striking loss of judgment as, striving for a sense of continuity with a less highly charged situation (the absence of bright color in the previous card), he declares that this card is "rather similar to the one before"—which it is not. His feeling of repulsion in response to these emotional stimuli now becomes apparent. He attempts to cope with this by minimizing it, but does not do a very good job in this regard, for his "repulsion" merely gives way, in his account, to a feeling of "irritation." In the face of strong emotional stimuli such as those represented in this card, then, Keitel experiences a loss of judgment and feelings of repulsion which, with some effort, he is able to moderate slightly. He finds emotions repulsive and irritating, and when emotionally aroused *he* no doubt becomes repulsive and irritating. It should also be pointed out that his initial comment, reporting subjective feelings rather than saying what the blot might be, reflects an egocentric and hysterical quality.

The dogs' and bears' heads to which he refers indicate remnants of an earlier vitality that was characterized by a simple, animal nature. The fact that he sees only the heads, however, suggests that he is not a whole creature, that he suffers from a more than ordinary separation between the intellectual and the instinctual—a point emphasized by the unusual reference to the animals' necks, the organs that separate the head from the body.

The white space on this card is generally regarded as background. Keitel is drawn to it, however, thereby revealing his considerable inner emptiness. His inability to rationalize it ("I don't know") points to his helplessness in dealing with this inner emptiness.

In the initial response he says that the red doesn't belong. In the inquiry, however, he says that "it's just the . . . normal color." He does not mention that the normal color is black, and it should be noted that the black parts of this blot are in fact flecked with red spots. Both remarks, then, evidence a denial of emotional responsibility, while the latter one could well indicate that much of his difficulty in handling emotional response centers around situations involving blood—in other words, around situations of violence.

CARD III

[Studies it, tilting head from side to side; then comments, stalling]
1. (68″) could be a sort of bird's head, kind of torn below, like bird's head and breast
2. (120″) spider legs below

INQUIRY

1. just the shape and feathery breast (upper black D)

Testing the limits: rejects suggestion of waiters, but accepts apes bending over. "But the red doesn't belong at all. You see, I'm an outdoor man, not a barfly."

2. exactly the shape of spiders' legs (D)

Most of Keitel's codefendants are able to see human figures in this card. But even after a considerable delay, Keitel produces instead the grotesque concept of a bird's head that is torn off at the breast. The response suggests a lack of substance as a human being that is quite extreme, as well as an intense experience of fragmentation, pain, and violence.

In the inquiry he describes the breast as feathery. Although this at first sounds like a sensitive use of shading, the feathery quality seems to arise from the shape of the edges, and the use of this shape as feathers indicates a phony sensitivity rather than any capacity for direct and genuine involvement.

His inability, even in testing the limits, to see human figures in this card, alongside his ability to see apes, reveals directly the primitive nature of his personal development. Again he asserts that the red does not belong, denying emotional involvement in the situation. The rather cryptic but apparently boastful comment that he is an outdoor man and not a barfly appears to rationalize his concept of apes and his rejection of waiters (whom he presumably associates with bars).

In his second response he tells us, in effect, what the "bird's head and breast" of his first response rest on. Where others are able to integrate the details of this blot quite readily, and to see the lower part as legs of people, he splits it off and sees the slender, weak limbs on which the predatory arachnid rests.

CARD IV

[mutters under breath, turns card over]
1. (55″) also a kind of birdlike insect; feelers and eyes above, torn wings, backbone—same class as bats and butterflies

INQUIRY

1. more a marine animal with big eyes and feelers; might be a picture taken through the water because of shading; looks dark in water (W)

Again there is a long delay before a response is offered, indicative of a cautious or depressed personality, or both. His behavior in turning the card over to see what is on the other side indicates a suspiciousness that at least borders on the paranoid. These reactions are to a card with great textural variety, strong forms and the suggestion of a dominant masculine figure. In the face of this rather foreboding presence, Keitel produces what is by far the most confused self-portrait evoked by card IV among this entire group of subjects. It is not just that the *form* of his concepts is extremely poor. Much more striking is the rapidity and fluidity with which he moves from one incongruous concept to the next—from a birdlike insect to a bat (with the feeble rationalization that a birdlike insect could belong to the same class as a bat), and then from a bat to a butterfly, lumping these two, also, in the same class before going on, in the inquiry, to say that it is more like a marine animal. This response suggests that when confronted by the stimuli represented by Card IV, Keitel experiences a striking loss in abstract thinking ability, an extremely poor capacity to generalize even at a fairly simple level, and an inability to hold on to a concept, which, taken together, seem quite psychotic.

The "big eyes" and "feelers" to which he points in the inquiry are further indications of his intense suspiciousness. He cannot respond to the shading on this blot in a way that reflects satisfying contact with other human beings: touch is not possible, contact is absent. There is only darkness and the insubstantiality of a picture taken through the water.

CARD V

1. (60″) Well, there's the head and wings, feelers and legs—but I've never seen a butterfly like that

INQUIRY

1. It's like looking down at a flying animal from my balcony; maybe a bat (W)

Even the conventional concept that Keitel produces here takes him an entire minute to arrive at, and, significantly, he does not present the concept as a whole but rather builds it up from its parts —and then quickly denies responsibility for what he has produced. Even a conventional situation, then, can initially be a disintegrative experience for him, one which he can generalize only with some effort and in a psychopathic way, denying responsibility for his perception ("but I've never seen a butterfly like that").

There is some improvement in the inquiry; he goes from an unreal butterfly to what he appears to accept as a bat. Again, however, his psychopathy manifests itself in the ambiguous "flying animal." It is unusual for a person to see a bat here in relation to his own position. Here, Keitel sees it in a way that emphasizes his own distance from and superiority to a creature that is (compared with a butterfly) relatively developed, instinctive, and alive. He is, then, distant from and, in an irrational way, superior to his own instincts. The element of irrationality here is present in the concept of "looking down . . . from my balcony." To say "seen from above," or something similar, would have been sufficient here. The concreteness of his being on his balcony carries the quality of cognitive confusion as well as of emotional distress.

CARD VI

1. (30″) the hide of a beast of prey—the middle line here—and spread out on the ground

INQUIRY

1. just like a stretched-out tiger hide; arms, tail below, kind of leopard texture; head missing (W)

In this card, so rich with textures, Keitel does not make use of the shading beyond a limp reference to a "kind of leopard texture" at the end of the inquiry. Initially, at least, he appears to see the blot as the leathery hide rather than the furry outside of the skin of an animal—and one which, moreover, is a beast of prey. Such limited capacity as he possesses for perceiving and responding to nuances of feeling in human relationships, accordingly, is used not in a merely manipulative but in a downright predatory way—and it is in this way that he also perceives others' attempts at expressing warmth and sensitivity toward him.

The hide itself has no apparent function. He says that it is "spread out on the ground," then changes this with the remark that it is merely "stretched out." With the same fluidity of thinking, the tiger becomes something like a leopard. Keitel's psychotic tendencies, already noted in Card IV, are again breaking through here—and it is indeed not surprising that the "head is missing."

At least some of Keitel's violence, it would appear, is associated with the need to deny internal conflict, as suggested by the reference to the "middle line" (with its implication of a search for symmetry). It will be noted that, with the exception of Card I, this is the fastest response in this record. Particularly in situations involving inter-personal relationships and their manipulative exploitation, then, his predatory and violent qualities are relatively accessible and close to the surface.

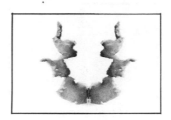

CARD VII

[Holds it near and far, turns, comments, stalls]
1. (80″) maybe a cat's fur—very poorly done, pieces hanging together—rabbit fur

INQUIRY

1. just the color and shading of cat's fur; rabbit's fur texture; a miserable job of skinning. I'm a hunter and nature lover (W)

The "feminine" qualities of this card, the challenge to feelings that it poses, and the nature of Keitel's response to it account for his stalling, and long reaction time before he is finally able to produce a response. Eventually, he gets over his block and expresses the residual, repressed and distorted nature of his feminine aspects by describing the blot as "maybe a cat's fur." He disapproves of the way that it has been depicted, indicating a lack of responsibility for the feminine side of his personality, and then goes on effortlessly and randomly to change his concept from a cat's fur to that of a rabbit—from the remnants of a creature with some conceivable dignity to those of the scurrying rabbit. There is no warmth or sensitivity indicated in this response, only the crudeness and brutality of pieces of fur ripped off an animal and hanging together in a meaningless way. He expresses disapproval of the way in which the animal has been skinned, adding that he is a hunter and a nature lover; if he were to shoot a rabbit or a cat he would do a much better job of skinning it. The notion of doing a good job of skinning a cat —and of being a cat hunter—suggests that he would kill at random and without purpose.

The fact that the texture he perceives lacks any definite form— it is merely pieces hanging together—and his emphasis on the miserable job of skinning underline both the crudeness of his reasoning and the primitiveness of his reactions to people's feelings.

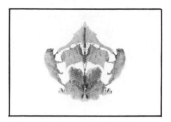

CARD VIII

1. (55″) dandelion bud prepared on a slide and enlarged
2. (120″) If fantasy goes to work one can see two animals with head, nose, legs

INQUIRY

1. just the colored drawing of a microscopic slide projection with natural colors in a botany book (W)
2. just the shape. They're in motion (usual D)

He sees the bud of a dandelion—a weed that contrasts strikingly with the exotic plants seen in this card by other subjects in this book—elaborately enlarged and displayed. Again the psychotic fluidity of his perceptions and reasoning becomes apparent, for what he initially refers to as a colored drawing then becomes the "natural colors" of the bud. Poor as the form of his response is, and vapid as his concept may be, a *colored* drawing makes more sense than his subsequent assertion that these are the *natural* colors of a dandelion bud. They are, of course, not by any stretch of the imagination the natural colors of a dandelion bud, and the response indicates the increasing inappropriateness of the manner in which his extremely vitiated feminine aspects manifest themselves. Unlike the responses of many of his colleagues, who see fantastic plants, orchids, etc., these aspects were, to begin with, expressed through a highly impoverished concept—the dandelion bud. Even his sentimentality is highly constricted; and even in this form he is unable to control it emotionally.

Even at the simplest level, then, his instinctual qualities are very weak and unintegrated with his emotions. He requires fantasy to see the two animals, and while he says that they are in motion he does not describe their motion or explain the terrain on which they are moving.

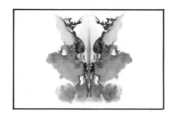

CARD IX

[Looks it over and throws arm up helplessly. *"Das ist ein tolles Ding!* (That's an amazing thing!)—The plant world ends here."]
1. (80″) eruption of a volcano with clouds of smoke rising out of the depths and becoming brighter clouds above
2. (130″) an animal with snout and eyes and beard; looks like an elk on one side, crocodile on the other

INQUIRY

1. The red is fire; green is dark clouds coming out of the crater and the sun is shining through the clouds on top, making them brighter (W)
2. just the features (inside detail in both greens) (di)

After a long delay and a dramatic display of helplessness which he attempts to rationalize by saying that "that's an amazing thing," Keitel acknowledges that "the plant world ends here." Even the extremely superficial and inappropriate sentimentality of which he was capable in his response to the previous card cannot be maintained in the face of his reaction to this card: for the volcano within him is erupting.

But just as there is something pathetic about his unwitting acknowledgement that he is unable to maintain even his superficial sentimentality, so too is there something pathetic about the volcanic eruption within him. At first glance, his response appears to be based primarily on a use of the colors in the card. The emotional challenge of the color is what has triggered off the explosive response. In his responses to Cards II and III, we saw that he was unable to use the red portions of the card; here he calls the pink part red. The volcanic fire, then, while it may seem red to him, is in fact merely pink—which is to say that it is very much less intense a fire than one would expect to find in a volcano.

The flames, moreover, are not merely pink where we might have expected them to be red; they are also extremely low. There is a lot of smoke but not very much fire, and it is apparently clouds rather than flames that are coming out of the crater. The fire in this man, then, is nearly out; what remain are the destructive effects of the explosion or eruption, mitigated—if indeed that is what they are— by the inappropriate sentimentality of the sun shining through the clouds at the top.

In the second response to this card he shows how remarkably able he is to recover from the eruption of the volcano. He shows a capacity to see the same blot area in different but appropriate ways, and to conceive of different interpretations for the same fact. But these indications of a flexible, differentiated mind are merely residual. His inability to explain why the details look like an elk and a crocodile (beyond making the dull and irresponsible statement "just the features") suggests that in his failure and loss of energy what may once have been a good and differentiated mind now emphasizes trivial differences without any real commitment.

CARD X

[almost rejected. Comments on colors, turns, studies, stalls. "It is entirely without relationship."]
1. (80″) some kind of flower in the orchid family, but nothing definite; gray stem, red leaves—the other things are inorganic

INQUIRY

1. The red belongs; there are such flowers, and it has the calyx shape; but the other things don't belong (attempt at W) (D)

His comment, after yet another extremely long delay, that the card is "entirely without relationship" is a reflection of his own disintegration, of the fact that he, too, is torn apart and fragmented.

Now the ostentatious, florid sentimentality that emerges rather earlier in the records of other subjects in this collection makes its appearance. In the course of this sentimentality he again misperceives color, describing the pink as red—the pallid as vivid—while seeking to emphasize his rationality by insisting that "the red belongs" and that "there are such flowers." In fact, the form is extremely poor—there are no red-leaved orchids—and for all the specificity of his description of the plant, he does not really identify it beyond saying that it is "some kind of flower in the orchid family." His ostentatious, arbitrary, sentimental flower is, then, as inappropriate and irrational as his own sentimentality; like the gray stem, it is basically dead.

SUMMARY

Keitel's entire defense at Nuremberg rested on the claim that he, as an army officer, was required to obey his superior's orders—his superior, of course, being Adolf Hitler himself. In one form or another this explanation of his conduct was repeated by some of the other defendants at Nuremberg and by witnesses—and it has since been echoed by historians. Von Blomberg, for example, testified at Nuremberg that it was "general knowledge that Hitler kept Keitel at his side because he was convinced of his unconditional soldierly obedience and loyalty" (IMT, XL, p. 409); while Jodl described Keitel as "an obedient and dutiful soldier, too soft and decent for Hitler, but upright, truthful and helpful" (IMT, XL, p. 422). He was regarded by Trevor-Roper as "a compliant puppet," by Telford Taylor as a "doormat," and by Wheeler–Bennett as a man of "complete acquiescence and subservient adulation" (Trevor-Roper, p. 122; Taylor, p. 13; Wheeler–Bennett, p. 429).

These views of Keitel, while containing an element of truth, beg the question of how he was able to commit himself so loyally to Adolf Hitler, of all people. And the fact is that while he sought to justify his obedient behavior by reference to the traditional German military code of conduct, Keitel on at least one occasion acted in gross violation of just that code. At the trial it was revealed that Keitel had issued instructions to have the French generals Giraud and Weygand caught and assassinated after their escape. Keitel felt extreme shame and embarrassment at this revelation—he was far more affected by it than by evidence of far greater atrocities for which he was responsible—because this was one instance in which the Prussian code of honor would have justified disobedience to Hitler's command (if indeed it was Hitler who had ordered Keitel to issue the instructions). So outrageous a breach of conduct was this considered to be that his fellow defendant General Jodl, who can hardly be considered a paragon of virtue, from then on "cold-shouldered" Keitel and would have nothing further to do with him (Gilbert, 1950, p. 229). Indeed, a further example of Keitel's real attitude toward the military code of honor emerged at Nuremberg. In September, 1941, Keitel had issued instructions regarding the treatment of Soviet POWs that were in brutal violation of the Geneva Convention and of established principles of international law. When this fact was drawn to his attention by Admiral Canaris of the Abwehr, Keitel wrote in a memo: "The objections arise from the military concept of chivalrous warfare. This is the destruction of an ideology. Therefore I approve and back the measures" (NCA., II, p. 536).

Keitel was, accordingly, something less than a rigidly correct German military officer who obeyed orders and kept his nose out of politics; he was a Nazi soldier who, when fighting inimical ideologies, could effortlessly suspend "the military concept of chivalrous warfare."

His Rorschach record contains many indications of the rapid and complete decline of his fortunes: his energy, as we saw, is very nearly burnt out, and his responses are marked by a great deal of cognitive confusion. The psychotic traits which we discovered in his record are not mentioned by either Gilbert or Kelley, however, and there are some indications of competent mental functioning during the time of his imprisonment which require consideration. Most notably, there is the long memoir which he wrote in his cell. While certainly not a great piece of literature—it is, in fact, marked by the extreme flatness of tone which we might have expected from his Rorschach record—it is a cogent, coherent, detailed, and well-constructed work that reflects Keitel's undoubted organizational abilities. It is difficult to believe, accordingly, that the psychotic trends which we observed developed during, and as a result of, his imprisonment. What seems more probable is that he possessed a capacity to function reasonably well *despite* those trends, which may well have existed in him at a much earlier date.

In addition to the extreme flatness and emptiness of his personality (Cards I, III, and IV), Keitel's record is marked by a strong prospensity to deny emotional responsibility—notably, as we have seen, in situations associated with violence. Here, then, is the psychological correlate of the defense which he offered at Nuremberg. (It is interesting to note in this connection that he blamed his wife's ambitiousness for his decision not to leave the army in the early 1930's and retire to the obscure comforts of life as a gentleman farmer [Keitel, p. 12].) Implausible as that defense was, it is also belied by other aspects of his Rorschach record, which contains numerous indications of a highly violent personality (Cards II, III, VI, and VII). Spurred on by his active paranoia (Card IV), his violence was not at all restrained, as it might ordinarily have been, by a capacity for sensitivity, warmth, or nurturance. Indeed, the feminine attributes of his personality were not only sentimental and ostentatious but fragmented, incoherent, and altogether vitiated (Card X).

While his Rorschach record enables us to establish that Keitel was not merely the obedient soldier he depicted himself as being, it does not offer us the chance of acquiring a detailed insight into his personality. To an extent, no doubt, this is because there was not very much detail to him: most who knew him regard him as an exceptionally cold, austere, distant, and impersonal individual. But there is at least one aspect of his personality which we can establish from another source and which does not show up in the Rorschach. "Rather than not go down at all in history," he told a friend, "I would go down as the greatest destroyer of all time" (Rauschning, p. 315). We see in this remark how his violence was coupled with an extraordinary (and extraordinarily revolting) ego-inflation. It hardly needs to be said that this ambitiousness represents an extreme compensation for an inner emptiness and mediocrity. And insofar as his Rorschach record conveys just these qualities of emptiness and mediocrity, its paucity of detail is an accurate reflection of Keitel himself.

10

Constantin von Neurath

Constantin von Neurath was born in 1873 into a well-connected family of the Wuertemberg nobility; his father was lord chamberlain at the court of that kingdom. Von Neurath joined the diplomatic service in 1901, fought briefly during the First World War before being invalided out of it as the result of a wound, and rejoined the diplomatic service with a posting in Constantinople. He remained there until 1916, when he was dismissed by the German Foreign Office for disloyally reporting his ambassador's love affairs to Berlin. He returned to Wuertemberg for two years as chief of the king's cabinet. He was appointed Minister to Denmark in 1919 and ambassador to Italy two years later. He served in Rome until 1930, when he was appointed ambassador to London. Two years later his friend von Papen summoned him back to Berlin to be foreign minister. Although not a Nazi, he remained in this post under Hitler until 1938 (when he was succeeded by Ribbentrop). As such, he played an important role in connection with Germany's withdrawal from the League of Nations in 1933 and the failure of the European disarmament conference of that year—events which were decisive in the sequence that eventually led to the Second World War.

At the Hossbach conference of November 5, 1937, Hitler disclosed to his principal aides his intention of eventually going to war. Von Neurath was so distressed that he suffered a heart attack on the spot and soon thereafter submitted his resignation. He was not so distressed, however, that he declined the numerous high honors and positions which Hitler now bestowed on him. All of these, though, were without real power or function. The Secret Defense Council over which he now presided, for example, appears to have consisted of nothing more substantial than the letterhead on which Von Neurath enjoyed writing his letters.

In 1939, von Neurath was appointed Protector for Bohemia and Moravia. Although he performed his tasks here with relative humanity and was clearly not liable for some of the brutalities carried out in his name, he was considered by the Nuremberg tribunal responsible for a number of excesses.

These, however, had failed to impress Hitler, who in September 1941 informed von Neurath that he had been too lenient in dealing with Czech dissent and that Heydrich (the "hangman" who was later assassinated by Czech partisans) was being sent to Prague to correct this deficiency. Von Neurath refused to work with Heydrich and went on leave; characteristically, however, he did not resign his position, clinging to its official prerogatives and status until October, 1943.

Von Neurath's culpability in Nazi crimes is indicated by the fact that he was found guilty on all four counts of the Nuremberg indictment; but he was the only one of the six found guilty on all counts to escape hanging. He was sentenced instead to fifteen years' imprisonment.

CARD I

1. (∧ 5″) angel figure without a head, seen from behind

INQUIRY

1. shape of angel with wings, standing (W)

This record at once seems highly unusual for this group of subjects. Where a large number of his colleagues see a subhuman figure, even an insect, von Neurath describes a superhuman angel. Although not an original response, this is an uncommon one in any group of subjects. He organizes the blot in an effective manner, thereby revealing that he has a good mind—albeit one which is not operating with much good judgment, as the stress on the absence of the head suggests.

An outstanding problem for him appears to be with femininity. He responds at once directly to the center portion of the blot, the part which is ordinarily seen as a woman. Instead of seeing her in these terms, however, he describes her as an angel. He is fascinated by the feminine but regards it as distant and unreal. The fact that the angel is seen from behind, moreover, indicates a low level of psychosexual development on his part—and an evasion of it. (A rear view minimizes the distinctions between male and female.) In turn, the headlessness of the angel also suggests that von Neurath is unable to bring his mind to bear in an integrated way on the problems aroused by his sexual identity.

There is some vitality, reflectiveness, and self-awareness in this subject, but—the angel is standing still rather than engaged in any kind of movement—there is also a certain passivity about him.

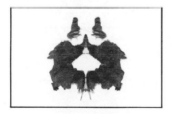

CARD II

1. (∧ 15″) two women or Chinese greeting each other

INQUIRY

1. women or Chinese with red turbans, hands together (W)

When human figures are seen in this ink blot they are ordinarily described as men. Von Neurath, however, sees them as women. It is apparent that the feminine plays a significant part in his life—unlike many of the other subjects in this group—but it often seems to emerge inappropriately, and just when masculine qualities are called for. He does however also distance himself from the feminine. It is unclear from the record whether we should understand these to be *Chinese* women. But in any event, the association of "women" with "Chinese"—or that which is remote and exotic—is readily apparent.

The two figures in this card are ordinarily seen in some kind of relationship of confrontation or conflict with one another—even if this is expressed only by depicting them as clapping hands. Here, however, they are shown greeting each other. By default, we have here an indication of the intense conflict within the subject, and of his aggressiveness toward others. These are frequently masked by superficial politeness and courtesy.

In general, his emotions do not overwhelm him: he ignores the lower red. The upper red is described by him as "turbans," rather in the way that many of his colleagues see a hat. The indication here is that his adaptive emotional response is tied to considerations of status rather than to genuine feeling.

CARD III

1. (∧ 20″) two men greeting each other, hat in hand—don't know what that middle thing is
2. (60″) could be a bow tie

INQUIRY

1. the black part just looks like that (W)
2. just the shape (Center D)

Testing the limits: gives red devils for corner red

Von Neurath evidences less obsequiousness than many of his colleagues—he does not describe two *waiters* bowing to each other, but rather two men greeting each other—so there seems to be a more intact sense of self than in some of the other subjects, although the superficial, formal quality is still apparent. There is something quite alive and refreshing about his quick and candid admission that he does not know "what that middle thing is." He takes the time and trouble to think about it and finally comes up with an adequate if not brilliant solution, identifying it as a bow tie. That object of adornment, found in a number of other records in this collection, betokens a certain superficiality in his emotional adaptation, and a quality of display: the emotions which he presents are a facade.

There is a somewhat depressive aspect to his statement, in the inquiry, that the *black* part looks like two men greeting each other. In general, however, he does not have an inordinate and ambitious need to come up with a spectacular generalization that includes every aspect of the card; he is quite willing to leave some parts out of his narrative. In testing the limits, he comes up with an appropriate integration of form and color, describing the top-corner red spots as red devils. Affect, then, conjures up in him a vision of evil incarnate. But he has to be pushed to this point. It is as though he recognizes that if he has to get involved with feelings, bad things are likely to come out. In general, he avoids this situation by staying with the black—for all its depressive qualities. The good form of this response indicates that his mind can continue to operate rationally even when, almost literally, the devil is brought out in him.

CARD IV

1. (∧ 20″) bear skin

INQUIRY

1. shape and appearance of fur—yes, long-haired fur (W)

By pointing to the shape and texture of the bear skin in the inquiry, von Neurath expresses some capacity to react in an appropriately sensitive way even in the face of the possibly gloomy and ominous shadowing of the blot. The poverty of his associates, however, is striking, and suggests a markedly depleted quality. The remark that the fur is long-haired appears to be a reply to the examiner's rather routine question whenever fur is mentioned, and may have no significance for interpretative purposes.

CARD V

1. (∧ 3″) a bat
2. (45″) a loaded donkey from behind

INQUIRY

1. the shape (W)
2. he is going away; poorly loaded (W)

In his characteristically terse fashion, he begins by giving a conventional response. The second response is, on the other hand, a good and original one, and indicates that he has a very high IQ. Nevertheless, he is merely a loaded beast of burden, and one which is frequently regarded with some derision. The pathos of this self-portrait is amplified in the response. He is a *poorly* loaded beast of burden, and evidently has trouble functioning even as a mere donkey. What is more, he avoids confrontation with his circumstances: "he is going away" from them.

A beast of burden, of course, does not load itself. It would seem that von Neurath was poorly prepared in childhood for the burdens of life—even for the burdens of life as a humble beast of burden—just as he is now not very effective in handling them himself. Whoever is supposed to be looking after him is evidently not doing a very good job of it. As a result, his burden is inappropriate and he is, so to speak, saddled with a lot of bad stuff. His dependence needs have not been taken care of and are not being taken care of—either by others or by himself.

The view of the donkey from the rear again indicates a low level of psychosexual development (see Card I); possibly this is one of the burdens that he is rather ineptly carrying.

CARD VI

1. (∧ 60″) clothes rack

INQUIRY

1. shape of pole with hooks (upper projection), and fur hanging on it
    —short-haired, woolly, like llama (W)

In Card IV von Neurath was able to respond appropriately and well to the textural qualities of the blot. Card VI is ordinarily easier in this respect. In this subject, however, it evokes the concept of a clothes rack. That is to say, he is riveted to the strongly phallic aspect of the top part of the blot; the fur which he mentions in the inquiry is something of an afterthought and is ineffectively integrated with the "clothes rack." Particularly in situations calling for masculine reactions, then, he lacks the capacity to respond well to nuances in human relationships. His masculinity—the pole—moreover, has "hooks" on it, which is to say that there is something spiky about it, and that it is associated with the inflicting of pain on others, and with his own experience of pain.

There is something very limp and passive about the way in which the fur is merely "hanging" on the clothes rack. From this it would appear that he experiences an inability to control his weakness, passivity, and dependence and is uncomfortable with his inability to control those feelings.

CARD VII

1. (∧ 60″) door hinges down here

INQUIRY

1. the shape (bottom center dr)

Testing the limits: Yes, with a lot of fantasy it could be two dancing girls

Until this card, von Neurath has used either the entire blot for his response or an obvious detail of it. In the present card, however, he virtually avoids the blot and rivets his attention on a small and unusual detail.

This card represents the challenge of femininity. Von Neurath, it will be noticed, does not distort this but, rather, attempts to keep away from it, only to end up by focusing on a detail which often, because of its intrinsic quality, evokes association with a vagina. But his focus is weak, and not very effective in its attempt to keep things together.

He is still remarkably preoccupied and disturbed, then, with problems of sexual identity. He feels woefully inadequate with regard to sex: he does not know whether he is really male or female, or which he would rather be. In testing the limits he gives expression to his desire to avoid the whole question, and can see the conventional image of two dancing girls only "with a lot of fantasy."

The images of hinges suggests features that were apparent in his responses to the previous two cards. Hinges have a hanging, dependent nature, and acquire movement and indeed significance only from the door to which they are attached. Here they portray von Neurath as an unimportant person who can become important only by attaching himself to some entity bigger than himself. An entity which has, in more senses than one, movement: movement which is mechanical and inanimate, not to say inhuman.

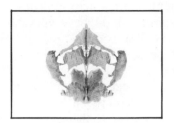

CARD VIII

1. (∧15″) two chameleons climbing up a plant

INQUIRY

1. just the shape—the bottom part might be the color of a flower, but otherwise color doesn't apply (W)

Once again we see the two chameleons, a depiction of the subject's instincts in the service of his opportunistic ambition. With good mental judgment, however, and without the sloppy sentimentality that characterized many of his codefendants, von Neurath is able to restrict the plant to an appropriate part of the blot, and to use the color only where it is most appropriate.

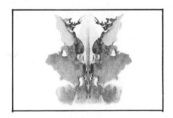

CARD IX

1. (∧ 60″) two deer

INQUIRY

1. shape of top part (D)

Additional: green part might be green bush

The lack of sufficient inquiry here makes it uncertain how he sees the two deer: his response might have very poor or quite good form quality. In light of the rest of this record, however, it is probable that the deer *are* well seen. It will be noted, though, that his response is confined to the deer and, in the inquiry, rather tentatively to the green bush. His good intellectual judgment as (probably) evidenced by the deer would thus seem to be exercised at the expense of an elaborate, imaginative response to the varied stimuli of the card.

The deer is a creature of the wild. While he can manage quite well for himself, he is extremely timid, particularly in the face of direct attack from other creatures. He is also vulnerable to—and a favorite target of—hunters. This self-portrait suggests great vulnerability in von Neurath along with a certain ability to survive in the face of attack.

CARD X

[*rejected*]
("Don't know what that could be")

INQUIRY

Testing the limits: recognizes rabbit head, but laughs: "That requires a lot of fantasy." Recognizes lions top center, but tends to reject suggestions like red blood smear, brown leaves; recognizes shape of dogs, alive but independent of color

Usually, the rejection of this card is based on an inability to generalize in the face of varied and complex emotional challenges. As we have seen, however, von Neurath has in previous cards been quite willing to respond to individual details and to forego the ambitious—and, with our subjects here, frequently unsuccessful—use of entire cards. Two possible reasons for the rejection of this card by von Neurath may be suggested. He can no longer put up with the piling up of emotional stimuli (this is the third colored card in a row) and therefore avoids them with a candid acknowledgment of his own inadequacy. Alternatively, his rejection of the card may be rooted in the fact that the scattered nature of the blot evokes his own fragmentation, to which he responds by avoidance.

In testing the limits he accepts an obvious concept—the rabbit—at the examiner's suggestion, but with the remark that "it requires a lot of fantasy." In fact, the rabbit's head does not require "a lot of fantasy," for it can quite readily be seen by many subjects, and von Neurath's comment indicates the intensity of his need to avoid making responses to the card. Even now his judgment remains intact, however. He is not unduly swayed by the examiner's suggestions, which he accepts and rejects on the basis of their appropriate form. His independence of judgment here is quite impressive.

SUMMARY

"Think much but say little," Constantin von Neurath, we are told, would advise his fellow prisoners at Spandau; "Feel much but show little" (Fishman, p. 143). Von Neurath's life, in both its emotional and vocational aspects, would have been a much different and better one if he had not lived it by the restrained and reserved code of the Prussian aristocracy. If he had expressed his beliefs more openly he would not have risen to such eminence as he did, and then paid a heavy price for his tawdry and tenuous achievement. If he had dealt more openly with his feelings, it is possible that his intelligence and vitality would have brought him to a more constructive resolution of his emotional problems. That he ruined his life was not because he was deficient in the qualities required for a well-spent life. Most people who knew him, whether German or Nazi or otherwise, considered him a pleasant, intelligent, and basically decent man; Hitler himself, as we have seen, regarded him as too lenient in dealing with the Czechs. And Davidson is no doubt right when he says that von Neurath could never have ordered the destruction of Lidice, because "he disliked violent reprisals and killings" (Davidson, p. 173). He was known, at least by the German underground, to dislike Nazism and the Nazis (ibid., p. 175). Unlike his fellow aristocrat von Papen, he did not possess some of the personality characteristics which, as we see from their Rorschach records, typify this group of Nazi leaders.

But there was one attribute which von Neurath did share in common with most of the Nazi depicted in this book: an inordinate opportunism. In the service of his ambition he could violate not merely the Prussian code of conduct but basic human decency as well. We saw, in the introduction to this chapter, how this trait manifested itself in him well before the rise of the Nazi movement in the priggish and altogether unpleasant report he sent to Berlin, ratting on the ambassador under whom he was serving. Later he would continue playing the same game under the Nazi regime. If the stakes were higher, the goal nevertheless was unchanged: what was good for von Neurath was all that really mattered.

He did not lose his ethical judgment entirely, however. Indeed, the quality of his moral judgment, in the face of Hitler, was rather higher than it had been in Constantinople. He recognized the wickedness—and the danger to Germany—of Hitler's decision to wage war, and he opposed it. He recognized, too, the wickedness and inhumanity of the kinds of repressive policies he was chided for not implementing in Czechoslovakia, and he refused to implement them. Given the strong pressures for conformity to the Fuehrer's will, and the high price for failing to do so, his independence of judgment was impressive (Card X).

Nevertheless, the rewards of going along were always just a little bit too enticing to this opportunist. If the German underground knew that he disliked Nazism, it "also knew that he would do nothing about getting rid of it. Instead, he would continue to serve in his uncomplaining, cautious way" (Davidson, p. 175). He might refuse to continue as Hitler's foreign minister, but he would eagerly accept the empty honors that Hitler showered on him thereafter. He would refuse to repress the people of Czechoslovakia as a cohort of "hangman" Heydrich, but he would postpone for more than two years his resignation from the office of protector of Bohemia and Moravia out of love for the perquisites of that office.

All this has been known about von Neurath for several decades. The Rorschach record, however, reveals the underlying causes of some of these aspects of the image which he presented to the world. It is noteworthy, for one thing, that his almost legendary courtesy and affability were a mask for and a defense against intense inner conflict and the aggression which, in him, was associated with it (Card II).

Even more interesting, however, are the frequent indications in his record of feelings of weakness, vulnerability, timidity, and unimportance (Cards II, V, VI, VII, X). He unwittingly depicted himself, in this record, as a mere beast of burden, and a poorly laden one at that. These feelings, it would appear, are associated with his unfulfilled dependency needs (Cards VI, VII); and these, in turn, would seem to be connected with the highly problematic sexuality that expresses itself repeatedly in his record.

Von Neurath felt inferior and therefore undernourished, undernourished and therefore inferior. He was a snob, a congenital name dropper (Card II: cf. Fishman, pp. 147–50). More fatefully, he sought to compensate for his inadequacy, and for his emotional undernourishment, by his opportunistic ambition. He would sell himself to Hitler despite his own better judgment, if he could thereby make himself feel that he was an important person.

11

Franz von Papen

On June 1, 1932, Franz von Papen was named Chancellor of Germany by the aging president of the Weimar Republic, von Hindenburg. The appointment was greeted with almost universal incredulity, in part because von Papen "enjoyed the peculiarity of being taken seriously by neither his friends nor his enemies" (Shirer, p. 230), and largely because of his manifest lack of political experience or qualifications.

Born in 1879 into an impoverished but aristocratic family, von Papen had risen rapidly in his army career—not because of his abilities, it is said, but rather owing to the social influence of the wealthy industrialist whose daughter he had married. His military service during the First World War was distinguished by a succession of comical blunders which belie his reputation as a master spy. After the Armistice he entered politics and, as a member of the Center (Catholic) Party, sat in the Prussian parliament from 1920 to 1928, and again from 1930 to 1932. He was known for his extremist nationalist and conservative views.

Von Papen remained Chancellor for little more than five months. His appointment was, in part, occasioned by the role he had played in undermining his predecessor, Bruening, who was also a member of the Center Party. Von Papen's disloyalty to his own leader had led to his expulsion from the party. The socialists and communists, meanwhile, were bitterly opposed to his appointment. The result was that von Papen had almost no political base from which to attempt to carry out his policies as Chancellor. He sought to strengthen his position by making concessions to the Nazis; these included the lifting of the ban on the SA (Hitler's brown-shirted "storm troops"), who promptly committed the most brutal excesses—including murder—and who were, equally promptly, given unconditional pardons by von Papen. In November, unable to muster sufficient support —the Nazis had polled only 32 percent of the votes in the election held that month—von Papen was forced to resign. He actively intrigued against his successor, von Schleicher, however, and sought to strengthen his own political base by strengthening that of Hitler. Most notably, in this regard, he played an important role in the negotiations which led a group of major German industrialists to give Hitler financial support. Von Schleicher was soon forced to resign, and on January 28, 1933, von Hindenburg again asked von Papen to form a government. Two days later he had done so. With only three exceptions, the new cabinet was identical to his earlier one. The exceptions, however, were notable, for the three new members were all members of the Nazi party and one of them was actually appointed Chancellor. Adolf Hitler had come to power. Franz von Papen, his Vice-Chancellor, was in large measure responsible for the fact that he had done so.

There is much evidence to suggest that von Papen believed that he would be able to use the Nazis as a pawn in his own struggle for power (Rauschning, pp. 135ff.; Fest, pp. 155ff.). In fact, the reverse turned out to be the case. In July, 1933, while Goering was suppressing all nonreligious Catholic organizations in Prussia, von Papen went to Rome and negotiated the Concordat with the Vatican (Shirer, p. 234). In June, 1934, in an attempt to assert his independence, von Papen gave an address at the University of Marburg condemning the excesses that were being perpetrated by the new regime. He was arrested, the assistant who had written the speech was killed, and for a while it seemed as if von Papen, too, would be executed. But with the remarkable staying power that characterized the man, he was released from prison and was allowed to remain on as Vice-Chancellor for two more months.

In August, 1934, he was sent to Austria as Hitler's special envoy, and two years later he was appointed ambassador to that country. He played a major role in the events that led to the annexation of Austria in 1938; and the following year he was sent as ambassador to Turkey, where he remained for almost the entire duration of the war; he was credited with having kept Turkey neutral.

In the Nuremberg trial and in his memoirs, von Papen depicted himself as a nationalist and a patriot who had always despised

Nazism and who served the Nazi regime in order to have the influence with which to minimize its excesses (von Papen, chaps. 23–25). He was acquitted by the tribunal.

CARD I

1. (∧ 10″) a butterfly

INQUIRY

1. head and feelers and torn wings; it's dead and mounted; just the form (W)

He responds promptly and conventionally but, on inquiry, reveals the experience of being a torn, fragmented and dead creature that is so highly characteristic of this group of subjects.

CARD II

[*laughs—stalls for time*]
1. (∧ 90″) footprint of a shot animal; but there's really no resemblance

INQUIRY

1. just the footprint, with blood from the wound; doesn't resemble any part of the animal (W)

Testing the limits: can barely see dancing figures

His remarkably long delay in responding to this card is clearly the result of a block caused by the strong emotional stimulus of the red color and the violence it represents to him. His response is itself extremely unusual. He does not see in this blot either two animals or two human beings, alive and active creatures that even many of his colleagues are able to produce as indications of some life and movement within themselves. Rather, he reacts with violent, excitable, and almost uncontrollable emotion to the red and then immediately denies all responsibility for it ("but there's really no resemblance"). He gives and takes away in a highly psychopathic fashion, committing himself to something highly specific and then promptly withdrawing from it.

The life of the creature is absent. Its vitality and strength are entirely gone. All that is left are the impress of its existence in the soil and the blood from the wound which it has sustained. The latter represents the split-off and autonomous effects of violence, of which he is both perpetrator and victim. Even in testing the limits he is "barely" able to see the dancing figures, an indication that even at a relatively superficial level merely the scantest liveliness exists in him.

CARD III

1. (∧ 60″) caricature of two men quarreling over a pot

INQUIRY

1. heads, feet, arms—like Secessionist art of 1900 (excluding red) (W)

Even in giving a safe and conventional response—which, however, it took him a full minute to produce—he evinces a need to distance himself from any commitment to what he has seen. It is, as he says, merely a caricature, and he makes no effort to explain in detail why it is so. His own personality is a caricature, in one respect because it is marked by contentiousness rather than genuine conflict. The two men are, after all, quarreling over a pot, as empty a container as von Papen himself appears to be. (The pot is seen with unusual frequency in this group of subjects.) He makes no attempt to justify in relation to the blot his depiction of the two men as quarreling. The arbitrary quality of this aspect of his response indicates that his conflicts, too, are arbitrary and not related integrally to any real issues.

He fails, too, to elaborate his reference to Secessionist art, thereby suggesting a rather pretentious identification with aesthetic values. The reference itself could imply a desire not to be identified with a group of men—his fellow prisoners—with whom he is in fact associated, as well as a yearning for the good old days ("1900") when his own life was in a far better condition than it is now. His exclusion of the red color from something which presumably resembles a painting indicates his tendency to exclude the affective aspects of creativity as well as of human relationships from his behavior and perceptions.

CARD IV

1. (∧ 40″) hide of an animal
2. (∧ 90″) crawling animal or insect

INQUIRY

1. shading gives impression of fur; could be long-haired because it's dark (W)
2. dead specimen of insect or crawling animal; by the shape (W)

His first response is an animal skin. His somewhat tentative use of the shading (initially he calls it a "hide," which could well be leather), and his remark that it merely "gives the impression of fur," however, indicate that he probably makes little or no use of his limited sensitivity toward other people for any but manipulative purposes. The skin and fur in this response have a dysphoric ("dark"), flat, sparse, and depleted quality. They—and he—have no purpose or goal, and no individuality. He lives, in a pale sort of way, in a pale sort of world.

Next, von Papen sees a crawling animal or insect. A rather retrogressive and lowly portrait of himself is, of course, indicated in this response. Even the amount of vitality suggested by the *crawling* of the animal or insect turns out, however, to be spurious, for it is dead. Thus the use of a term of movement is ambiguous and reflects a psychopathic ability to give an imitation of vitality where in fact there is none. It is also common among psychopaths to describe this card as an insect. All in all, then, this response indicates that von Papen is a primitive and unevolved creature, not even, in some sense, alive.

CARD V

1. (∧ 20″) same thing—butterfly, or something like that [not satisfied]

INQUIRY

1. mounted specimen, dead; just the shape (W)

He gives the extremely conventional response of a butterfly but again does not commit himself even to this safe and ordinary concept ("or something like that"). The fact that he refers to the butterfly he saw in the first card is noteworthy. He has seen three other cards and four other concepts since that first response but is nevertheless able to say that the present card is "the same thing"—without even specifying what it is the same as. What happens between two similar events evidently has no special reality for him; he denies differences and distinctions, is unaffected by experience, and prefers instead to leap for safety to the repetition of an earlier mode of behavior. The flatness of his response—and of his existence—is underlined by the fact that the butterfly is a mounted specimen, and dead. It is, moreover, characterized by a quality of display ("mounted specimen") that would appear to be, for him, the most positive attribute of the familiar experience to which he is repetitiously drawn.

CARD VI

[*more stalling for time*]
1. (∧ 90″) some kind of insect with head and feelers

INQUIRY

1. either a specimen or an X-ray photo of the insect; upper part with wings (D)

Another long delay occurs as he struggles to respond to this card, with its strong shades and its contrast between the phallic upper portion and the undifferentiated and fluffy lower section. In his response he is drawn to the masculine aspect—which, however, he describes in negative terms. That is to say, his masculinity has a helpless, demeaned quality—it is merely an insect—and feels exposed ("X-ray photo"). Altogether, this is a very unimposing self-portrait of a man who was a cavalry officer and a master spy. He is quite unable to integrate aspects of femininity into his masculine self, but the latter, too, is vague, weak, helpless, and vulnerable.

This is the third time in this short record that Von Papen has focused on a head, and the second time that he has identified feelers. These responses indicate a strong emphasis on control functions and an anxious, even paranoid, searching out of his environment. It will also be noticed that he nowhere refers to bodies—as if the central part of a person, the part where the vital activities of the organism are taking place, does not exist in him. His rationalizing or control functions, we may see from this, are empty substitutes for substance and individuality.

CARD VII

1. (∧ 30″) torn clouds—but clouds don't look like that; not so black
2. (90″) two fauns looking at each other

INQUIRY

1. general effect of the lighting—but that black center strip doesn't belong (W)
2. just the faces and headdress and arms—they're laughing (upper ⅔ D)

Von Papen's personality has all the diffuse quality of clouds, with their formlessness and absence of clear boundaries. Moreover, they are, as he is, characterized by a destructive and destroyed quality: they are "torn." Characteristically, he denies responsibility for the concept he has produced. He is drawn in depressive fashion to the black color, which he emphasizes twice and whose appropriateness he twice denies. This response indicates an inability to deal with his own depressed feelings, except through denial.

In the second response, he gives, for the first time, an expression of good intelligence, for he manages to produce a concept which in itself explains some of the incongruous details of this blot. While appropriate in this sense, however, the concept of the fauns indicates a neglecting and even distorting response to the feminine aspects of his personality. The fact that the fauns are laughing is unusual, but it is, for fauns, an appropriate response, though it is somewhat arbitrarily imposed on the shape of the blots. Despite this element of arbitrariness, however, the indications are that this subject responds to his feminine aspects, and to those of other people, at a high intellectual level, even though the response is marked by the primitive and bestial attributes of fauns, which are, in intrinsic quality, quite similar to Goering's "half-man, half-animal" response to the same card.

Again, he does not identify bodies. The laughter of the fauns indicates a compensation for depression, while their headdress reflects von Papen's concern with status and display.

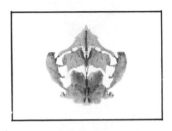

CARD VIII

1. (∧ 30″) two animals crawling up a tree

INQUIRY

1. just looks plantlike from shape and color, but there are no red animals—that's just the shape (W)

His failure to say what kind of animals he sees indicates his distance from his instincts and the noncommittal nature of even the most safe and conventional expression of them. Their movement is, moreover, hesitant, with a certain insidious and creepy quality ("crawling"), and does not appear to be effective in the service of his ambition. While intellect and emotion are integrated in this card ("shape and color"), the former involves poor judgment and the latter inappropriate feeling, for neither in shape nor color does the "tree" much resemble a tree. The "plantlike" quality he refers to in the inquiry is vague and weakly conceived, and indicates the undifferentiated manner in which his "feminine" qualities can emerge. His insistence that there are no red animals shows him being somewhat concrete in his thinking, as if he felt it necessary to emphasize that he can recognize the most obvious aspects of reality.

CARD IX

[rejected]

There is no indication of how long he took before rejecting this card, though he probably did so quickly because no time lapse is recorded. This *is* the most difficult and most frequently rejected card, and, with its profusion of diverse stimuli, it represents the most complex sort of life situation. Without the energy or courage to attack this complexity, and without the guidelines of obvious form, he simply avoids the entire situation.

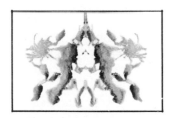

CARD X

1. (∧ 40″) an anatomical picture, perhaps

INQUIRY

1. Well, I'm not well versed in anatomy [doesn't explain] (W)

He makes a mild recovery in this card: he is at least making *some* effort, even if it is in a noncommittal ("perhaps") way. In essence, though, he is covering his inability to deal with this complex situation by a false show of scientific knowledge. He withdraws from this commitment, too, with an apparently modest remark which is really a way out of responsibility for his concept. Color, in anatomical drawings, is arbitrary and serves the sole function of enabling the student to separate closely interwoven parts of the body. The use of this concept here indicates a primitiveness, phoniness, and lack of substance in his response to emotional challenge; he does not even acknowledge any use of the color in his concept.

SUMMARY

"Urbane, dapper and by nature and upbringing a gentleman, he was also essentially well-intentioned," one historian has written of von Papen (Wheaton, p. 135). Von Papen shared this opinion of himself: he was, he declared, a man who had lived "according to the best of my ability in the service of God and my country" (von Papen, p. 545). Surprisingly, the psychologist at Nuremberg saw von Papen in roughly the same terms. He was, says Gilbert, a man drawn to Hitler in the belief that he represented the imperiled traditional values of Germany with which he himself identified. Subsequently, however, he discovered that Hitler posed the greatest threat of all to those values, and at that point he turned against him (Gilbert, 1947, p. 166). Gilbert saw in von Papen no signs of a violent personality, and appears to have felt no reason to challenge von Papen's remark to him that "shooting isn't in my line" (Gilbert, 1947, p. 120). Kelley, for his part, referring to von Papen's "well-integrated, and not at all emotional" character, declared that "his basic personality must be considered as entirely normal, except for his inability to abide by the accepted code of honesty and loyalty" (Kelley, 1947, p. 118).

In fact, the differences between the Nazi program and ideology, on the one hand, and those of the German conservative nationalists as represented by von Papen, on the other, were minimal. "Papen spoke on the radio," Goebbels noted in his diary in August, 1932, "a speech that sprang from beginning to end from our ideas" (quoted in Fest, p. 156). The agreement between the two parties, Fest observes, "went far beyond tactics, not merely negatively in a common antagonism to democracy, liberalism and all freedom, but also positively in the vision of an authoritarian, nationalist class order with militarily orientated structures and the idea of a national community welded into a single disciplined entity" (ibid.). And Rauschning points out that the German nationalist viewpoint "was in essence merely a politically more moderate but fundamentally equally as nihilistic a doctrine of force as that of the National Socialists" (Rauschning, p. 286).

The political similarity between the two groups is paralleled by the psychological similarity between von Papen and many of the other subjects in this volume. It is worth noting that the psychiatrists and psychologists who examined von Papen evidently had a higher opinion of him than he of them. In his memoirs he recalls the "disagreeable" visits of "the gentlemen who called themselves psychiatrists":

> It was their duty, apparently, to determine our sanity, though few of them gave the impression of having any genuine scientific qualifications. If they had, people like Goering and Ribbentrop would certainly have been fascinating subjects. Instead, we were called upon to undergo intelligence tests, together with silly problems like explaining what we saw in certain abstract splodges of ink (Papen, p. 547).

The latter task, he adds, "was above my head, and I asked to be excused." Fortunately for our purposes here, he *did* take the test, and the results enable us to identify the psychological correlates of the major aspects of his career.

"The man of true spirit," von Papen had declared in his famous Marburg speech in 1934, "is so full of vitality that he sacrifices himself for his convictions" (quoted in Fest, p. 160). Von Papen's Rorschach record provides us with psychological grounds for agreeing with Fest (ibid.) regarding the spuriousness of von Papen's famous protest against Nazi excesses, for his record is of a man strikingly devoid of vitality and thus incapable of real conviction. The torn wings of the butterfly he sees in Card I are those of a torn and fragmented human being; the grotesque concept he offers in response to Card II shows the extent to which his vitality and strength are absent, and indicates that even at a relatively superficial level only the scantiest liveliness exists in him. This impression is confirmed in his response to Card IV, which, indicates not only that he lives in a pale sort of way in a pale sort of world but that even the slight (and psychopathically ambiguous) suggestion of life in him is of an extremely primitive sort. His response to the masculine stimulus in Card VI is indicative of a helpless and demeaned man whose masculinity and potency are symbolized by the image of an insect.

This limp, drained quality in von Papen could not possibly have coexisted with any real conviction in anything. The most definite aspect of his personality is its violence. Not only is he far from being a man to whom shooting is something alien, but a proclivity for and the experience of violence is so strongly present in his personality that it has destroyed both his vitality and his strength (Card II); further indications of his destructive—and destroyed—personality are manifest in his response to Card VII. The attributes which might have inhibited the violent and destructive aspects of his personality, moreover, exist only in distorted and vitiated form. His limited sensitivity to nuances in human relationships is used primarily for manipulative purposes (Card IV), and his "feminine" aspects are vague, weak, helpless, and vulnerable and altogether unintegrated with his masculine side (Card VI); indeed, they are also characterized by primitive and bestial qualities (Card VII).

His lack of vitality may have precluded the possibility of any real conviction in the man, but it did not preclude a concern with status and display (Card VII). Anxious, suspicious, and exposed (Card VI), he was nevertheless capable of great ambition. The insidious and essentially weak quality of his ambition (Card VIII) went hand in hand with what we have already noted as the manipulative use of such capacity as he had for sensitivity to nuances in relationships. "He proved to be the kind of traitor beside whom Judas Iscariot is a saint," von Schleicher is reported to have said of him (*Current Biography,* 1941, p. 652). On three successive occasions his close personal aides were murdered by the Nazis, but this did not deter von Papen from further cooperation with the latter. From a psychological standpoint, the fact that he was not a fanatically loyal Nazi cannot be explained by any ethical considerations on his part but chiefly by his inability to remain loyal to anyone or anything.

We have also seen, however, that his instincts are not very effective in the service of his ambition, and that he would frequently respond to situations involving his ambition in a way that was emotionally inappropriate and deficient in judgment. Both his friends and his enemies, we have noted, were unable to take von Papen seriously—though they surely erred in underestimating his capacity for treachery—and the miscalculations that marked both his military and his political careers entirely justified them in this. "What are you worried about?" he replied to colleagues who expressed concern over his alliance with Hitler in 1933. "In two months we shall have Hitler squeezed into a corner so that he squeaks" (quoted in Fest, p. 157). A man capable of such colossal miscalculation could hardly succeed in any sustained effort. As a mere caricature of a man, however, whose internal and external animosities and conflicts reflected no real conviction (Card III), failure in any undertaking was not a matter of much moment to him. As the French ambassador to Berlin during von Papen's chancellorship so acutely remarked, he was a man who would "pick up every gauntlet, accept every wager. If he succeeds in an undertaking he is pleased; if he fails, it doesn't bother him" (quoted in Fest, p. 153).

This observation mirrors not only the empty and purposeless nature of von Papen's loyalties and commitments—if we can indeed call them that—and the mindlessness of his antagonisms, but also his inability to be affected by experience (Card V)—as his continued support of the Nazi regime, despite its frequent poor treatment of him, amply attests.

12

Joachim von Ribbentrop

Joachim Ribbentrop had an adventurous youth that belied the conventional, middle-class character of the family into which he was born. The son of a retired army officer, he was sent to school in France by a wealthy aunt, and then worked at a variety of jobs in Switzerland, England, Canada, and the United States, returning to his native country soon after the outbreak of World War I. A brief stint in the army earned him the Iron Cross for bravery in action. After a few months of active service, however, he was withdrawn from the army and inducted into the German intelligence service. He spent the rest of the war, first in the United States and then in Turkey, working under von Papen.

After the war, Ribbentrop entered the wine business. He soon married the daughter of a wealthy champagne grower and, as a partner in his father-in-law's firm, began playing an increasingly prominent role in Berlin society. Although he had been known as a socialist and pacifist, he now joined the exclusive *Herrenklub*, where industrialists and aristocrats met together to plan Germany's future. In 1926, he signaled his new place in the world by arranging to be adopted by his wealthy aunt, and thereby acquiring the aristocratic "von" before his surname. He had many Jewish friends during this period, and was a frequent attender at the Rothschild salon. Nevertheless, in 1928 he joined the Nazi party.

It was at Ribbentrop's luxurious home in the Berlin suburbs that the final negotiations for Hitler's cabinet were conducted late in January, 1933. Ribbentrop was appointed Reichskommissar for Disarmament and, in this position, negotiated the Anglo–German Naval Agreement of 1935 on terms highly favorable to Germany. He also represented Germany at the conference which ratified Hitler's militarization of the Rhineland. As head of the so-called Ribbentrop Bureau, he created a rival to the Foreign Office, and was frequently called on by Hitler to perform activities at which the more traditional diplomats still balked. In 1936 he was appointed ambassador to England, where his most notable accomplishment was the tremendous scandal caused by his *"Heil Hitler!"* salute to King George. Even while ambassador to England he negotiated the original anti-Comintern treaty with Japan. In February, 1938, he returned to Berlin as the new Foreign Minister. He played a notable role in the negotiations which led up to the Munich Pact, but his most striking achievement was, of course, the Molotov–Ribbentrop agreement in August, 1939, by which Germany and the Soviet Union agreed not to attack each other and to divide Poland between themselves. This infamous pact, however, indirectly signaled the end of Ribbentrop's importance in the Nazi hierarchy. It made the Second World War inevitable and, as a consequence, relegated diplomacy to the sidelines. Ribbentrop, bitterly disliked by most of the other major Nazi leaders, was unable to carve out any new sphere of influence for himself. He tried to reestablish himself by using his good offices to urge Germany's allies to speed up the extermination of their native Jewish populations. As such, he was found by the Nuremberg tribunal to have participated in crimes against humanity. These nefarious efforts, however successful they may have been, did not regain for him the power he sought. On May 1, 1945, he was dismissed from his post by Hitler's successor, Admiral Doenitz. He was found guilty on all four counts of the Nuremberg indictment and sentenced to death by hanging.

CARD I

1. (10″) As I've already said,* that is something like a crab

INQUIRY

1. shape of body, small claws (omits outer projection) (W)

Additional: Could also be a night bird from Dante's *Inferno*—fantastic figure—dark gray–black, like bat

His immediate reaction is to make clear his sanity and his recognition of the continuity of reality by reminding the examiner of what the latter already knows. The possibility that he might give a different response from the one he had given previously does not enter his mind, evidence that he was an unimaginative and dogmatic man. The self-centered response ("As *I've* already said") to the compelling stimuli of the card is a notable feature which, while not psychopathic in itself, alerts us to the possibility of psychopathic responses further on in the record.

The creature depicted in the first response is poor form, revealing poor judgment at the outset; as an armored, aggressive marine animal it indicates the primitiveness and bellicosity of the subject's personality. He ignores the winglike outer projections of the blot, with their potential for ascent to a somewhat higher level of being. And while the claws he identifies are consistent with the crablike animal of his concept, they are *small* claws. Pronounced though his aggressive and destructive tendencies may be, they are evidently not very potent.

In his additional response he shows an improvement of form, rising—for the concept is a conventional one—with some effort only to the level of the ordinary. The reference to Dante's *Inferno* is pretentious, for it is wholly arbitrary and unsubstantiated. Like so many

---

* This is a retest. Ribbentrop's original Rorschach record is not available.

of the subjects in this collection, he adds a remark dissociating himself from responsibility for his own concept ("fantastic figure"). The response also points to deep depression ("night bird . . . dark gray–black").

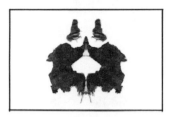

CARD II

1. (10″) harlequins doing a wild dance

INQUIRY

1. They are clapping hands. [Examiner: "Happy?"] No, grotesque; a mummer's dance. Top part is heads, independent of color (W)

His efforts to compensate for his experience of failure and loss are wild and unreal and have a strong element of display, and they are quite unsuccessful in making him feel "happy." Although it is common among this group to see clowns in this card, it is unusual to find that the color is not used to describe their hats, red being an appropriate color for clowns' hats. Used in that way, the red spots indicate a capacity for adaptive emotional response, albeit one which is superficial and connected with status considerations rather than with genuine feeling. Ribbentrop evidently lacks this capacity for adaptive emotional reaction (see also analysis of additional response to Card VIII).

Mummers specialize in mime. In this subject, then, grotesque display substitutes for direct communication.

CARD III

1. (15″) two waiters
2. (40″) a butterfly in the middle

INQUIRY

1. the shape. [Examiner: "Lively?"] Well, yes, a little crazy (W)
2. just the shape (D)

In his depression, the subject alternates between apathy and agitation (the "wild dance" of Card II), though the former quality seems to be more pronounced in the record as a whole. He does not elaborate his concept of the waiters, but presumably could have related it to the blot if he had been asked to do so. Instead, he is asked an interesting and unusual question by the examiner: are the waiters lively? His reply is most unusual: the waiters are "a little crazy." While craziness is appropriate to dancing harlequins or mummers, it is decidedly inappropriate to waiters. There is no rationale for this response nor any attempt to justify it, and his remark indicates a breakthrough of his own craziness from deep within him.

A certain amount of "craziness" can be a sign of vitality and flexibility. If his is elicited only by his current situation of imprisonment, or in that more general aspect of him which is a servile waiter rather than a clown, then he is evidently a man who is otherwise so flattened, rigid, and devoid of spontaneity and the ability to tolerate it, that he can very easily become crazy if something breaks into his rigidity.

The "butterfly" detail in the middle of the card is a very frequent response in the general population. But while six members of this group see the equally popular "bow tie," with its implication of decorative facade, Ribbentrop is the only one who calls it a butterfly. In his anxiety and depression he lacks the concern with self-display that many of his colleagues still maintain. By not using its color, however, Ribbentrop fails to take advantage of an opportunity for easy surface adaptation. He is, therefore, not merely a depressed man but one who avoids emotional involvement as well.

CARD IV

1. (15″) fur hide, hanging on the wall—from Africa

INQUIRY

1. long-haired fur (W)

He has some capacity to respond to nuances of feeling in human relationships, but he experiences them as decorative ("hanging on the wall") and also exotic, primitive, and remote ("from Africa"). He uses that capacity, therefore, for manipulative purposes rather than to establish real human relationships. The response also provides some indication of a sense of loss of control over his feelings ("hanging").

CARD V

1. (10″) Here I said a butterfly or bat—a night animal

INQUIRY

1. night animal, because it's dark and the form is grotesque (W)

Again, as in Card I, he asserts his sanity and his recognition of the continuity of reality, in addition to exposing his unimaginative and dogmatic qualities. The butterfly is a conventional, popular response. But he proceeds with great alacrity from that light, delicate creature to the highly depressive "night animal." Depression, in his personality, is accompanied by an experience of grotesqueness. He is depressed because of his grotesqueness, and grotesque because of his depression.

CARD VI

1. (3") again a hide

INQUIRY

1. short-haired; a little fantastic, but looks like a hide (W)

Two features which have appeared in previous responses are manifested again here: namely, his dull, sparse, depleted quality and his tendency to deny responsibility for his own concept.

CARD VII

[*rejected*]
["I don't know what that is—it doesn't convey anything to me"]

Testing the limits: yes, could be two women with a lot of imagination; (∨) yes, two dancers without heads; top part are capes, grotesque dance.

Unlike some of his colleagues, Ribbentrop does not even have the energy and capacity to see the feminine qualities of this card as grotesque or distorted, but rather removes himself entirely from situations in which they are evoked. He is very much more demanding of realism and accuracy in the representation of female than of male figures (cf. Cards II and III), so that when two women are pointed out to him he can see them only with "a lot of imagination." Imagination, along with other "feminine" qualities (as we are calling them in this volume) such as creativity, lightness, and sensitivity, is among the more prominent qualities that he lacks.

When he is shown the dancers he sees them—but without their heads. Feeling and thought are disconnected in him; and when his feminine aspects are forced to operate they lose their heads and become grotesque in their counterdepressive efforts. Covered by capes, moreover, they lack individuality and are well protected against exposure.

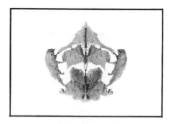

CARD VIII

1. (5″) right and left are skunks; otherwise, I don't know

INQUIRY

1. They're climbing up a tree; independent of color (D)

Additional: could be butterfly below, but only the shape of one. Flags in the middle; only the form

His peremptory and authoritative quality ("right and left are . . .") regarding the obvious rapidly deteriorate into a limp and helpless "I don't know" in the face of emotional challenge. He is capable of being authoritative, moreover, only about the peripheral. We leave to the reader's increasing familarity with the Rorschach technique the elaboration of the meaning of Ribbentrop's self-portrayal as a climbing skunk.

In the inquiry we encounter a number of instances of a pattern that has been manifested in earlier responses. He identifies concepts which fit their colors extremely well, but denies use of the color and relies instead merely on the form. It is as if he is both using and not using the color. He is close to the pull of an old, easy adaptive function—he was probably a good host, was able to take others' feelings into account, and was capable of a friendly manner—but now must block himself off from it altogether. His natural tendency to respond in an easy, adaptive way is now coupled with a need to block off emotions altogether out of a great fear that if he gives in to these he will be overwhelmed by a morass of crazy and grotesque feelings and lose all emotional control.

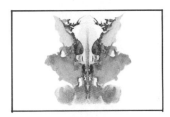

CARD IX

[*rejected*]
["doesn't convey anything—you must have an awful fantasy for this"]

Testing the limits: cannot see sea horses

In the face of the complex life situation represented by this card, he withdraws altogether. The underlying horror of his fantasy ("awful fantasy") emerges here and explains his inability to respond to this card. So far as he is concerned, however, this is not his fault at all, for *the card* "doesn't convey anything."

CARD X

[*rejected*]
["Doesn't convey anything. What would you want? How it looks? I can't say—it has nice colors"]

Additional: The blue might be a polyp by the form, not the color

Testing the limits: cannot find rabbit's head until pointed out

His comment expresses not just withdrawal but extreme regression and an inability to cope. Pathetically, he asks the examiner, here representing authority, for directions about something he has already been doing. This is a frightened and infantile appeal for direction, and for structure. Even the little comment he is now able to make, "It has nice colors," has a pathetically regressive and appeasing quality to it.

Eventually, however, he ends up with a polyp—an octopus. He began his record with a crab and ends it with an octopus: in his condition of disintegration he can see only an alarming beast that sucks in, envelops, and consumes its prey. It is hardly surprising, then, that he is unable to see the mild and unaggressive rabbit in this blot.

SUMMARY

Ribbentrop's Rorschach record is notable for its flatness and constriction, even among this collection of uncommonly flat individuals. Some of this depleted quality, no doubt, is to be explained by the extreme emotional disarray in which Ribbentrop found himself at Nuremberg. "The panic and disintegration that Ribbentrop manifested," Gilbert writes,

were quite extraordinary. At times it resembled agitated or comatose depressions. His mental processes were generally so retarded and confused (in spite of his high IQ) that he could hardly give a rational account of his activities. Every vestige of dignity, not to speak of pride, was gone. . . . He could not sleep without daily sedatives. At times he felt too incapacitated physically to come to court. As the evidence of war crimes was presented, Ribbentrop's guilt anxiety knew no bounds. He offered to be cut to pieces or thrown over a cliff if he had really had any responsibility for those things (Gilbert, 1950, pp. 192–93).

Evidence of extreme depression and anxiety is abundantly present in Ribbentrop's Rorschach record (Cards I, II, V, X); so, too, is the very thin line that was keeping him from falling into the abyss of insanity (Cards III, X). The record is that of a man with primitive, aggressive qualities (Cards I, X) who formerly possessed some capacity for easy, adaptive emotional response (Card VIII) and whose feminine attributes were virtually nonexistent (Card VII). We also see him as a rather ludicrous and servile person (Cards II and III), manipulative (Cards IV and VI), and a skunk (Card VIII). This adds up to a picture of a man who is not only depressed, but also psychopathic.

Ribbentrop "barely eked out eight uncertain and mediocre responses (about the same on retest)," Gilbert writes, "so that an analysis of the record would not be profitable" (Gilbert, 1950, p. 192). Yet, although Ribbentrop's defenses were indeed shattered by his recent experiences—not the least traumatic for him being the fact that the Fuehrer to whom he had been so completely devoted had not even mentioned him in his will, and had designated Seyss–Inquart as Foreign Minister (Kelley, 1947, p. 112)—it is by no means to be taken for granted that the record presented here is profoundly different from the one he might have produced at a more felicitous period of his life.

It would appear that almost everyone who knew Ribbentrop considered him to be a weak, stupid, and pretentious person. "Of all my sons-in-law," his wife's mother said of him, "the most foolish became the most prominent" (Kelley, 1947, p. 95). And Goebbels, explaining the contempt which most of his colleagues in the Nazi leadership felt for Ribbentrop, remarked that while each of them had at least one praiseworthy quality, the foreign minister had none (Fest, p. 178). When Hitler justified his selection of Ribbentrop as ambassador to London on the grounds that he knew many of the leading figures in British social and political life, Goering, who had protested the appointment, replied, "Yes, but they know him, too."

Ribbentrop's pretentiousness was legendary: underneath it was a profound mediocrity and sense of inferiority. On his famous trip to Moscow in August, 1939, he was struck by the "strong faces" of Stalin and his henchmen. It was Ribbentrop's great desire, Fest suggests,

> which he pursued beyond the limits of the ridiculous, to appear himself as "a man with a strong face." Hence the forced toughness which he assumed; the artificial, screwed-up pose of the statesman filled with cares for the future; the laboriously furrowed brow; in short, all the Caesar-like grimacing which, in all his high-falutin obtuseness, so often verged toward *buffo* comic opera. Eyewitnesses said he almost fell on the rails of the Gare des Invalides when he visited Paris in 1938, through holding his head high, as he always did. The vanity, the provocative self-assertion and continual self-dramatization, were merely the reverse side of his very ordinary personality (Fest, p. 178).

Ribbentrop was fanatically devoted to Hitler, who, no doubt considering this a proof of the man's high abilities, declared him to be a "genius" and a "second Bismarck" (Fest, p. 178). And just as he showed complete loyalty and obedience to the Fuehrer, so, too, did he demand "from his employees the same attitude which he himself [took] toward the Fuehrer" (Kelley, 1947, p. 108). He would, he warned, personally shoot any subordinate who contradicted his instructions (Schwarz, p. 191). Ribbentrop's sense of authority was, then, completely bound up with Hitler. He submitted completely to him and, in the microcosmic world of his own Foreign Ministry, played the role of Fuehrer.

Significantly, one of Ribbentrop's few quarrels with Hitler was over a trivial circumstance, one involving a minor question of status:

> In 1941, Hitler and I had a disagreement. It was really a very simple sort of thing—over a decoration. I had a decoration for service in the Foreign Office, and Hitler was bringing out a new decoration which would have made mine only a second-class one. Really, it wasn't very important. However, we argued and I lost my temper and stated that if my opinion wasn't good enough, I would resign (Kelley, 1947, p. 101).

In the service of his consuming need for status and display, Ribbentrop could also be unboundedly ruthless. Grunberger reports that Ribbentrop acquired his magnificent country estate in Fuschl, Austria, by the simple expedient of having its previous owner committed to Dachau and murdered there (Grunberger, p. 94).

Ribbentrop was, then, a grotesque person—truly a skunk—but he was not a very real person. He was, says Schwarz, like an actor who "plays in reality only the outer attributes of the role, not its essence. The actor is naively convinced that by concentrating on the attributes and making them dazzling, everybody will believe themselves to be face to face with the real thing. . . . It is the cliche of a mind incapable of following its own organic law and therefore escaping into stage effects. If Hitler is the reincarnation of Knipperdolling the Anabaptist, Ribbentrop is just a half-baked Cagliostro." (Schwarz, p. 292).

The salient features of Ribbentrop's personality, as the world knew it, appear, then, to have been compensation, both gaudy and sinister, for his inner emptiness; there was very little of a person underneath the actor's makeup. Hence the vacuity of Ribbentrop's Rorschach record is probably an accurate reflection of the vacuity of the man himself, not just after his denouement but in the years of his ascendancy as well. His Rorschach record reveals him in all his emptiness, stripped of the vainglory which he used to mask the coldness and banality of his being and deprived of the sustaining identification with Hitler through which he compensated for the weakness of his personality.

13

Alfred Rosenberg

Alfred Rosenberg was considered to be a Baltic German—he was born in Reval, in Estonia—but it has been suggested that there was little if any German blood in his veins; indeed, it may actually have been the case that he was of partly Jewish ancestry. The son of a cobbler, he studied architecture at Riga and Moscow, and was in Moscow during the Russian revolution. In 1918, at the age of 25, he moved to Germany, settling in Munich. There, he joined the secret Thule society, a nationalist organization that dabbled in occult practices and specialized in paranoid myths about Jewish, Freemasonic, and Bolshevik conspiracies.

Rosenberg soon became an acknowledged authority on these subjects. His literary output was prolific; its substance is indicated by the titles of some of his books: *The Tracks of the Jews Through the Ages* (1920); *Immorality in the Talmud* (1920); *The Crime of Freemasonry* (1921); *The Morass: A Plague in Russia* (1922), and so on. He played a notable role in the dissemination of the notorious forgery *The Protocols of the Elders of Zion*, the purported records of a world Jewish conspiracy. In 1930 he published his masterpiece, *The Myth of the Twentieth Century*, which, next to Hitler's *Mein Kampf*, was considered the most important text of the Nazi movement. The book is characterized by fantastic racist theories of history and society, all presented in a tone of pretentious profundity that is quite incapable of concealing the extreme poverty of its author's intellect.

His accomplishments earned him the status of chief ideologist of the Nazi party, and the post of editor of its official newspaper. With Hitler's accession to power, Rosenberg sought to gain control of German foreign policy in his capacity as head of the Nazi party's foreign political office. His ambitions in this regard were frustrated, however, by the opposition of, successively, von Neurath and Ribbentrop, and by his own political and administrative ineptitude. He had to settle instead for a host of splendid but largely empty titles such as "Deputy to the Fuehrer of the National Socialist Party for the Entire Spiritual and Ideological Training of the Party." In reality, Goebbels, as Minister of Propaganda, played a far more important role in propagating the Nazi ideology, and Rosenberg's boast that he possessed "sovereignty over the judgment of all intellectual institutions" in the Third Reich (quoted in Fest, p. 170) reflects his vainglory rather than the reality. This is not to say, however, that Rosenberg became an obscure figure. In his capacity as editor of the *Voelkischer Beobachter* and through his addresses to major Nazi rallies (Burden, pp. 24ff.), he contributed substantially to the Nazification of German society.

In 1941, possibly because as a Balt he was considered familiar with these regions but possibly also because Hitler and others considered him a boor and wished to get him away from Berlin, Rosenberg was appointed Reichsminister for the Eastern Occupied Territories. His powers, however, were "pathetically limited from the outset":

> Goering, as General–Supervisor of the Four-Year Plan, Himmler as Special Commissioner in the Army Operational Zone, Chief of Police and Reichsfuehrer of the SS as well as Reich Commissar for the Consolidation of the German National Identity and responsible for resettlement measures, Sauckel as Commissioner for the Labor Force, and finally the Wehrmacht High Command: all these ate away his authority to the point where little was left but the title. . . . the function of his office . . . was visibly reduced to writing pleas which no one read, memoranda which were circulated only within his own office, protests which no one took notice of any more: a forgotten man at the head of a forgotten institution. Despised, tricked and ridiculed, finally in autumn 1944 he resigned. (Fest, pp. 172–73).

Rosenberg appears to have opposed a number of the more brutal activities of Nazi forces in Eastern Europe, including the murder of

Russian prisoners of war. He was, however, deeply involved in other brutalities, most notably those connected with the extermination of Jews. For these crimes, he was sentenced to death by the Nuremberg tribunal and executed.

CARD I

1. (∧ 15″) same as last time*—beetle with spread-out wings

INQUIRY

1. It is the feelers and torn wings and the body shape of the beetle— more dead, or mounted (W)

The possibility that he might give a different response from the one he had given previously does not enter his mind, evidence that he was an unimaginative and dogmatic man who, at least in this situation, finds it necessary to make apparent his sanity and his recognition of the continuity of reality.

In the first response he sees a beetle rather than a butterfly, indicating thereby a low level of personal development. The "spread-out wings" give an impression of liveliness, or at least of life. This impression is negated, however, in the response to the inquiry. The beetle is "more dead" than alive, and its wings are torn and thus incapable of flight. The response reveals not only a disintegrated and fragmented self but an imitation of life by something which actually has no life—a psychopathic characteristic that has been noted in a number of other responses among this collection of subjects.

---

* This is a retest. Rosenberg's original Rorschach record is not available.

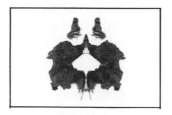

CARD II

1. (∧ 5″) two clowns with red caps clapping hands, one foot up, elbows out

INQUIRY

1. black costume with red dunce caps and red socks—just caught in the middle of a movement (W)

While not an original response, this is a reasonably well inte-grated image and reflects the above-average intelligence shown in many of these records. There is, however, a certain arbitrary quality in the description of the red as, respectively, dunce caps and socks. The response, moreover, also contains an element of display—viz., the clowns performing—and implies that the integration and appro-priateness suggested by the combination of form and color exists, in fact, only on a rather superficial level.

What is more, clowns cannot be considered entirely responsible for their actions, and these are particularly foolish clowns, in their dunce caps. The additional remark that they are "just caught in the middle of a movement" reinforces this dissociation of the person from his own actions.

It is, of course, extraordinarily interesting to note that the philoso-pher, so-called, of the Nazi party describes himself, albeit unwit-tingly, as a dunce. The response contains a number of more direct references to Nazism. The "one foot up" is suggestive of the Nazi goose step, in its own way as absurd a disfiguration of the human being as clown. And it is very difficult indeed to resist the inference that the movement in which the subject is caught up, ludicrously and irresponsibly, is the Nazi movement.

It will be noticed that the clownish figures are clad in black, but with certain red appendages to their costume. In the Nazi uniform a red sleeve band displaying the swastika was worn on otherwise black clothing: the red is, in a striking way, integrated with the black, but it is an arbitrary integration, and the vitality and brightness represented by the red are, quite literally, worn on the sleeve. That is to say, they are only superficially adaptive emotions and are poorly integrated with the depressiveness of the black, and possess a strong element of display besides.

Here, then, is a self-portrait of a Nazi: depressive and with poorly integrated compensatory qualities that give a largely spurious impression of vitality; comical and even stupid; and not responsible for being in the appalling society which he has joined—he is "just caught in the middle of a movement."

CARD III

1. (∧ 12″) two withered old men, standing by a pot, holding on, pulling apart
2. (40″) two red torches

INQUIRY

1. two men in tuxedos (usual W)
2. just flickering red light—not really red lamps—torches (D)

In the first response to this card he describes himself as a withered old man in whom there is a strong element of formality and facade ("tuxedo"), and who is engaged in a meaningless and self-contradictory activity ("holding on, pulling apart") that suggests intense but empty inner conflict. The second response indicates that some of his emotional response is still present, for all that it is "flickering." It is a positive sign that, unlike many of his colleagues, Rosenberg does not describe the red as "bloody," and that the torches do indeed throw some light. But the torches, with their strong connotations of display, are not really part of himself (they are unconnected with the "two withered old men"), and the capacity for emotional response to others that they represent is not only tenuous ("flickering") but rather superficial as well.

CARD IV

1. (∧ 5″) long-haired, soft fur rug before a hearth

INQUIRY

1. the shape and shading of a fur rug (W)

Rosenberg's response to this card appears to be quite out of character with the rest of his record. If this is a spontaneous and untutored response it indicates an unusually appropriate and adaptive sensitivity and an awareness of nuances in human relationships: the hearth, moreover, suggests relatively intact areas of warmth in this man. On the other hand (and this *is* a retest), Rosenberg may have learned the "correct answer," as it were, from implications he detected in the inquiry to his response to this card when he first took the Rorschach. If that is the case (and only the discovery of the original record would answer this question), then his "correct" reply here would be a very strong indication indeed of psychopathy. In any event, the kind of sensitivity implied in this response can be used either for establishing genuinely adaptive relationships *or* for manipulative purposes instead.

CARD V

1. (∧ 5″) a bat, just about to fly away

INQUIRY

1. has the pointed head and massive wings of a bat. [Examiner: "Color?"] Yes, it is dark, as in nature (W)

In this conventional response he shows rather poor judgment, for the head in the card is *not* pointed and the wings are *not* massive. Even in quite ordinary situations, then, his intellectual capacities can fail him.

The fact that the bat is "just about to fly away" sounds arbitrary. (Why isn't it just landing? He offers no explanation.) Presumably it means that he is seeing it from behind. Since sexual identity is much less readily ascertained from the rear, the tendency to see rear views, especially when no justification is offered in relationship to the details of the blot, suggests a relatively undeveloped psychosexual identity. The dark color of the bat, described in response to the inquiry, could be indicative of a depressive mood; however, it was made in response to a question by the examiner.

CARD VI

1. (∧ 5″) a rug—soft fur

INQUIRY

1. shape of stretched fur—shading shows soft fur (W)

Compare the discussion of Card IV. The concept "stretched," seen in so many of these records, suggests the strain involved in the subject's adaptive efforts.

CARD VII

1. (∧ 5″) two little boys talking to each other

INQUIRY

1. they are porcelain figures, not really alive

Testing the limits: re the dancing figures, "No; there are vertebrae, though."

The figures here, although not depicted as females, are far less distorted than those provided by many other subjects in this volume. In the inquiry, however, the two little boys talking to each other lose their aspect of vitality and communication and become mere porcelain figures, suggesting that the child, in this man, (his child-like inner qualities) is unreal and without actual vitality. Porcelain figures, it will be recalled, frequently capture a certain movement and liveliness of form. They are, as Rosenberg says in response to Card II, "caught in the middle of a movement."

In testing the limits, Rosenberg is still unable to see the dancing female figures and only perceives the vertebrae. In doing so, he reveals the bareness and poverty of his inner life and its weakness and debilitation, as he does in the "two withered old men" of Card III.

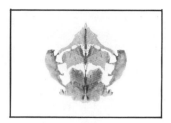

CARD VIII

1. (∨ 10″) two field mice climbing down a tree—if you ignore the color

INQUIRY

1. red leaves on top, but the animals are independent of color—the rest is branches and trunk (W)

There are two remarkable features to this response. In marked contrast to a very large proportion of all subjects and to his code-fendants in particular, Rosenberg turns the card upside down and sees animals climbing *down*. Far from seeing either fierce beasts or opportunistic chameleons, he identifies field mice, which are among the most timorous of animals. His instinctual qualities, then, are not harnessed in the service of his ambition (as would be suggested by animals climbing up); rather, his instincts are vitiated by an experience of profound failure.

The intensity of his need to depict the animals as climbing down —and hence the intensity of his feelings of failure—is made clear by the fact that with the card upright the rest of the blot can indeed be seen as a tree of fairly reasonable form; turned the other way around, however (so that the animals are climbing down), the tree has hopelessly *bad* form.

This man could evidently suffer very bad lapses of judgment and entertain very irrational notions, which were occasioned at least in part by his inability to deal appropriately with emotional stimuli. What is also remarkable, however, is the plausibility with which he presents this completely irrational description of a tree. It is only on careful examination that one discovers its extremely poor form; yet there is nothing tentative about the way in which he points to the tree and its leaves, branches, and trunk. He must have been a talented con artist. This ability to present a completely irrational idea or to perform a completely irrational act in an apparently innocent and persuasive fashion—the ability to disguise the inappropriate as appropriate—is strongly associated with psychopathy.

CARD IX

Comment: "This is one on which I couldn't see anything."
1. (∨ ∨ 30″) at best, two crabs crawling out of a mixture of red and blue plants

INQUIRY

1. The crabs should really be darker, but otherwise it's more the impression from color than form (W)

The initial comment shows a certain ability to admit his own limitations. Yet he makes a determined effort (this is by far the longest reaction time in this record) to respond to the card and finally does so. He recognizes but does not completely give in to his weakness; this, at least, is the initial impression conveyed by his response.

His intellectual output and judgment continue to be poor, however. He becomes very sloppy and inappropriate in his identification of color (the blue to which he refers is actually green), and he is unable to distinguish between pastel and stronger shades. These features indicate a considerable lack of differentiation in the intensity of his emotions, as well as something of a "things mean what I say they mean" quality.

The armored, aggressive, unevolved crab in this card has extremely poor form and suggests a lapse in rational judgment. While he has a sense of the inadequacy of his concept, he attributes it to a very minor and peripheral aspect of the response—why, after all, *should* the crab be darker?

We see him, then, as a man with extremely poor self-critical faculties. He puts on a show of subtle and sensitive awareness of his own limitations, while at the same time riding roughshod over reality and generalizing the components of the blot in an extremely poor fashion. While this may to an extent have been a diversionary tactic aimed at concealing his limitations from others, it is probable that by this time he had also managed to conceal them from himself as well.

As in many other records in this collection, we note here the expression of his "feminine" impulses, his feelings, merely in terms of undifferentiated and unidentified colored plants.

CARD X

1. (∧ 3″) animal pictures on a coral reef, with sea horses and crabs and green snakes

INQUIRY

1. long red strips of coral; form and color of gray sea horses; shape of crabs but not color (W)

The organization of this card into an underwater scene is at first glance an appropriate and lively combination of emotion, impulse, and imagination. If one looks only slightly below the surface of this apparent image, however, something close to chaos appears. The only colors he uses are the misnamed red (which is actually pink), the gray of the sea horses, and the green snakes. With no recognition of their inappropriateness in this setting, he includes the snakes on the coral reef. We have then, in this response, a thin facade of intellectual control and appropriate emotional reaction which only very inadequately covers flatness and disintegration.

SUMMARY

Alfred Rosenberg, one of the Nuremberg prison psychiatrists wrote, was "the culmination of everything brutal and vicious in the Nazi Party" (Kelley, 1947, p. 50). The prosecution at Nuremberg depicted him as among the most important of Nazi criminals —"there was not a single basic tenet of the Nazi philosophy which was not given authoritative expression by Rosenberg," it asserted (NCA, I, pp. 120, 130)—and the judgment handed down by the tribunal in sentencing him to death was that he was guilty of all four counts in the Nuremberg indictment.

Both historically and psychologically, these assessments are questionable. The racial doctrines which Rosenberg enunciated at such length and with so much pretentious obscurity did indeed establish him as the philosopher of the Nazi party. But it is doubtful whether his books were, in fact, widely read—his fellow defendant von Shirach dubbed him "the man who sold more copies of a book no one ever read than any other author" (Kelley, 1947, p. 44)—and while he was obviously influential, he was surely considerably less so than Goebbels and Hitler himself in the dissemination of Nazi propaganda. There is also, as we have seen, much evidence to suggest that his role in the formulation of policy was never great and diminished rapidly (Fest, pp. 172–73; cf. Rauschning, pp. 191–93; Shirer, p. 942; Broszat, pp. 24–25). And although it was established beyond doubt at Nuremberg that he knew about and participated in measures for the extermination of Jews and others, the fact is also that he opposed the murder of Russian prisoners of war and sought, as a matter of policy, to win over the peoples under his control to the Nazi cause instead of alienating them by repressive measures (Shirer, p. 952; cf. Fest, p. 174).

Rosenberg's record, then, hardly justifies Kelley's description, though it is surely sufficiently incriminating to have warranted the judgment and sentence handed down by the tribunal at Nuremberg. From a psychological standpoint, moreover, his lack of consideration for human values was not primarily and possibly not at all the product of an inner need to commit violence. His Rorschach record reveals some capacity for tenderness, human concern, warmth, and similar qualities, although in an undifferentiated and attenuated form, and it does not show him to be a sadist or a brutal, destructive, violent person. In this rather specific sense, there is in fact a measure of truth in Doenitz's surprising remark that Rosenberg "is a man who would not hurt a fly" (Gilbert, 1947, p. 274). Even in the earliest days of the Nazi movement, he did not participate in the street-gang violence in which almost all his colleagues indulged, and during the First World War, as well as in the 1930's, he kept well away from any kind of soldiering (Dutch, pp. 85–86; Rosenberg, p. 26). Evidently it was by no means only toward the end of his life that he was a timorous "field mouse" (Card VIII); the quality would appear, rather, to have been a permanent feature of his personality. How, then, are we to account for the brutality and violence which he publicly advocated and sought, in his inimitably heavy-handed way, to "philosophize" about? And how are we to account for his participation—if only at an administrative level—in mass murder?

"German beauty," Rosenberg declared, with characteristic bombast, in his *Myth of the Twentieth Century*, "means inward law" (quoted in Dutch, p. 91). Yet "inward law"—that is, inner order and accountability—was precisely the quality that Rosenberg lacked. His internal disorganization profoundly affected both his emotional and his intellectual functioning. The "torn wings" of his response to Card I introduce us to a personality whose disintegration and fragmentation were long-standing features rather than merely products of his present misfortunes. The inner conflict revealed in his response to Card III is intense but empty and trivial, rather like the cluttered desk of a very minor bureaucrat. And while his intelligence was somewhat higher than that of many of his colleagues (Card II), we see repeated indications of the failure of his intellectual judgment, even in quite ordinary situations. He was, after all, the man who, on a goodwill mission to England in the 1930's, placed a swastika wreath on the Cenotaph in London (Zeman, p. 61).

Rosenberg's overriding personality need, it would thus appear, was for the "inward law" that would compensate for his inner emotional and intellectual chaos. Both his internal disorganization and his efforts at compensating for it were projected on to the external world. This process began to come to the surface some time during his early adulthood.

As we have already seen, Rosenberg was in Moscow, studying architecture, during the fateful year of 1917. By his own acknowledgment, however, the dramatic upheavals of the Russian revolution left but a scant impression on him (Rosenberg, pp. 20ff.). He proceeded with his own studies and produced his thesis design—for a crematorium in Riga!—without apparently experiencing the chaos all around him as a mirror of his internal disarray. Leaving Russia for reasons connected with his wife's health rather than with the political situation, he traveled west and arrived in Germany a few days after the Armistice ending the First World War had been signed. "I left my homeland behind me," he wrote, "in order to gain a fatherland for myself" (Rosenberg, p. 29).

It is apparent that he was drawn to Germany in large measure out of a need to live in an ordered society. After the upheavals he had witnessed all around him during the previous year, such a need might ordinarily be considered natural, and his efforts to satisfy it healthy. In fact, however, it would seem that the intensity of his need in this regard was rooted not in an objective assessment of the external world—whose turmoil, as we have seen, left him unaffected while he was in Moscow—but rather in the process of pro-

jection of his own inner turmoil onto that external world which began at about this time. Possibly the mounting social and political
chaos all around him contributed to his sense of disarray, which
quite probably was established in him in early childhood, but the
important point for an understanding of Rosenberg would seem to
be that some time after leaving Moscow he began to experience
that chaos as a projection of his own chaos. It was now, too, that
the process of transferring his internal needs for order onto an
external, political situation began to take place. He would counter
the inner disarray of his "homeland" with the structure and authority of the "fatherland."

What he found, instead, was a Germany on the brink of revolution, a revolution which seemed to threaten "the delicate structure,"
as he called it, of "her industry, commerce and population" (Rosenberg, p. 30)—just as it threatened even more "the delicate structure" of his own being. In other remarks about his arrival in Germany we find indications that his depressive qualities (Card II)
were associated with his experiences of disarray:

> Strange how empty memory can be sometime. In spite of all
> attempts to remember certain details, I can recall no specific
> episode of the trip. . . . Only this much I remember: that our
> entrance into Berlin was sad, that the houses looked twice as
> gray; and that at the entrance to our hotel revolutionary pamph-
> lets were immediately pressed into our hands (ibid.).

The Nazi doctrines that Rosenberg would at a somewhat later
stage in his life begin to articulate rather clearly reveal his attempt
to use a political restructuring of the world as a compensation for
his own, inner lack of structure. "Internationalism," he declared,
with reference to both communism and democracy, "destroys the
foundations of the ability to think and feel" (Burden, p. 52). The
narrowest, most automated nationalism would be its substitute, his
defense against the weakness of his own ability to think and feel.
Moreover, democracy, as he was fond of saying, turned nations
into "masses of unrelated individuals with no political unity," while
socialism "stirs up organizations and groups to revolt against each
other" (Burden, p. 51). The arbitrary and rigid monism of the
fascist state would counter the fragmentation and intense—but substanceless—conflict within his own being.

"So life pulled me and I followed," Rosenberg reflected regarding the course of his life. "I saw myself amidst the interplay of
forces with all their confusing aspects" (Rosenberg, p. 30). By
controlling the interplay of forces he would resolve the confusion in
the world—and in himself. And for all his passivity—"I followed";

"just caught in the middle of a movement" (Card II)—and despite his renunciation of responsibility for the grotesqueness into which he allowed himself to be led, it is clear that Rosenberg *did*, in his own perverted way, seek to bring order and structure into the world—and into himself. He did not just follow; he also pulled.

"It belongeth also to the judgment of the . . . sovereign power," Hobbes had written (*De Cive,* VI, 16), "to set forth and make known . . . what is good and what bad; and what he ought to do, and what not." As a Nazi, Rosenberg identified himself with a movement that sought to acquire such power; as a leading ideologist of that movement, he hoped that his own crazy and confused thoughts and feelings would be imbued with sovereign power and hence given structure—not because they inherently possessed it, but because the power of a total state would proclaim that they were, indeed, structured. Accepted as truth by an entire nation, his "philosophical" constructs would become true. Sanctioned by the institutions of the state, his fragmented and disorganized mind would acquire the appearance of stability and structure.

Hannah Arendt has convincingly demonstrated that the Nazi state, despite its appearance of extremely rigid and unitary structure, was in fact organized along far more irrational and evanescent lines than is generally supposed (Arendt, 1958, pp. 395ff.). But the shifting, inchoate disarray of Rosenberg's own personality was too great even for the Nazi state to accept; the "things mean what I say they mean" quality of his mind surpassed both the desire and the ability of his colleagues to reshape the world. If he unwittingly revealed himself to be a clown and a dunce (Card II), the philosopher of the Nazi party was considered no better than such by his associates. "The buffoon," his deputy on the *Voelkischer Beobachter* called him, "the crackpot ninny"; while Goebbels would rather wittily refer to Rosenberg's Ministry for the Eastern Occupied Territories ("Ostministerium") as the *Cha-ostministerium*, the Ministry of Chaos (quoted in Fest, pp. 166, 173).

Rosenberg's advocacy of and participation in acts of extreme violence were not, accordingly, rooted in an intrinsic propensity for brutality. Rather, they reflected the violence which must ensue when a personality that is highly disorganized and a mind that is guilty of frequent lapses in rationality seek to rearrange the world along their own disorganized and irrational lines.

Alfred Rosenberg, then, had the energy and ambition to set the world in order—as he conceived of order—but he utterly lacked the capacity to do so, precisely because his own world was so disordered. The profound experience of failure evident in his Rorschach record (Card VIII) was by no means primarily the result of the collapse of the Third Reich. Long before its collapse, he had failed miserably within it. Even more profoundly, however, he had failed all through the course of his life in his attempts to give structure and substance to his personality. The pretentiousness and arrogance for which he was noted among his fellow leaders in the Nazi party (e.g., Fest, pp. 166f.) and, equally, the lofty destiny that he proclaimed for the Aryan race could never have been effective or even persuasive compensation for his feelings of disorganization, emptiness, and failure.

14

Fritz Sauckel

In the spring of 1942 Germany's labor shortage had become acute, and Adolf Hitler turned to his old comrade from Munich days, Fritz Sauckel, to remedy it. The new Plenipotentiary General for the Utilization of Labor had come a long way from his humble proletarian origins. Born in 1894, the only child of a postman and his seamstress wife, Sauckel left school at the age of 15, working as a seaman and at various odd jobs before joining the Nazi Party in 1923. He remained an uneducated man—he never read books, he told the Nuremberg tribunal—but he was a highly effective administrator. These gifts would soon make him "the greatest slaver of all time" (Davidson, p. 506).

Captured Nazi documents give a vivid impression of the assiduousness with which Sauckel rounded up hundreds of thousands of people in the occupied countries for work in German factories. The brutality of his methods shocked the Reich Minister for the Occupied Eastern Territories—Rosenberg—who demanded of Sauckel: "It must be avoided that lines in front of theaters be arrested bodily and be brought from there directly to Germany. . . . Men and women including youngsters from 15 years on up are allegedly picked up on the street, from the market places and village festivals, and carried off." Recruiting methods are used, Rosenberg went on to complain, "which probably have their origin in the blackest period of the slave trade. . . ." (Bernstein, pp. 213–14).

At other times his methods were more subtle. In France he trained female agents "who for good pay went hunting for men and liquored them up—in the old days it would have been called shanghaiing—in order to dispatch them to Germany" (Bernstein, p. 216). Of five million workers brought to Germany, fewer than 200,000 according to Sauckel's own estimate, came voluntarily (ibid.).

The conditions under which they were brought to Germany were terrible. Jammed together in freight cars, they sometimes went for days without water. But their life in the factories was frequently still harsher. They worked in the clothes they had been picked up in, were fed meat from tubercular animals, and were obliged to work even when sick. At night they frequently slept in flooded cellars or unheated barracks and even in ash bins and baking ovens. There is no telling how many thousands died of exhaustion, malnutrition, or disease (Davidson, pp. 509ff.).

Found guilty on counts three and four of the indictment (war crimes and crimes against humanity) Sauckel was sentenced to death. He was executed on October 16, 1946.

CARD I

1. (∨ 5″) skeleton and bones
2. (∧ 35″) kind of bug

INQUIRY

1. mammoth skeleton by the shape (middle DS)
2. middle part has shape of bug (D)

Even for this group of subjects the lifelessness, emptiness, and flatness indicated by the "skeleton and bones" concept are extreme, and suggest a striking inability to come up with a rational generalization even in a conventional situation. Arbitrarily, grandiloquently, and beyond any common sense the skeleton is then described as "mammoth." The flatness and irrationality of the concept are strongly suggestive of psychosis; and the attempt to compensate for its vacuity by blowing it up to "mammoth" proportions fails completely.

The "kind of bug" indicates an extremely low level of development; as does Sauckel's inability to maintain the grandiosity—wholly irrational and without foundation as it is—of his "mammoth" skeleton.

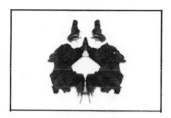

CARD II

1. (∧ 30″) fantastic butterfly
2. (40″) lampshade
3. (50″) dance pose

INQUIRY

1. black butterfly with red tips (W)
2. shape of white space (S)
3. black Spanish mantilla, white dance dress, spinning toe dance (DS)

The butterfly concept for the whole of this card is not very bad form, but it is rather childish. Here, as in the previous card, one of his problems seems to be a marked inability to see the card in terms of two sides in relationship to one another. Such responses, even if they are only the two clowns which many of his colleagues can see, indicate an ability to see that there can be two sides, and that there can be conflict in relationships—and in oneself. Sauckel, instead, makes an unbrilliant effort at generalizing the whole. He does so in a way that is psychopathic, attributing his inability to justify the concept by referring to its "fantastic" quality. It would seem that the "red tips" of the butterfly are also quite irrational, and are included in his response for no better reason than that there happens to be some red on the card. As with so many of the subjects in this book, we find the depressive emphasis on the black coupled with a peripheral, arbitrary, and unintegrated emotional adaptation. His use of the red, however, is considerably more meaningless than is the red cap worn by clowns in many of the other responses to this card in this collection.

In the second response Sauckel goes out of the field, leaving the substance of the stimulus situation, and retreats into the white background, as though to make something substantial out of it. The lampshade is not bad form, but it is a subtle way of retreating from the liveliness of the card, from its two-sidedness, and from its depressive qualities. He seeks light and suggests that it is there, when there is, in fact, nothing.

In the third response he uses the white space and adjacent details for a quite original and rather beautiful image. The excellent quality of the form and its creative originality serve not only to show the high intellectual potential of this man (of which there is hardly any other evidence in his record), but also to underline the schizophrenic aspects of his personality: the veering between very bad and very good form is a hallmark of schizophrenia.

His response on inquiry involves a black/white contrast, suggesting not only his depressive qualities but also his simplistic, black/white moral view—which, again, is in contrast with the fine quality of his creative concept here. The fact that his concept is located largely in the white space again emphasizes the lack of substance in the man. The position and figure–ground reversal of his image demonstrates the lack of connection with any positive feminine qualities that he might have (note the rejection of Card VII).

It will be noted that he goes from the live, but still, image of a dance pose into a "spinning toe dance." It appears that ego-alien forces are taking over inside him. The circumstances under which this occurs seem to be those in which he is suddenly challenged by intense emotional stimuli, by potential conflict and intense depressive feelings. He is unable to reject this situation out of hand by going on to the next card—possibly because this combination of stimuli is too intense for him. So he leaves the situation symbolically, going into the empty space and using the remnants of a good mind to produce an intellectually superior idea. In the process, some of the feminine side of his nature, and his highly undeveloped emotions, comes close to taking him over and leaving his conscious purpose behind.

CARD III

1. (∧ 15″) two fops in tailcoats, greeting each other, hat in hand

INQUIRY

1. just the shape of the black part; red doesn't belong (W)

This is the first response in which he is able to recognize the two sides of the card and establish a relationship between them. But the two "fops in tailcoats" are individuals concerned with form rather than with substance. They are rather ridiculous, distorted, showy, and frilly: formal, superficial persons engaged in formal and superficial activity in which considerations of status ("hat") are emphasized. His reference to the "shape of the *black* part" again calls attention to his depressive qualities. But he is unable to deal with the emotional stimulus of the red and declares that it does not belong, thereby heightening the sense of substanceless formality and foppishness in his concept—and in his relationships with others and within himself.

CARD IV

1. (∧ 5″) could be hide of a bear

INQUIRY

1. symmetrical hide, hairy edges (W)

The frequently mentioned bear hide is made quite unusual in this response by the failure to use the highly fitting light and dark shading of the blot to suggest a furry texture. Only the "hairy edges"—a concept based on the shape rather than the texture of the blot—suggests that this is a bear hide. The qualities of sensitivity to feelings and awareness of and responsiveness to nuances in human relationships are absent in Sauckel; they do not even exist on the edges of his personality. He emphasizes the symmetry of the blot and thereby indicates, once again, the strength of his need to deny inner conflict.

CARD V

1. (∧ 3″) a bat

INQUIRY

1. shape of head, wings, etc. (W)

Very quickly, Sauckel gives a conventional response. In the inquiry, he points to the head and wings in an appropriate manner. In this conventional situation he performs adequately and almost unnoticeably. The only remarkable thing about this response, in terms of his own record and of the others in this collection, is its lack of remarkability.

CARD VI

1. (∧ 15″) X-rayed body
2. (35″) turned leg of a stool

INQUIRY

1. may be lung X-ray with windpipe in the middle
2. shape of upper black part (D)

Further response to shading further exposes Sauckel. Not only is there no aware, sensitive, comforting, protecting, relating part in him, but he lacks even the covering of his own skin. The contrast between the tops of Card III, who were all surface, and the X-rayed body of this response, in which the insides are exposed with no adaptation and no individuality, reflects the strong contrast between Sauckel's facade and the extreme flatness and emptiness within him. His X-ray is not even of a part of the body which has bones in it, but merely of the lungs, which are full of air. The use of the shading in this card in this manner, apart from the specific content of his concept, indicates concern with status and position. His representation of something which is normally three-dimensional on a flat plane suggests that his concern with status and position focuses on the trivial.

His second response, the "turned leg of a stool," is another example reflecting the best qualities of his intelligence. We guess that although in the inquiry he says *"shape* of upper black part" he did use the shading here and, if questioned further, would have pointed to its black, shiny quality. That he cannot respond to the soft, furry texture but does to what is hard and shiny points to a compensatory hardness in his reactions to human feelings that is quite extreme.

Unlike many of his colleagues, then, he responds to the phallus-like shape at the top, and does so in an intelligent and rather unusual concept. It should be said, however, that the turned leg of a stool is the end product of the skillful use of mechanical devices; it is also inanimate and, in Sauckel's concept, more decorative than functional. These, then, are attributes of his masculinity. A turned object, moreover, is identical from all points of view—more so, even, than something which is only symmetrical. From whichever side you look at this man, he is likely to be the same.

CARD VII

[*rejected*]

In Card III the color did not belong; in Card VII the whole thing does not belong. The shading of this card and its many "feminine" qutlities are things he does not have the energy or desire to handle. Unlike many of his colleagues, he cannot even distort it into something grotesque.

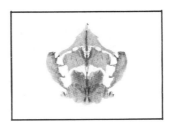

CARD VIII

1. (> ∨ > 30″) futuristic attempt at a tree, with two wolves at sides; bottom doesn't belong

INQUIRY

1. shape of wolves at side; top looks like treetop; don't know about the rest; not real—no perspective (D)

Sauckel provides a new addition to the collection of traditionally vicious animals that appear in this group of records by bringing in wolves. He shows reasonably good judgment by not making the rest of the blot into a tree simply because the top of it happens to look like a tree top. He rather contemptuously disposes of the mediocrity of the concept by criticizing the attempt of the producer of the blot rather than by finding a better solution, a psychopathic trend found repeatedly in these records. He mentions no movement in the wolves; they are vicious animals, but he gives them an unvital quality. He is disconnected from his instincts; and the total absence of animal movement in this entire record makes clear Sauckel's lack of connection with any genuine impulse life in himself or in others. This is common among psychopathic personalities. Such persons are often thought of as dominated by their animal instincts—being brutal and cruel because their aggressiveness and their instinctive reactions are not under control. Actually, it is far more typical to find in psychopaths the repression of any connection with a breathing, living creature within, a failure to realize in oneself, or in others, the experience of pain, love, joy, or even hate.

A final comment in this card sums up, better than we can, an important aspect of this man's personality: "not real—no perspective."

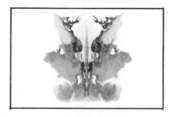

CARD IX

1. (∧ 12″) two gnomes in a fairy tapestry; stage designer's fancy

INQUIRY

1. shape of gnomes on top, but a scene painter probably just threw green and red paint on below

Even his fairy tapestry is not peopled by light, delicate, and benificent fairies but by distorted and deformed gnomes. The grandiose, finely worked, laboriously detailed setting of his life has only the deformed, gnomic self as a focus. But even that setting is spurious. The tapestry is not, it turns out, a tapestry, but rather a stage setting. He cannot, then, even briefly, sustain an image of his emotional life as differentiated, finely wrought, and the result of creative development ("tapestry"); he is, rather, revealed as a creature of meaningless emotionality, whose emotions are thrown around in a clumsy and careless way. His emotions are irrelevant to the situation ("probably just threw . . ."); they are mere surface coating with no meaning and no perspective.

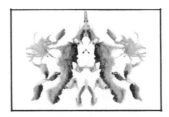

CARD X

Comment: "This is crazy—all imaginable colors."
1. (∧ 30″) I'm not an anatomist—it's a fantastic conglomeration of colors
2. (∨ 70″) fantastic blossom, but too many colors; maybe a big flower here

INQUIRY

1. maybe something anatomical—I don't know (W)
2. green calyx and red blossom (D)

In the face of the varied, complex, emotionally charged, and not easily organized stimulus material of this card, Sauckel, like so many of his colleagues, is disconcerted, disorganized, and unable to respond in a way that can convince him that he can do something rational with the situation. So he characteristically projects the craziness aroused by the emotional challenge and the struggle within him onto the outer situation ("This is crazy . . .").

Immediately thereafter he attempts to go as far away as he can from all this churning emotion to the scientific detachment and intellectualization of an anatomical concept. But this effort to defuse the emotional charge of the situation does not reflect any genuine control. The only thing that suggests anatomy in this card is the variety of its colors, which in anatomical charts are arbitrary and serve the purpose of distinguishing the parts; as such, they bear no integral relation to the forms with which they are associated. So even this veiled effort, which by his own recognition ("I'm not an anatomist") lies beyond his abilities, represents a phony, superficial reaction rather than a response to the intense emotions which are clearly aroused in him by this card.

The flowery, sentimental blossom common to so many of these subjects appears in his second response. Confused by the variety of emotional stimuli, he attributes his inability to structure what he sees to defects in the external situation ("fantastic . . . too many colors"), for which he denies any responsibility. The misidentification of color in an arbitrary way to fit his concept of a big flower is quite striking, particularly when he describes the achromatic part as a *green* calyx. Because he has decided that this is a calyx, he arbitrarily changes the gray to green. The pretense of scientific detachment, poorly sustained as it was, that he displayed in the first response is now replaced by the psychopathic show window display quality of his flowery, sentimental, and inept performance here.

SUMMARY

The sparseness of this personality is extraordinary, even among this collection of highly undeveloped persons. His lack of substance is revealed in response after response: in the "skeleton and bones" and "kind of bug" concepts of Card I; in the lampshade of Card II; in the "fops" of Card III; in the emptiness of the X-rayed lungs of Card VI; and in the messy stage designer's fancy of Card IX.

We see Sauckel as a person unable to acknowledge conflict within himself (Cards I and II), possessed of a simplistic moral view (Card II), and entirely devoid of sensitivity to nuances of feeling in human relationships (Cards IV and VI). His masculine attributes have a hard, mechanical quality, while the feminine side of his personality is almost nonexistent, except insofar as he can express an ostentatious sentimentality in an extremely inept, unstructured, and irrational way (Cards IX, X). He is cut off from connection with any genuine impulse life (Card VIII), and even by the standards of his colleagues in this collection his emotional adaptation is inept and superficial (Card II). His one moment of insight, inadvertent as it was, reveals him as a person who is "not real—no perspective."

We have seen that schizophrenic and psychopathic qualities were present in his personality. He registered a merely slightly-above-average intelligence on the modified Wechsler–Bellevue test devised by Gilbert and had the third lowest score in the entire group (above those of Kaltenbrunner and Streicher [Gilbert, 1947, p. 31]). In fact, however, as we have seen, he could at times rise to a superior level of intellectual performance (Cards II, VI). No doubt it was this capacity, erratic though it may have been, which enabled him to function as an effective administrator.

Like other individuals in this group, but to a more marked extent than most of them, Sauckel sought to compensate for the vacuity of his being with grandiosity and ego inflation. We see his concern with status and position, and his trivial and inept performances in connection with it, in a number of his responses. His very first concept, the flat and desiccated skeleton and bones, is magnified into a "mammoth" skeleton. This effort is not only marked by considerable irrationality (he offers no justification for this grandiose concept so that we are left wondering how the *shape* of a mammoth skeleton differs from that of an ordinary one) but fails in being either imposing or impressive. So, too, with the elaborate tapestry in Card IX, which, almost at the moment of its conception, degenerates into an extremely sloppy stage backdrop, without depth or substance, onto which a painter "just threw . . . paint."

Sauckel was not a "violent" man. Even within the inner circle of the Nazi leadership he neither justified nor extolled the brutal excesses connected with the slave labor program. Instead, he simply denied that those excesses occurred and went so far as to uphold his activities as a model of enlightened conduct. "I myself report to you," he once wrote to Hitler, ". . . that never before in the world were foreign workers treated as correctly as they now are being treated, in this hardest of all wars, by the German people." It is true, he acknowledged, that the foreign workers were less than enthusiastic about their servitude. This was a source of considerable vexation to him: "These occupied territories are indeed not able to exist unless they produce the things which Europe wants from them, and since the planning of production for the whole of Europe is done exclusively and solely by Germany, all these nations are indebted to Germany alone and to nobody else for the fact that they have bread and work" (Bernstein, p. 217).

We saw in his response to Card X a psychopathic show window display quality—a tendency to believe the truth of phony statements and postures and to ignore the realities which they belie. Sauckel was evidently able to live with the responsibility of managing one of the cruelest systems of slave labor ever devised by telling himself and others (including Hitler, who must have wondered why Sauckel thought it necessary to treat foreign workers so well!) that it was not cruel. The mere statement transformed it into a beneficent system. "Aside from Kaltenbrunner," Bernstein says of Sauckel, "he was the most persistent and least accomplished liar in the dock" (Bernstein, p. 217). Sauckel was not lying to the judges at Nuremberg any more than he was lying to Hitler: he was merely describing reality as he wished it to be and therefore decided it was. "He was really confident that he would not be executed," Kelley reports (1947, p. 196). Seen in his cell a few moments after he learned of his death sentence, he told Gilbert, "I have been sentenced to death! I don't consider the sentence fair. I have never been cruel myself. I always wanted the best for the workers. But I am a man, and I can take it." Then he started to cry (Gilbert, 1947, p. 433).

15

Hjalmar Schacht

Hjalmar Horace Greeley Schacht—his father had lived in the United States and was a great admirer of the American journalist—is generally considered to have been the leading German economist of the century. His lack of scruple in applying his talents became apparent at a relatively early point in his career. Financial administrator of Belgium during its occupation by Germany in the First World War, he issued large quantities of forged bank notes to pay for the supplies bought by the German occupation forces. It appears that he was implicated in some unofficial financial scandal during this period and, under pressure, resigned his post in Belgium and entered private banking in Germany. The terrible inflation of the German mark after the First World War provided Schacht with an important political opportunity. Appointed Reich Currency Commissioner, he succeeded in bringing the inflation under control in a dramatically short time; he then threatened to resign unless he was appointed president of the Reichsbank. Despite the unanimous opposition of the directors (based, apparently, on his record in Belgium), he was appointed to that post and remained in it until 1930, playing a leading role in the complicated negotiations over the reparations payments which Germany owed to its enemies of the First World War under the terms of the Treaty of Versailles. When the Reichstag accepted a plan which Schacht considered disastrous (the so-called "Young Plan") for a new structure of reparations payments, he resigned from the Reichsbank and began to mobilize the financial support of leading German industrialists for the Nazi party. After Hitler gained power he rewarded Schacht's efforts by reappointing him president of the Reichsbank, and, in August, 1934, he made him Minister of Economics.

While all historians are agreed that Schacht played a decisive role in engineering the recovery of the German economy in the 1930's and thus making possible the financing of German rearmament, Schacht's relationship with Hitler and his commitment to Nazi goals are matters on which no final determination seems possible. Abroad, Schacht was regarded during the 1930's as one of the most civilized members of the Nazi elite, a moderating influence on Hitler's extremism. Schacht claimed that his resignation from office in 1938 was out of opposition to Hitler's plans for war. As he frequently pointed out, he never joined the Nazi party, and his hostility to Hitler during the war years finally landed him in a concentration camp. Nevertheless, the prosecution at Nuremberg presented evidence to suggest that Schacht's resignation may have stemmed from causes other than those he described and that he continued to supply the Nazi government with advice and support even after his resignation. And while it would appear that he opposed some of the cruder measures against the German Jewish business community, he also played a role in devising other steps against it.

In any event, Schacht was a survivor. He survived Hitler's hostility and he survived the Nuremberg trial—where he was acquitted, despite much public protest in Germany and abroad. He was also acquitted in several German denazification proceedings in the postwar years.

CARD I

1. (∧ 2″) a bat
2. (20″) tanned hide; an animal skin without the holes
3. (60″) [covers sides] The center could be two men with one arm around each other and one hand held up, taking an oath
4. (120″) Egyptian mummy inside

INQUIRY

1. the shape (W)
2. the shape of an opened hide (W)
3. They're swearing brotherly love and eternal allegiance to the Versailles Treaty (D)
4. The head is missing, but the rest is exactly the shape of a wrapped-up mummy (lower half, inner center) (D)

After a very speedy and laconic recognition of the conventional situation ("a bat"), Schacht produces a response which is most uncommon here (though not to Cards IV and VI). The hide is poorly seen; that it is tanned indicates that it is leather rather than fur. This points to a simulation of the mere outlines of adaptive, sensitive response, with minimal control or judgment. His reference to holes in connection with this skin suggests a denial of the emptiness to which he is drawn. In his third response, he shows a surprising degree of concreteness in his need to actively cover the sides of the blot in order to see the center. It is as if he must actively and aggressively deny the "wings"—with their suggestion of soaring, light, and delicate qualities—in order to see the two men to whom he refers. This part of the blot is most often seen as a single, female figure. The form of Schacht's concept is good and has original qualities, and he accounts well for the upper details of the blot. The bitter and gratuitous sarcasm of his response reflects not only an outwardly directed hostility but a much deeper *self*-loathing, as well as cynicism and dishonesty.

The portion of the blot which Schacht uses for the mummy is not infrequently seen as the lower part of a woman's body. The mummified quality of his femininity, and of the vital, instinctual aspects of his whole self, is evident in this response.

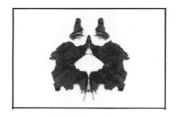

CARD II

Comment: "red ink . . . a little harder"
1. (∧ 5″) two circus clowns clapping hands, with red caps
2. (60″) white space is hanging lamp, with crystals below
3. (90″) fantastic animal profiles

INQUIRY

1. They have red caps and red socks and black gowns, dancing (W)
2. shape of white lampshade, shining down, and glass crystals (pink inner slit of red) attached to pull cord (Sd)
3. outside contour of black (de)

His immediate response to the emotional excitement implied by the "red ink" is to distance himself from it in an intellectual, rationalized fashion. Very quickly, however, he sees the circus clowns, with their red caps and socks and black gowns, which are so common among this particular group of subjects, and whose intrinsic qualities have been discussed elsewhere.

The emotional stimulus here, even when dealt with in the superficially adaptive manner of his first response, is evidently too strong for him to continue to confront it directly; he therefore leaves the substance of the blot, drawn to the inner emptiness of the white space and by a need to impose some structure on it. His emphasis on the fact that this is a *hanging* lamp points to his helplessness in the face of ego-alien forces within him.

For a man of his high intelligence, the flat, obsessive quality of the third response is noteworthy. Profiles can be seen in numerous places at the edges of any of the Rorschach cards, and to point them out is, for a man of Schacht's capabilities, a banal and rather trivial thing to do. He describes them as fantastic, moreover, and does not specify what kind of animals they are. Once again, then, we discover one of this group of subjects responding in a psychopathic way by not taking responsibility for his own concepts.

The sequence of his responses to this card shows him escaping from the emotional challenge of the "harder" red, first into the emptiness of the white space and then to a meaningless periphery of the situation.

CARD III

1. (∧ 10″) two gents greeting each other, bowing to each other, hats off to each other
[Examiner: "You have more imagination than some of your comrades."
Schacht: "Please don't call those criminals my comrades."
Examiner: "Well, more imagination than the others, then."
Schacht: "Yes, so much imagination that I even imagined at first that Hitler was an honorable man of peace. But so did Chamberlain."]
2. (50″) red bow tie
3. (80″) lobster and claws
4. (> 120″) a fox running and looking behind

INQUIRY

1. just the black part (W)
2. shape and color (D)
3. It's alive (lower gray D)
4. has that shape, and he's running pretty fast (corner red D)

This intelligent man again surprises us by the banality of his responses: here he presents a concept, including elements of formality, obsequiousness, depression, and concern with status, that we encounter frequently in this collection of records. Under the circumstances, the examiner's comment is perhaps somewhat surprising; Schacht's dissociation from the other defendants in the trial and his reminder that even Hitler's subsequent enemies had formerly been deceived by him echo aspects of his defense during the course of the trial.

He gives a conventional response to the easy, popular, center red portion of the card. The lobster concept is of a rather marginal form quality; the primitive quality of this animal, and Schacht's emphasis on its claws, point up aspects of Schacht's own personality. Although his comment in the inquiry that the lobster is alive may be a response to a routine question by the examiner, Schacht's willingness to attribute vitality to the aggressive, grasping, and primitive parts of his nature, while other parts of him seem so dead, is of interest. In the fourth response he uses his good mind and imagination but also seems to sum up his entire character from one point of view as a sly, cunning animal who is frequently pursued because of his predatory habits.

CARD IV

Comment: "Hmmm, a weird thing ['*eine tolle Sache*']"
1. (∧ 20″) could be a spread-out hide [dismisses it as too simple];
   outside of animal fur of a primeval animal
   (∧ > ∨) [tries to improve on it]

INQUIRY

1. [wants to improve on it] monster with bird head striding toward
   you; it's the fur texture and shading

His immediate response to this strongly and darkly shaded card is to comment on its weirdness. He then goes on to identify the usual animal skin, but from there proceeds in a process of retrogression, in both judgment and feeling, that is quite extraordinary. The initial concept sounds like a nice, adaptive feeling response, but he then emphasizes the primitiveness of the animal, thereby indicating the primitivity of his adaptive sensitivity. Evidently considering this inadequate— too banal, perhaps—he turns the card sideways but is unable to improve on the concept. In the inquiry, still trying to "do better," he produces an incongruous image of a monster with a bird's head. His initial sensitivity, primitive as it was, shifts to the malevolence and narcissism (for the monster is alive and striding toward him; see discussion on page 231) of this incongruouous monster.

CARD V

1. (∧ 4″) of course, a butterfly or a bat . . . not much fantasy here

INQUIRY

1. just the shape of a typical bat (W)

It is unusual, among this group of records, to learn that there is "not much fantasy" involved in seeing this as a butterfly or bat. In a simple way, Schacht reveals a flexibility of mind in indicating that this could be either creature.

CARD VI

1. (∧ 5″) also a tanned hide . . . but . . . [not satisfied] . . . a rug before a bed
2. (50″) also a flying insect . . . a night butterfly with feelers and feathers

INQUIRY

1. hairy, woolen hide, shows woolen texture (W)
2. It's flying (upper D)

He initially stresses that this is a tanned hide but proceeds to give it a more resilient texture; even then, however, it lacks the softness and differentiation of the richer "fur" response that is more often given to this blot. In common with Goering, he relegates this object to the bedroom. His sensitivity to nuances of feeling in human relationships, then, is not very great and is used primarily in the context of sensual enjoyment.

As a self-portrait, the "night butterfly" is that of a deeply depressed creature. Only two details on the butterfly are identified. One is its feelers, depicting Schacht's searching out of his environment. The other is its feathers. Now, not even "night butterflies" have feathers, and this detail is not only inappropriate but irrational. Feathers on creatures who do not grow them naturally are used for adornment and decoration. We have here, then, a self-portrait of Schacht as an insignificant and depressed being who displays himself irrationally with highly inappropriate decorations.

CARD VII

1. (∧ ∨ ∧ 20″) two dancers waving scarves above . . . charming
2. (∧ 60″) snow on branches . . . settled in the angle formed by branches
3. (80″) horns of reindeer . . . not too good
4. (110″) girls' heads about to kiss each other, with hairdo and feathers here

INQUIRY

1. (usual W)
2. the shading and texture of snow piled on branches (W)
3. just roughly the shape (W)
4. shape of top part (D)

Although this card ordinarily lends itself to the concept of two women, it is relatively unusual to find this response in the present group of subjects. However, the record contains too little information as to the way in which the dancers are seen to enable us to make much of a judgment about the response or to say anything of interpretive significance. In the second response, the shading, which is ordinarily seen as soft and fluffy, evokes the wintry image of snow-covered branches. This is a lifeless image in which the underlying structure appears only minimally related to the surface appearance, and which, in its whiteness and coldness, reflects the profundity of his depression and his compensatory covering up of his sensitivity and pain.

The third concept is indeed "not too good," and reflects a certain poverty of control in Schacht, for if he does indeed recognize it as a poor concept he could well keep quiet about it. Evidently, he is so drawn by the minimal resemblance of this blot to the organs of aggression and defense that he is impelled to give the response despite his recognition of its inadequacy. In his final response he again sees females but this time only their heads, even though the card lends itself to a fuller image. The figures he sees are childish—they are arbitrarily described as girls when they could just as well be women—and there is also a childish quality to their kissing gesture.

The widely contrasting images of Schacht's responses to this card suggest two sides to him which rarely came together and which were certainly not integrated—a childish and poorly developed softness, on the one hand, and a hard, aggressive, cold, and rigid quality, on the other.

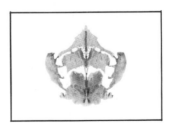

CARD VIII

Comment: "That's tough."
1. (∧ 10″) a blossom
2. (30″) two chameleons crawling up on flower; could be mice but lack tails; if seen alone they might be bears, but that's too big in relation to the flower
3. (120″) Christ on the cross, with loincloth; arm, head to side
4. (180″) small xylophone
5. (> 220″) reclining dog looking back

INQUIRY

1. red and brown orchid (lower part of blot) (D)
2. just the figure (shape) (D)
3. (faint outline inside right blue patch, apparently well seen) (di)
4. shape (Dr)
5. (left appendage of orange) (Dr)

After an unusual "that's tough," in which he takes responsibility for his difficulty in responding to the card, he immediately makes use of the color in combination with the form and commits himself to a specific concept. This suggests a considerably more appropriate and in some ways less superficial adaptation than is found in many of these records. However, it should be noted that the concept itself is that of an orchid, which, with its qualities of flashy display, is common in this group of subjects.

Schacht then goes on to describe the chameleons seen by such a striking proportion of individuals in this collection. There is not much energy left in the service of his opportunistic ambition, however, for the chameleons are merely crawling. His acknowledgment that they could be bears or mice reflects once again (cf. Card V) his capacity to see a situation from more than one point of view—though we should note that this capacity exists here in the context of opportunistic ambition. His response does, moreover, contain striking evidence of irrationality. Almost the only detail that lends itself with any degree of appropriateness to a chameleon is the lizardlike tail—but Schacht says that the chameleons lack tails! His use of the tail as the fourth leg on the mice is, in fact, appropriate—though he says they could not be mice because they lack the tails which are *required* for the chameleon concept and are less necessary for the mice concept. The bears are an improvement on the chameleons, but there is a striking degree of concrete thinking in his remark that they are too big in relation to the flower. In fact, for his initial flower ("blossom . . . orchid") responses he used only the lower third of the blot. He cannot, as is frequently done, use the entire center portion of the blot to depict an object up which the bear is climbing. There is thus a stimulus-bound quality to his thinking, a rigidity in clinging to earlier perceptions that are no longer appropriate.

The highly original and apparently well-seen "Christ on the cross," occurring in response to a faint outline deep within the shading, suggests a very deeply hidden but important image of himself as a martyred savior. From this grandiose concept he shifts to the triviality of a small, tinkling, toylike instrument. The record does not disclose the location or form quality of this response, and we are therefore unable to comment further on it. The reclining dog is unusual and well seen. When this detail is used it is usually merely for the head of a dog or similar animal. Schacht, however, is able to see the entire body, suggesting resources for connecting himself to his instinctual side. However, the passive position of the animal indicates the relative unavailability of vital energies for constructive purposes.

CARD IX

1. (∧ ∨ ∧ ∨ 50″) floor lamp and red lampshade
2. (> 80″) a shot rabbit's head
3. (∧ 140″) wizard with pointed hat, stretching out hand
4. (∨ 200″) caterpillar eating green leaf
5. (260″) two Dutch girls with blue caps and green aprons, holding hands
6. (320″) white speck is South America
7. (380″) gargoyle

INQUIRY

1. The base is missing, but the center line and red lampshade are there (D)
2. (inside detail in green) (di)
3. outline of upper right piece (orange detail, D)
4. shape and color (edge orange and green) (Dr)
5. (part of green just below pink, well seen original response) (Dr)
6. (S)
7. (edge of green facing lower left corner of card) (de)

Instead of rejecting the card or responding to it with an overambitious and unsustainable generalization, Schacht responds with a series of concepts that range from relatively poor to brilliant. He quite appropriately takes his time, freely turning the card several times without assuming that the situation represented by the card must be dealt with in the manner in which it was originally presented to him. The floor lamp and shade is a reasonably appropriate (i.e, adaptive) form–color combination. However, the essential poverty of his effort to throw some light on a difficult situation is impressively under-scored by the absence of the lamp's base. Where others frequently see the head of either a deer or a crocodile, Schacht sees that of a shot rabbit. The implied violence of this concept reflects Schacht's ex-perience as both victim and perpetrator: if he is a rabbit he is also a fox (Card III), which frequently preys on rabbits. The third response ("wizard") is good form and again reveals an element of compensa-tory grandiosity in Schacht. The precise location of the caterpillar and green leaf are not clear, but this is probably a good, adaptive combination of form and color; again we see that there are good intel-lectual and emotional resources still available to Schacht, but they are portrayed here in a concept which is primitive and trivial and in-volves destruction. The two Dutch girls are a brilliant and original response which involves movement and color and a positive experience of femininity. This concept, too, suggests resources of intellect and feeling that are still present, though, as we have seen from other re-sponses, they are barely if at all utilized.

There are very few details in any of the Rorschach cards which lend themselves to a good geographical response. With impressive intelligence, Schacht has found one of these. Escaping into the empty space, however, he no doubt reveals a yearning to join some of his erstwhile comrades in that continent. The gargoyle of his final re-sponse reflects the ugliness of Schacht's present experience and of his experience of himself.

CARD X

1. (∧ 35″) fantastic devils dancing, two on each side
2. (75″) young animals
3. (130″) pelvic girdle on human skeleton
4. (160″) rabbit's head
5. (180″) Venetian lions
6. (200″) bird's nest
7. (220″) mussels

("can't make much of the red . . . let's try it this way. (∨) Too much confusion")

INQUIRY

1. shape of dancing figures, one is waving torch (outer blue D)
2. alive, looking at each other (D)
3. the shape (mid-blue D)
4. the shape (usual bottom center D)
5. statues, just shape (inner yellow D)
6. shape (side gray D)
7. brownish mussels (D)

The extent to which Schacht is stimulated both to greater productivity (in the number of his responses) and to a far higher level of original and creative thinking by the colored cards suggests that he was highly dependent on emotional stimulation from his surroundings for his accomplishments. On the one hand, this can have a positive meaning, in the ability it bespeaks to respond not merely emotionally but also intellectually to external emotional stimuli. On the other hand, such a personality quality, when this pronounced, suggests an extraordinary degree of vulnerability to outside influence.

Except for the excellent form and vital quality of his first response, with its embodiment of extreme evil, Schacht seems by now to have burnt himself out in the face of the relentless continuation of emotional stimulation, which no longer leads him to newer heights of originality but rather, after the first response, to an unrelieved series of flat and banal responses. The location of the animals cannot be ascertained from the record and so no judgment regarding their form quality is possible; but, it should be noted that the animals are unspecified and that they are merely looking at one another. The pelvic girdle concept is reminiscent, in its flatness and emptiness, of many of the responses of his colleagues; the rabbit head is conventional; the lions, while of good form quality, are statues rather than live animals; and although the bird's nest is probably also good form it would appear to be merely an empty and abandoned one. His final response, although it continues to use color adaptively, is nevertheless a concept involving one of the most primitive and immobile forms of submarine life. His effort to do something with the pink—which he mislabels red—comes to nothing; he lacks the energy to deal with any but the palest pastel and achromatic colors. His attempt to achieve a new view of the situation ends with a direct portrayal of his current experience of confusion.

SUMMARY

We have seen how indignantly Hjalmar Schacht dissociated himself from the other defendants at the Nuremberg trial (Card III). As we mentioned in the introduction to this chapter, the question of Schacht's commitment or lack of it to the Nazi cause, and of his responsibility for the excesses committed by the Nazi regime, remains unresolved. Schacht frequently attempted to persuade his audiences of his impeccable anti-Nazi credentials by reminding them that he had been thrown into a concentration camp in 1944. If he did indeed believe that this proved his point, we can only regard it as an instance of his insensitivity to facts, for—as faithful Nazis from Roehm to Goering had discovered—even the most loyal and steadfast follower of Hitler could incur his terrible wrath and be doomed to death. (Goering escaped execution in the confusion of the last days of the Reich.)

Whatever the biographical facts of Schacht's life, however, and whatever the real responsibility he bore for the catastrophes which followed in the wake of Hitler's rise to power, it is evident from his Rorschach record that he shared many of the psychological characteristics of his fellow defendants. Like a large proportion of them, he sees the circus clowns in Card II and uses the red features of the blot in a superficially adaptive manner for caps and socks; like so many of them, he responds with an image of formality, obsequiousness, and concern with status in the image of two men greeting each other in Card III. The showy display of sentimentality indicated by the orchid concept in Card VIII and the opportunistic chameleon of the same card are also distinctive responses repeatedly found in this collection of records. It is, indeed, worth noting that while poor form quality is found in a variety of Schacht's responses, and not only in those which are similar or identical to those of other Nazis, some of the poorest forms are found in the "typically" Nazi responses in his record—as, for instance, in the use of the lower red for socks in Card II. More generally, Schacht also shares with his colleagues qualities of aggression (Cards III, VII, and IX) and of flatness and emptiness (Cards VII and X). As with the majority of them, moreover, Schacht's capacity to respond sensitively to nuances of feeling in human relationships was minimal. Indeed, his performance in this regard is striking even by the standards of this group. In Card I we found indications of nothing more than a simulation of the mere outlines of adaptive, sensitive response; in Card IV, his adaptive sensitivity degenerates into the monstrous, malevolent, and narcissistic qualities of an incongruous beast; while in Card VI we have a rug whose texture appears to be woolen rather than furry and whose function is relegated

—as was, no doubt, Schacht's limited sensitivity to nuances of feeling in relationships—to the bedroom. Although Schacht was capable of a positive experience of femininity (Cards VII and IX), the feminine aspects of his personality would appear to have been overwhelmed by his qualities of rigidity, coldness, and hardness (Card VII).

In these notable respects, then, Schacht shared much in common with the other members of the Nazi elite whose records are included in this collection. This circumstance will hardly come as a surprise to readers who have viewed his protestations of innocence with skepticism. What is surprising, however, in this record of the "financial wizard" of Nazi Germany (cf. Card IX), are the frequent indications of considerable irrationality that we have noticed. He gives evidence of concrete thinking in both Cards I and VIII; shows poor control in withholding what he has already recognized to be a "not so good" concept in Card VII; and comes up with irrational concepts and reasoning in his "feathered" "night butterfly" in Card VI and in his chameleons and mice in Card VIII. We leave it to economic historians to identify the ways, if any, in which these qualities—interspersed as they are with frequent indications of an excellent mind—were reflected in Schacht's economic policies in the 1920's and 1930's.

"Talented, believes he is meant for great things," Schacht's high-school teacher wrote of him when he graduated (Peterson, p. 19). Qualities of grandiosity have been noted in Schacht's Rorschach record (Cards VIII and IX), but we have also seen how poorly sustained they are. "Christ on the cross" in Card VIII is followed by the "small xylophone"; the wizard in Card IX by a caterpillar eating a green leaf. It has frequently been suggested that individuals seek power to compensate for low-self-esteem. The frequent indications of self-loathing and insignificance in Schacht's record, notably in Cards I and VI, would seem to suggest that this may indeed have been the underlying motivation behind his quest for power.

16

Baldur von Schirach

Baldur von Schirach's ancestors had migrated to the United States during the nineteenth century—his great grandfather lost a leg at Bull Run and was a member of the honor guard at President Lincoln's funeral—and although he was born in Germany (in 1907), he regarded himself as "three-quarters American" (Schirach, p. 13). Nationalist sentiment ran high in his family. His elder brother, Karl, committed suicide in 1919 "because he did not wish to live on after Germany's great misfortune" (Schirach, p. 15), and he himself considered as the turning point of his life the time when, at the age of 17, he read the notorious anti-Semitic work *The International Jew*. A meeting with the rabid Nazi anti-Semite Julius Streicher, editor of *Der Stuermer*, won him over to the Nazi cause; he entered the University of Munich because he knew that the headquarters of the Nazi party, and Hitler himself, were located there. His student activities gained him the leadership of the National Socialist German Students Union; in 1931, Hitler, whose close personal friend he had now become (Schirach would marry the daughter of Hitler's personal photographer Hoffmann), appointed him Reich Youth Leader of the NSDAP and, in June, 1933, Youth Leader of the German Reich.

Under Schirach's tutelage, the Hitler Jugend first absorbed all other German youth organizations and was then transformed into an instrument for the indoctrination of German boys and girls in the service of the Nazi cause. By a special agreement between Himmler and Schirach, the SS recruited into its ranks chiefly members of the *Streifendienst* branch of the Hitler Youth.

In 1940 Schirach was sent to Austria to be the governor of the Vienna *Gau*, one of seven districts into which Austria had been divided after the *Anschluss*. The appointment was a demotion; hitherto responsible directly to Hitler, Schirach was now the subordinate of Frick, Minister of the Interior. ("He has not shown any political sense and is no grown-up Nazi," Goebbels complained of him [Goebbels, p. 362], and it may be that his demotion followed Hitler's growing exasperation with Schirach's propensity for writing bad poetry and indulging in high-flown romantic expressions.) Although the deportation of Viennese Jews to the extermination camps had begun well before his appointment, the Nuremberg tribunal found that Schirach had actively participated in the deportations after becoming Gauleiter of Vienna, probably in full knowledge of the fate which awaited the Jews.

Found guilty on count four of the indictment ("crimes against humanity"), Schirach was sentenced to twenty years' imprisonment.

CARD I

[approaches problem cautiously; doesn't answer until he's sure]
1. (∧ 40″) a bat

INQUIRY

Additional: Now I can see two Santa Clauses with Christmas trees under their arms

1. It's the painful gray tones, but it's mostly the shape and it's alive. If it was colored I would have thought of a dancer. The outside specks are only the mess from the airbrush; the white spaces just don't belong (W)

Additional: Now I can see two men with helmets raising gloved hands

Cautiously, without qualification or elaboration, he gives a conventional response to the novel situation. His relatively slow response to the first card contrasts strikingly with the fast times of his subsequent reactions. In general, his is a quickly reactive and resourceful mind.

The depressive quality of the gray seems much more acute than in other records in this collection—it is actually "painful" in its grayness. In confronting this deeply depressing situation, he evidently lacks the ability to see the form and movement of a dancer (which is often seen in this card), except insofar as he is able arbitrarily to inject colors that are actually not present. Behind the depressive mood, then, there is a quality of vitality which at present he is unable to summon up for the task of rescuing himself from depression. He now tries to detach himself altogether from involvement in this situation. His attention is caught by the tiny specks, to which he lacks any imaginative association and which, he compulsively informs us, "are only the mess from the airbrush." There is a covert, paranoid quality to this remark, as if he is saying that he knows that this is not really an ink blot, since ink blots are not made with the use of an airbrush. Next, he is drawn in a no less compulsive way to the white spaces. He cannot handle them (they "just don't belong") and must negate them, something which he must frequently have done with reality.

Once he is familiar with a situation he is able to express a great many qualities that initially he was too cautious to permit. The two Santa Clauses are excellent form and an original response. Unable to quite see the dancing figure, he provides us with a more static symbol of gaiety and magic.

The center portion of the blot, usually seen as a single female figure, now becomes two men in a highly ambiguous position with obvious aggressive qualities. Why are their hands raised? Are they just entering combat, are they surrendering, or are they greeting someone (perhaps even in a *"Heil Hitler"* salute)? Schirach is evidently very cagey about directly expressing his anger and aggression. Substituting the epitome of masculine aggression for the delicacy of a female dancer, he reveals extreme problems in psychosexual identity. Evidently, aggression is a compensatory substitute for the delicate female whom he also sees but denies.

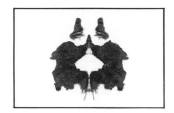

CARD II

1. (∧ 13″) two grotesque dancing men clapping hands with red turban and red boots, red waistband shimmering through . . . happy motif

INQUIRY

1. Clearly just the shape, but the color gives the impression of gaiety. I forgot to mention that they had white beards; yes, I saw that originally. No, blood would never have occurred to me. On further observation, they're holding a glass together (W)

He elaborates the concept, ordinary for this group of subjects, of grotesque men with red hat- and footgear. With his good intellect he makes the hats seen by others into turbans, and the image of red boots is rationalized as part of a happy motif. He also notes the red within the black, something that is rarely commented on, and if he is somewhat arbitrary in using only some of these specks for the waistband and ignoring the others, his sacrifice of some precision in favor of an imaginative response is not extreme.

Having thus integrated form and color, however, he remarks in the inquiry that it is "clearly just the shape" which has provided the concept. His controlling and containing ego functions are split off from the appropriate adaptive emotional response in the initial concept, and he renounces all responsibility for his emotional reaction, for his happiness and gaiety. We see, then, his emotional reaction become autonomous; his adaptive relating to other people's feelings disappears under our very eyes and becomes an egocentric and irresponsible expression of feeling that no longer involves responsibility for human interactions.

The "white beards" are most unusual. Looking at the card, the reader will see that it is quite a trick to do a partial reversal of the figure and background that brings *part* of the white into the figure and leaves part of it in the background. Involving as it does issues of black and white, this shows that Schirach was good at shifting his views on ethical matters in rather strange and clever ways and manipulatively.

His capacity to concentrate with interest and flexibility of intellect and to see a situation from different points of view is reflected in the "further observation" that the dancing men are holding a glass together, a concept which increases the atmosphere of conviviality and is probably an improvement in form. The compensatory quality of this conviviality should, however, be noted. The white color of the beards is close in meaning to the use of black as the expression of a depressive mood—here by the emphasis on its opposite. It reflects the quality of intense denial with which he expresses his profound depression.

CARD III

1. (∧ 15″) caricature of two men in coattail dress holding a pot; waiters, maybe. Behind them on the wall are red ornaments and in the middle something like a butterfly ornament. Corner ornaments are like something similar falling down. Whole thing is like an illustration for an E.Th.A. Hoffman [author of fantasies] story. It's fantastic because they don't have human heads

INQUIRY

1. Main figures are alive but the background figures are not. The pot is shiny, metallic, but they're putting a cloth over it, perhaps because it's hot; the waiters have white aprons with white strings around their waists and white ties and high collars (W)

The combination, by now quite familiar in this collection of records, of caricature and formality, subservience and high social status, appears here; as does the empty container, without meaning or function, which we have also encountered frequently. The emotionally highly charged red is described as ornamental, and even the center red, offering the relatively easy and adaptive butterfly response, is made still more superficial by being described in the same terms. The corner red, unidentified except as an ornament, represents an un-adapted splash of meaningless emotion; that it is falling down indi-cates that Schirach is experiencing ego-alien forces in himself against and through which he feels impotent. The emphasis on the fantastic nature of the concept shows him substituting fantasy for responsibility for the specific forms he has seen. The psychopathic nature of this evasion of responsibility is underlined by the fact that the waiters do not have human heads—a concept for which he offers no explanation or justification—and by the fact that he does not specify what kinds of heads they do have (e.g., birds' heads). This response also indi-cates a strong split between the head and body, between thinking and feeling. We can be sure that Schirach's thoughts were frequently highly inappropriate to his actions and feelings, and to the situations in which he found himself.

In the inquiry we find him using the shading for something hard and metallic rather than soft and comforting, which suggests an ex-treme hardening of his own feelings against those of warmth and sympathy. The image of the waiters covering the pot with a cloth is extremely unusual, perhaps particularly so in its use of the white for the cloth. We have here the image of a cover-up: he is using empti-ness, withdrawal, and nonparticipation (the white space) as a cover for his hot pot.

His further use of the white space as aprons, while not unique, is highly unusual; and it will be noticed that he apparently has no recog-nition of the perfectly appropriate black color of the waiters' outfits, a circumstance that is heightened by his need to explain the division between the upper and lower portions of the blot, which is ordinarily glossed over. It is as if he is ensuring that the white nothingness is securely tied around him. This emphasis on the white suggests a de-gree of flight from depression that borders on the unrealistic, to say the least. He is, of course, also using the white apron, devoid of sub-stance as it is, to keep himself clean and unsoiled.

CARD IV

1. (∧ 8″) fantastic animal god with powerful legs and slit eyes and a
    kind of widow's peak on his forehead. Gives impression of fur.

Belongs to Rococo period . . . dance pantomime in a Rococo festival

INQUIRY

1. Form is strong, but texture is also clear; it is soft, deep fur with animal skin on soles; probably a dancer carrying animal skin over him for festival dance (W)

A monster figure is frequently seen in this card among the general population. Schirach differs from many of his colleagues in seeing what is by implication a powerful masculine figure. His father, we may suspect, was physically present in his life but psychologically distant and frightening. That threatening father has become a monstrous side of himself, a bestial god covered by an exaggerated exhibition of sensitive understanding which is rather overtly inappropriate, too (fur being quite inconsistent with Rococo texture). In the inquiry we see how, in his counterdepressive effort ("dancer"), he hides behind a veneer of sensitivity and warmth. The reference to the soles of the feet reflects his need for something to stand on.

CARD V

1. (∧ 8″) first impression, like a bat
2. (30″) two figures in *Midsummer Night's Dream* or *Merry Wives of Windsor* . . . Shakespeare, in any case. [Shows he has Shakespeare book with him in cell.] The figures that dance around Falstaff in the last act of *Merry Wives of Windsor*

INQUIRY

1. It's alive; the shape and darkness give impression of a bat, but the goat's feet don't correspond (W)
2. Horns and fat central figure suggest Falstaff; rest are light wavy figures hidden behind his cloak . . . just vague forms (W)

The very common bat appears here, the emphasis on its darkness reflecting once again the depressive qualities in Schirach. Most unusual are the "goat's feet," which must come straight from his inner mythology because there is no justification for them in the blot and they are very rarely thus identified. An association with a faun or satyr is thus suggested, indicative of the bestial, lower aspect of this otherwise flying creature.

The second response is unusual and interesting. It is based on a genuine acquaintance with Shakespeare rather than the empty cultural name-dropping found in other of our records. The Pan theme of the goat's feet in the previous response is continued with the concept of horns on the figure. He is fascinated by and identifies with a figure that combines elements of the god of nature and the woods, on the one hand, and bestial sexuality, on the other. But there is also something of a Falstaffian absurdity about him. The vague forms hidden behind his cloak continue the theme of a cover-up; there appears to be a striking contrast between what he shows and what he conceals, the former being convivial and cheerful, the latter shadowy, elusive, and possibly sinister.

CARD VI

1. (∧15″) a wall decoration . . . a large animal fur
2. (35″) wooden rod or table leg
3. (60″) something feathery behind
4. (120″) part of a brick wall with gate or fountain in the middle; yes, a fountain in the distance with water gushing up . . . a definite scene in depth

INQUIRY

1. furry texture, probably tiger skin because of shading on legs (W)
2. polished black wood (upper center D)
3. gray tone (D)
4. definite vista; fieldstone wall because of mottled tones, like Max-

field Parrish; angle of perspective at bottom (lower portion of card) (D)

As is so frequently the case among this group of subjects, the animal fur is seen as decorative rather than as serving any useful function of warmth or protection, thus indicating a showy, manipulative use of his capacity for sensitivity to nuances of feeling. Somewhat arbitrarily, he identifies this as the skin of an extremely aggressive animal, the tiger, an indication of his own strongly aggressive qualities. (For discussion of the second response, cf. Sauckel, Card VI).

The variation in his use of shading in all the responses to this blot is remarkable. It indicates his great emotional versatility and unpredictability. It was probably very difficult to predict when he would be soft and when hard, when polished and when insubstantial in responding to other people and in the use he made of his sensitivity.

It is difficult, in the fourth response, to be sure of the areas in which he saw the various details of his concept. Here we encounter still another variation in his use of shading, this time to emphasize distance and perspective rather than close and sensitive relating. The hardness of the stone wall seems quite inappropriate and arbitrary for the textures of this card; combined with a view of the distance, it seems to indicate a confusion between what is near at hand and what is out of reach. Combined with the inanimate movement of the water, these elements of his vista response all give the impression of a sense of failure, the experience of a loss of control over his life, and a clinging (which may have been of real help to him) to his artistic interests. The vapid and sentimental quality of Parrish's illustrations reveals the *timbre* of his view of his life.

CARD VII

1. (∧ 6″) two women with coquettish hats looking back at each other
2. (60″) impression of snow or sugar . . . texture of something baked with fancy icing

INQUIRY

1. (upper two-thirds) (D)
2. from shading and texture; icing or snow has fallen on it (W)

Schirach is one of the few in this group to see two women here and to see them well and in a reasonable activity. Thus he shows more of an acceptance of his feminine qualities than many of his colleagues, but this is only potentially positive, for we have seen the walls which he erected against the expression of his softness and tenderness in Card VI.

Similarly, he follows up his first, positive concept with that of snow or sugar over something baked. Underneath the fancy icing, he is baked and hard. The snow, moreover, contrasts strikingly with the baked object—the one cold, the other with at least a semblance of having been prepared for nourishment; and even the icing sugar is decorative rather than nourishing. His use of the texture for snow or icing thus represents a point even further along the continuum of his compensatory denial of warmth than the hard wood and stone of his responses to Card VI. It should also be said that there is nothing in the intrinsic properties of the lower portion of this card to suggest "something baked," which is entirely a projection of his own qualities.

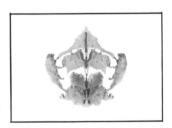

CARD VIII

1. (∧ 20″) two animals standing on a mountain grasping the gray and blue parts, perhaps bears; gives strong impression of heraldry . . . animals on a coat of arms . . . pleasantly shaded colors but no real construction

INQUIRY

1. They're balancing on one foot, holding on to coat of arms, climbing up (W)

His good intelligence comes to his rescue in the face of the strong emotional stimuli of this card. He sees the animals in a way appropriate to the form of the blot and to his total concept of a coat of arms (although he does not commit himself to the point of specifying the kind of animals). However, he is unable to integrate the colors with his symbol of inherited family importance and can make only a pale remark about the "pleasantly shaded colors." The most striking aspect of his response is the depiction of the animals, in their ambitious climb to the top, balanced precariously on one foot while holding on to the symbol of nobility, a concept whose meaning we invite the reader to elucidate for himself or herself.

CARD IX

1. (∧ 11″) orchid
2. (40″) something Oriental . . . Chinese dragonlike figures above and green jade . . . a Chinese vase for burning incense with smoke rising in the middle
3. (180″) mysterious animal with round head and slit eyes and green protectors before the face, blowing out red smoke . . . very artistic

INQUIRY

1. shape and color equally; orange flower, green leaves, pink blossoms (W)
2. The brown is bronzelike and the green is jadelike, but there is no surface texture; just the color. (upper ⅔) (D)
3. Brown suggests horns, center bulge the face with eye spaces; pink clouds on bottom are smoke (W)

Like most of his colleagues, Schirach is readily able to express his "feminine" qualities in the form of the sentimental and ostentatious orchid. His second response is considerably more impressive in its intellectual and creative qualities. This is a beautiful, original, and detailed concept in the face of strong and variegated stimuli which lead many of his colleagues into irrationality or else into rejecting the card. However, we should note the *exotic* context in which this concept is presented, which suggests that Schirach's creative capacities as well as his ability appropriately to combine control and spontaneity in adaptive and nonbanal ways were all far from availability in his daily experience. The amorphous and inanimately moving smoke —all that is produced by this lively container—contrasts his best capacities and the vapid nature of some of his final productions.

The third response represents a sudden regression to an arbitrary and psychopathic level. Indeed, the psychopathic quality of this response is more directly revealed than in any of his previous responses. He sees a completely unreal figure which he describes in great detail and which looks exactly like Card IX, but which involves no commitment to any reality. This highly elaborate creature is engaged in a vapid and meaningless activity—blowing out red smoke—and reflects what seems to be a not altogether highly developed artistic appreciation. The "very artistic" figure, indeed, is rather frightening and ominous. Ugly, essentially blind ("eye spaces"), and emitting red smoke, it is covered by a cold ("jadelike") green, masklike veneer of artistry. Three times in this record Schirach sees horns. These are defensive and aggressive weapons of the hunted male animal as well as the symbol of the cuckold—the foolish, unaware victim of betrayal.

CARD X

1. (∧ 10″) Whole thing is a page out of a fairy-tale book
2. two mountains with two little animals on top, with big eyes and open mouths
3. two blue devils running and laughing toward the mountain, waving leaf
4. mole on each side
5. green dancers bending their backs, holding ornament with horns
6. two yellow lions or dogs sitting, looking up
7. king's cape and crown
8. tree trunk behind the birdlike figures
9. (360″) Brown spots below are only decorative

INQUIRY

1. fairy tale because of color; all are figures in story (W)
2. just the shape (pink strips with gray figures on top) (D)
3. color is cheerful even though they are devils (outer blue and green) (D)
4. alive but sleeping (top gray) (D)
5. mostly the movement (lower green) (D)
6. form is very pronounced (D)
7. wouldn't have thought of a king's cape if it wasn't blue (center) (D)
8. (top center) (D)
9. Perhaps they belong to the mountain (D)

Schirach combines his good intelligence with his capacity for spontaneous emotional response in a good, whole response to this sometimes difficult card. But the fairy-tale setting puts all this into unreality. And although he says in the inquiry that they are all pictures in a story, there is no story. Rather, there is a cast of characters, some ugly, some attractive; some aggressive, some passive; some well portrayed (e.g., the good form and original thinking of the blue devils, who, like Schirach, cover an evil nature with a cheerful exterior) and some extremely inept (i.e., the execrable judgment shown in the poor form of the pink strips used as mountains). But there is no direction and no plot. Is this the story of the life of this brilliant but misdirected—or undirected—man?

SUMMARY

Baldur von Schirach had trouble standing on his own two feet; somehow, they did not seem to "correspond" (Card V), and often he would find himself, in a precarious way, "balancing on one foot" (Card VIII). It is as if reality was for him as artificial and transitory as that on the stage of the German National Theater at Weimar, of which his father was director.

What we might ordinarily think of as reality was, evidently, frequently more than Schirach could bear to face. "I have expressed my feelings so many times before to you," Henriette von Schirach wrote to her husband in 1950, "but you have always preferred to ignore them as being distasteful. Reality has always been distasteful to you" (quoted in Fishman, p. 77). That this letter concluded with the announcement that she intended to divorce her husband as soon as possible does not, we believe, invalidate her comments about him.

The attraction of Nazism for Schirach probably lay precisely in the opportunity he discovered in it to escape from the reality of his own experiences and emotions. In March, 1925, when he was still only 17 years old, Schirach was introduced to Adolf Hitler. Overcome by this experience, he ran home and wrote a poem which, in rough translation, reads as follows:

> Many thousands of you are behind me,
> and you are me, and I am you.
> I have had no thought
> that did not heave in your hearts;
> and there is no word I speak
> which is not at one with your desire;
> for I am you, and you are me
> and we all believe, Germany, in you.
>
> [*Ihr seid viel Tausend hinter mir,*
> *und ihr seid ich, und ich bin ihr.*
> *Ich habe keinen Gedanken gelebt,*
> *der nicht in euren Herzen gehebt.*
> *Und forme ich Worte, so weiss ich keins,*
> *das nicht mit eurem Wollen eins,*
> *denn ich bin ihr, und ihr seid ich,*
> *und wir alle glauben, Deutschland, an dich.*]
> (Schirach, pp. 22–23)

The flight from one's self suggested by this poem is surely extreme, even for an adolescent, as is the self-negation of its author's complete identification with the object of his adoration, Adolf Hitler. Schirach grew up—if he can be said to have grown up—to become a professional youth leader. But he did not grow beyond his self-escaping flight from reality and his identification with the idealized person of Hitler. Instead, he created a colossal organization in which the youth of Germany would be molded in the same image as he. The aims of the organization were stated in direct and unambiguous terms by the Fuehrer himself in an address to Nazi youth leaders:

We must be dominated by one will, we must form one unity, we must be held together by one discipline; we must all be filled with one obedience, one subordination. For over us stands the nation. You must practice today the virtues that nations need when they wish to become great. You must be loyal, you must be courageous, you must be brave, and among yourselves you

must form one great, splendid comradeship. Then all the sacrifices of the past that had to be made and were made for the life
of our nation will not have been offered in vain. (quoted in
Fest, p. 231).

Under the guise of a trite and romantic idealism, then, and in the
embrace of a camaraderie that was spurious because it was predicated
on the anonymity of its participants, the individual would renounce
his identity and autonomy; he would, in Schirach's highly telling
phrase, learn to "believe in the impossible" (Fest, p. 233).

Schirach's Rorschach record provides us with a number of indications that help to account for the particular bent of his personality—
an orientation which, in the service of his beloved Fuehrer, he sought
to impose on the entire youth of Germany. We see his propensity for
negating reality in Card I: significantly, he is able to recognize it, but
then, unable to handle it, he negates it with the assertion that it does
not belong. More generally, we see how his thoughts were frequently
highly inappropriate to his actions and feelings and to the situations
in which he found himself (Card III). Busy, detailed, and highly
intelligent though his life was, it was also without purpose or direction and was characterized by striking inconsistencies of both moral
and intellectual judgment—a life too jarringly confusing, perhaps, to
be lived with any reasonable degree of harmony with reality (Card
X). Particularly his most elaborate productions, reflecting the exercise of his considerable imagination and intelligence, seem devoid of
purpose and substance (Card VIII).

We see too, in this Rorschach record, evidence of great emotional
variability and spontaneity. He is, quite clearly, capable of warm,
sensitive, and tender feelings, but as soon as they are aroused he
must beat a hasty retreat from them, negating and denying them with
a display of hardness and even brutality (Cards I, VI, VII) or, as in
Card III, covering them up by emptiness, withdrawal, and nonparticipation. His "blue devils" in Card X, "cheerful even though they are
devils," reflect one aspect of his variability, for there is ample evidence
in this record of aggression (Cards I, IV, IX, X), masked by a superficial bonhomie (Card V). But the reverse is, in a sense, also true, for
much of his hardness and brutality was a defensive withdrawal from
his more tender and, as we are calling them in this volume, feminine
qualities. This withdrawal, as we saw in Card I, was associated with
severe psychosexual problems. There is no direct evidence that he
was homosexual, but the rumor that he was is certainly consistent
with the evidence in the Rorschach. His response to Card IV, moreover, could indicate that his relationship with his father, whom he
perceived as a distant and frightening person, contributed to his
psychosexual problems.

17

Artur Seyss-Inquart

In 1892, when Artur Seyss-Inquart was born in Stannern, Moravia, the Sudetenland was a part of the Austro-Hungarian empire. Seyss-Inquart went to Vienna to study law, and at the outbreak of the war he joined the Austrian army. A bad wound, which left him with a life-long limp, led to his discharge in 1917. After the establishment of an independent Czechoslovakia he left his home, intending to settle permanently in Vienna and to work for the unification of Germany and Austria, a cause in which he had become an ardent believer. A highly intelligent man, he had a successful law practice and, in 1930, entered politics. He was regarded as a loyal Austrian by Kurt von Schuschnigg, his wartime friend who had meanwhile become Chancellor of Austria. In fact, although not a member of the illegal Austrian Nazi Party, Seyss-Inquart was actively working behind the scenes with von Papen and others to undermine Austria's independence; he was, indeed, the first quisling. Schuschnigg appointed his friend State Councilor in 1937 and Minister of Interior and Security early in 1938. In the latter position he played an important role in the events that led up to the annexation of Austria. A few days before that event Schuschnigg resigned and, at Hitler's insistence, was succeeded by Seyss-Inquart. The new Chancellor now at last joined the Nazi party and a few days later, after the formal annexation of Austria by Germany, became the governor of the new province and a general of the SS.

In May, 1939, Seyss-Inquart was appointed to Hitler's cabinet as minister without portfolio. Four months later, after the conquest of Poland, he became Deputy Governor-General of that country, serving under Hans Frank. His responsibilities appear to have been connected primarily with the political and economic consolidation of Nazi rule over Poland. "The chief guiding rule for carrying out German administration," he told his subordinates, "must be solely the interests of the German Reich. A stern and inflexible administration must make the area of use to the German economy, and, so that excessive clemency may be guarded against, the results of the intrusion of the Polish race into German territory must be brought to mind" (NCA., vol IV, p. 322).

Seyss-Inquart's exemplary service to the Third Reich in Poland led to his appointment, in May, 1940, as Reich Commissar for the Netherlands. For five years he was, in effect, the absolute ruler of Holland. The Nuremberg tribunal found that in this position he had been "ruthless in applying terrorism to suppress all opposition to the German occupation, a program which he described as 'annihilating' his opponents. In collaboration with the Higher SS and Police leaders he was involved in the shooting of hostages for offenses against the occupation authorities and sending to concentration camps all suspected opponents of occupation policies" (quoted in Gilbert, 1947, p. 446). He also played a major role in the rounding up of Holland's Jewish population for shipment to extermination camps in the east.

Found guilty on three counts of the indictment, Seyss-Inquart was sentenced to death. He was hanged on October 16, 1946.

CARD I

1. (∧ 35″) vertebrae

INQUIRY

1. three vertebrae—shape of center part (D)

Unlike most other subjects in these records, Seyss-Inquart meets the novel situation represented by the first card by attending to an obvious detail rather than attempting to generalize. Drawn to the center, he ignores the wings and sees instead bare bones. There is a cautious poverty of concept indicated in this response. The preoccupation with the backbone suggests great inner weakness.

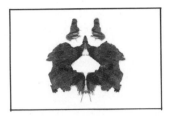

CARD II

1. (∧ 20″) grotesque dance

INQUIRY

1. two figures with red caps and socks and black gowns and they're clapping hands (W)

Like many other subjects in this group he does not identify the sex of the figures he sees, thereby indicating an evasion of his own psychosexual identity. The black gown mentioned in the inquiry indicates a depressive mood, while the movement of dancing represents an attempt to counteract the depression. The dancers—one of his self-portrayals—are grotesque.

He uses the red stimuli, however, in a reasonably integrative, adaptive, and appropriate way, suggesting that in his grotesque and depressed world there is a capacity for adaptive emotional response, even if only in a context of status and display. The integration of form and color in the response suggests a reasonably functioning mind that is not as dried out as those of some of the other individuals we are examining; while the clapping hands indicate more vitality than is generally found in this group. The red socks, on the other hand, are arbitrary. "They are down there, so they must be socks" is how the reasoning seems to go, and there is no effort to justify this response in terms of the form. There is, accordingly, a propensity in this man to remake situations to accord with what he rather arbitrarily decides they should be.

CARD III

1. (∧ 25″) similar to the one before, but salon style—in tailcoats
2. (60″) This belongs to the vertebrae in the first figure
3. (70″) red bow tie

INQUIRY

1. two men bowing, paying compliments to each other, hat in hand; just the shape of the black part (W)
2. shape like a vertebra and belongs to the first card (lower D)
3. grotesque shape, but bright red bow tie (D)

The formal, artificial images of the first concept offered here indicates an evasion of the substance of human relationships, and of the substance of his own psyche, in favor of superficialities. The vertebrae he sees in the next response, while not bad form, suggest an effort at imposing continuity ("this belongs to . . . the first figure") where there is, in fact, none. He is fragmented in his inner being, and his efforts to counter this are inappropriate and ineffectual.

The bow tie which he then identifies is an easy, popular, and adaptive response—but he then goes on to declare that it is "grotesque." It is as if he views even the most conventional things through distorting lenses, experiencing grotesqueness both in his inner being and in his social adaptation where other people would see something quite ordinary.

CARD IV

1. (∧ ∨ ∧ 20″) hide of a beast of prey—furry texture; head with glass eyes, whiskers

INQUIRY

1. hairy hide and the shape of the head is very clear, even if you turn is (> tries reflection picture); could be dark reflection in water, too (W)

He is able to combine form and furry texture in an appropriate fashion, suggesting an awareness of the nuances of people's feelings. That awareness, however, is used for manipulative, violent, and destructive purposes, for the fur belongs to a beast of prey. He betrays not the slightest need to justify this arbitrary description, which is so completely a projection of his own predatory violence rather than a perception rooted in anything in the blot itself that we must attribute a delusional quality to this response.

While this beast of prey is able to use its sensitivity to human feelings only for destructive purposes, its ability to discriminate between appropriate and inappropriate victims is minimal. It stares at the world through unreal and unseeing glass eyes, a primitive, predatory creature that is unable to distinguish between friend and foe and thus presumably attacks anything and everything within its range. He is gratified by the clarity of a very ordinary perception, and is reassured by it ("very clear").

In the inquiry, and elsewhere in his record, Seyss-Inquart often sees one half of the blot as a reflection of the other half, a response indicating considerable self-involvement and narcissism. The fact that in this case the reflection could be a *darker* version of the upper part suggests that the deeper recesses of his being contain even more predatory violence than his more external self.

CARD V

1. (∧ ∨ 10″) butterfly with feelers
2. (∧ 15″) bat

INQUIRY

1. mounted, as in a collection (W)
2. stylized, not alive (W)

The butterfly and bat responses here are conventional and safe, though the feelers, as the only detail he mentions on the former, indicate a suspicious searching out of his environment. The fact that the butterfly and bat are described as mounted in a collection and stylized indicates his own inner deadness. But there is also a display quality in the responses, suggestive of what Phyllis Greenacre describes as a "show window display" (cf. p. 279) concept of personality.

This feature, a characteristically psychopathic one, reflects an assumption that "you are what you appear to be." It indicates a tendency to assume that if you act in a friendly way toward a person you really do have friendly feelings toward him, and that having the intention to do something is the same as actually doing it.

CARD VI

1. (∧ ∨ ∧ ∨ > ∧ 70″) If you take off this projection [covers it], it's a fur hide

2. (> 80″) This way it's interesting—a scene reflected in water with trees, house, field, and woods, all reflected in water

INQUIRY

1. has the shape and texture of fur (D)
2. The dark shading inhibits the fantasy, because it's tragic; but it has the shape of a reflected scene; trees (feathery projections), house (small indentations), field (grayish expanse), woods (dark areas) (W)

There is a long delay before he responds to this card, and he turns it around a number of times. The projection which he has to "take off" (c.f. Goering, Card VI) before he can recognize a fur hide in this blot is a fairly obvious phalluslike image. This negation of his masculinity is a clear indication of impotence. It could betoken actual sexual impotence, though we have no way of knowing if he was impotent but in any case it points to deep psychic weakness and helplessness. This must be denied at all costs, and efforts are made to compensate for it by violent and manipulative behavior in which he uses his capacity to recognize the nuances of others' feelings.

In the second response, he sees a reflection, indicative not only of his narcissism but also of an emphasis on symmetry. This emphasis, present to a very marked degree in the responses of Ernst Kaltenbrunner, is indicative of a need to deny the difference between the two sides of a person—i.e., to deny inner conflict.

The vista response here suggests a concern with his own status and position in life. The inquiry reveals a genuinely tragic quality in this connection, a dark, tragic loss in his own life and of something that might have been. This is the self-portrait of a man who, as it were, knows that he has sold his soul to the devil and who recognizes that he could have done something much better with it instead. His sense of tragedy has a quality of genuine insight and a high intellectual level. In this dark, tragic world he inhabits he has a great need for a home, that is to say, for security and protection. This need, we must assume because of the individual quality of the response and the rarity of such responses in these records, is not just a product of his present dangerous circumstances, but has been a feature of his life for a much longer time.

CARD VII

1. ($\wedge$ $\vee$ > $\wedge$ 50″) symmetry suggests dancing; two people dancing
2. ($\vee$ 80″) two people running away from something, grabbing hat with hand and jumping or dancing away
3. ($\vee$ 115″) white space stands out, but I don't know what it is—stone monument, maybe

INQUIRY

1. children's dance with feather cap and skirts in motion (W)
2. impressive dance of flight, better than the other (lower $\frac{2}{3}$) (D)
3. outline of some kind of monument (S)

The vitality, intelligence, and individuality suggested by his ability to use all of the blot in an appropriate manner in a human movement response makes all the more striking his remark that "symmetry suggests dancing." Alongside an able, flexible, and intelligent mind there is a highly irrational component, here called into play by the need to deny inner conflict, possibly in a context of counterdepressive efforts ("dancing") in particular.

The second response is either highly original and creative as a flight of imagination or else represents a complete breakdown in his judgment. The record does not make at all clear the visual basis for this response, and it is not possible for us to determine precisely what the features were that he was using. He is, however, in flight and, as the dancing suggests, compensating thereby for his depression; and he is fleeing in a way which is either brilliantly clever or quite irrational—or, conceivably, both!

In the third response he expresses his need for flight in another modality, by departing from the substance of the ink blot to the white space. In this equation of elements of emptiness, hardness, and memorialization, he is saying that the emptiness inside him can only be, and is, filled by means of a stone-hard, cold monument, with its connotations of both death and inflated self-importance.

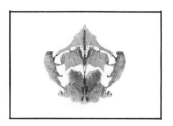

CARD VIII

1. ($\wedge$ $\vee$ $<$ 25″) a reflection again; an animal climbing from one object to another and reflected in the water [offers same thing in different positions]
2. ($\vee$ 80″) If you cover the animals [does so], it is a flower with leaves here and blossom here—maybe an orchid

INQUIRY

1. Shape of climbing animal is very distinct; colors don't have much to do with this
2. The colors play an important part in this conception (W)

The emphasis on the identity of the two sides ("a reflection again") indicates once more both his narcissism and his inability to tolerate internal conflict. Again, too, there is the popular response of a climbing animal, indicating the harnessing of his instinctual drives in the service of his ambition. His comment that the shape of the animal is "very distinct" once more reflects his banal satisfaction at finding the obvious to be obvious.

In his second response we find an instance of concrete thinking, for he has to cover the animals before he can identify the flower. As with so many of his colleagues, the "feminine," emotional side of his nature can be expressed only in the vague, undifferentiated, and sentimental image of a flower, blossom, or orchid.

CARD IX

(∧ ∨ ∧ ∨ >) Comment: "Can't get a reflection picture out of this . . ."
1. (∧ 70″) could be sea horses
2. (∨ 85″) fantastic plant picture; has flower, leaves, roots, but exaggerated

INQUIRY

1. approximate shape (D)
2. red blossom and green leaves, but roots are not so good (W)

Once again he strives for the symmetry and narcissism of a reflection, but this time he fails to achieve it. But he shows good judgment in acknowledging his inability here, and a sound recognition of his limitations.

The sea horse, which we have already encountered in other responses, is a primitive and undifferentiated animal that in some respects resembles a far more advanced one. He goes on to produce the plant picture so characteristic of this group of subjects and, hardly less characteristically, absolves himself of responsibility for it by saying that it is fantastic and exaggerated. It is notable that the parts of this plant that do not show—i.e., its roots—are "not so good" in comparison with the sentimentalized part that does.

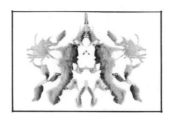

CARD X

1. (∧ 50″) profile with pug noses—can't organize all the details
2. (∨ 80″) a bridge between two cliffs—an ice bridge in a mountain crevice

INQUIRY

1. shape of the edge here (center red edge) (de)
2. The blue is icy, but the red does not belong—it is very grotesque, not very good (center pink and blue D)

The "profile" is a response which, when seen as here at the very edge of the blot, reveals a tendency to substitute form for substance and externals for solidity, and a need to remain on the periphery of things. These characteristics are indicative either of a wish not to, or of an inability to, commit oneself, and are associated with a great deal of anxiety.

The second response is a poignant portrayal of his current situation. The ice bridge, if one looks at the blot, is very poorly anchored now, its connections with the cliffs on either side being in large part eroded; the center of the bridge, too, is badly eroded and is near the point of collapse. Even at the best of times, however, the bridge was slippery and potentially treacherous as an "ice bridge," and it spans the dangerous gorge between two "grotesque" cliffs.

He is having a genuinely tragic experience of his own condition. He recognizes much of the reality of what he is, has done, and is about to face, as is indicated by the appropriate and adaptive quality of the form–color integration in the ice bridge. He has not only a sense that "we have failed" in reference to the Nazi adventure but, more acutely, a sense of anguish over the recognition that he has thrown away all the good things that his own life might have been. He is a man of considerable talent, high intellect, and artistic qualities that, somewhere along the road of his life, got submerged. Even if the ice bridge does not collapse while he is on it, or even if he does not slip off it, there lies ahead of him merely—and terrifyingly—another cliff of grotesque red experiences.

SUMMARY

Artur Seyss-Inquart was a highly intelligent, well-educated, and cultured man, and a pious Catholic. He was considered a respectable and basically decent man, too, even by some of those whom he betrayed; and there are responsible historians of the Nazi era who concur in this judgment. Kurt von Schuschnigg, the Chancellor of Austria and a long-time friend whom Seyss-Inquart did not scruple to overthrow at Hitler's behest, was convinced that the barbarism associated with the annexation of Austria "would probably never have occurred" had Seyss-Inquart been "able to have his own way" (Schuschnigg, 1971, p. 48). He was, says Brook-Shepherd, a "well-meaning Austrian tool of Hitler's," and his "treachery was the result of his actions rather than their motives" (Brook-Shepard, pp. 151, xxiii).

It is true that on several occasions during the events that led up to the annexation of Austria Seyss-Inquart showed himself reluctant to carry out the instructions he received from Berlin. It is this reluctance that has been interpreted as a mark of his basic decency and patriotism; in fact, though, it was probably rooted in his deep inner weakness and helplessness (Card VI). He was a firmly committed Nazi long before he joined the Nazi Party. If he had followed "a path which is not comprehensible to the masses and also not to my Party comrades," he wrote to Goering in July, 1939, he knew that he was doing so to "serve the Fuehrer as a tool in his work" (Davidson, pp. 455–56).

Lest this be considered a purely self-serving statement, it should be recognized that the succession of major positions to which Seyss-Inquart was appointed conclusively establishes that Hitler and Goering, at least, considered his credentials impeccable. And far from expressing regret at having allowed himself to be misused as the Fuehrer's "tool," Seyss-Inquart went to the gallows an unrepentant Nazi. "I do not feel that I have to be ashamed of anything I did," he told his interrogators at Nuremberg (NCA, vol. VI, p. 541).

Finally, to dispel any doubts that not even the most barbaric excesses were alien to this man, it is worth recalling his record of brutality as Deputy Governor–General of Poland under Frank and as Reich Commissar of the Netherlands. It was under his administration, for example, that 80 percent of Dutch Jewry—including Anne Frank—were rounded up and deported to extermination camps in the east, and that many Dutch civilians were shot as hostages or for opposing the occupation of their country.

Just as his career was that of an exemplary Nazi, so too did his personality resemble, in a number of its salient respects, those of many of his fellow defendants at Nuremberg. His self-portraits in the Rorschach are those of a primitive and undifferentiated person, empty, flat, and dead inside, with a strong need to deny inner conflict and a readiness to be delighted by the clarity of—and hence a strong need for—the obvious. Like many of his fellow Nazi leaders, he was a man who evaded the substance of relationships—and the substance of his own personality—in favor of superficialities; like them, his awareness of nuances in human relationships was used primarily for manipulative purposes; and like them, his feminine aspects, as we are calling them in this volume, existed only in the form of crude and undifferentiated sentimentality. Although possessing somewhat more vitality and intelligence than most of his colleagues, he was a deeply depressive person and suffered from striking lapses of judgment. Like many other Nazis, moreover, he sought to compensate for his inner emptiness and depressiveness by identifying with hard, cold, dead, and ego-inflating monumentality such as the Nazi movement was so adept at creating (Card VII).

Finally, like many of his colleagues, Seyss-Inquart had strong propensities for violence. He experienced even quite ordinary situations as grotesque; his predatory destructiveness, it would appear (Card IV), was scarcely able to distinguish between friend and foe, between genuinely threatening and innocent situations. As a beast of prey, he looked at the world through unseeing glass eyes, ready to lash out at anything and anyone who came close enough. And even greater violence and destruction appear to have existed in the deeper and more inaccessible parts of his personality (Card IV: "could be dark reflection in water").

In a psychopathic way, he was able to conceal at least some of his violence from himself and from others by the *appearance* of decency. There was a "show window display" quality to his personality (Card V). His show of hesitation during the events that led up to the *Anschluss* could persuade not only the Austria government but possibly himself, too, that he was not a thoroughgoing Nazi but at worst merely a well-meaning tool of Hitler. Grotesquely, he was able to assert his humanity even in the midst of issuing orders for the "annihilation" of those opposed to the Nazi regime. Speaking to his subordinates in Holland, he assured them, "We remain human because we don't torture our opponents: we must remain hard in annihilating them" (IMT, IV, p. 326). Here, in truth, we find the extent of this man's "decency": since he was merely *murdering* his opponents and not torturing them, he could persuade himself that he remained human. The fact that he was, in fact, *also* torturing them—the Gestapo was hardly unknown in the Netherlands and he, as Reich Commissar and an SS general, could not, to say the least, have been oblivious to its existence under his jurisdiction—could be negated for him by the mere *statement* that "we don't torture our opponents"! Seyss-Inquart, it would appear, was a mass murderer with a clear conscience.

At least part of his propensity for, and experience of, violence and destruction had its origin in a deep sense of homelessness and rootlessness (Card VI). We may be sure that this, in turn, was associated in part with his experience as an *Auslander*, a foreign-born German living in a somewhat equivocal situation in the Sudetenland. We have already noted that he left his home after the establishment of Czechoslovakia and, in Austria, worked for the unification of that country with Germany. His motives in doing so, however, were only in part nationalistic ones. Later in life he would contrast the emphasis on the *state* which had existed during the days of the Hapsburg Empire with that on *nationality* which had arisen after the establishment of Czechoslovakia. His primary preference was clearly for the former, though he was surely not unaffected by national sentiments. But his need was not so much for the identity that a home would provide as for the security and protection he could gain from it: he needed an authoritarian state more than a nation.

This view derives added plausibility from the consideration that underlying Seyss-Inquart's ferocious violence, there was a marked element of weakness, helplessness, and impotence (Card VI). This element, which may again in part be associated with the experience of growing up as a member of a minority community, was to a very limited extent compensated for by his narcissism (Card IX) and his enjoyment of status and display (Card II). But we may also quite reasonably assume that experiences of weakness and impotence generated a great deal of anger and violence and that these in turn were used to compensate for the weakness and impotence. The delusional quality we noted in him (Card IV), made all the more striking by his frequent indications of gratification with the clarity of the obvious, would have enabled him to invest his expressions of violence and destructiveness with much self-gratifying compensatory value.

But neither his delusional qualities nor his propensity for "show window display" could shield Seyss-Inquart entirely from the grotesqueness of his being and his life. And while this can be of no satisfaction to those who survived the collossal brutalities for which he was responsible—let alone to those who did *not* survive them—it deserves to be noted that Seyss-Inquart, for all his claims that he had nothing to be ashamed of, went to the gallows with a genuinely tragic sense of the stupendous horror and failure that his life had turned out to be.

18

Albert Speer

Albert Speer was born in 1905 into one of the leading families of Mannheim, where both his father and grandfather were prominent architects. After completing his own training in architecture, Speer was appointed to a minor teaching post at the Institute of Technology in Berlin–Charlottenberg, where he struck his superiors as rather mediocre and with a tendency to be "showy" (Speer, p. 32). He joined the Nazi Party in January, 1931, and was engaged by the Party to redesign one of its major buildings in Berlin, but ran up such large cost overruns in doing so that for about a year he was offered no further Party work.

After Hitler's rise to power, however, Speer was commissioned to design the decorations for several large Nazi party rallies and soon thereafter became Hitler's architect. Hitler's architectural ambitions were on a pharaonic scale: he sought to "bring a beauty to Germany such as no other nation has ever known" (Chelminski, p. 72). Speer's position in the Nazi hierarchy, accordingly, was considerably more important than might ordinarily be assumed in the case of an architect. Hitler, it would also appear, had a deep affection for Speer, whom he regarded as a "fellow artist" (Shirer, p. 1118).

In February, 1942, Speer succeeded Todt as Reichsminister for Armaments and War Production. Among the other positions he held in the Third Reich were those of Inspector General for the Rebuilding of Berlin (which Hitler intended would be lovelier than Paris); Prussian State Councilor; General Plenipotentiary for Armaments in the Office of the Four-Year Plan; Reichsleiter; Chief of the Nazi Party Technical Office; and member of the Reichstag. He was a holder of the Golden Party Badge of Honor, the highest Nazi decoration. As the war drew to a close, however, he disobeyed Hitler's order for a scorched-earth policy. He also claimed to have plotted the assassination of Hitler and the Nazi leadership (Shirer, pp. 1097, 1103–4).

Unlike most of his colleagues, Speer pleaded guilty at Nuremberg and was sentenced to twenty years' imprisonment. Since released from Spandau, he now lives near Heidelberg in the considerable comfort made possible by the sale of his memoirs.

CARD I

1. (∧ 35″) like a bug—but I don't know any bug that looks like that

INQUIRY

1. center part looks like a shelled bug because of the shape; not alive (center D)

There is an unusually long delay before the first response is offered. While this indicates cautiousness in the face of new situations, it should also be noted that the long delay results only in an emotionally flat statement. The subjects in this book, unlike Rorschach subjects generally, frequently see a rather low form of insect life in this card, and a bug is a particularly marked example of this: it does not even possess the wings of a beetle, let alone the attractive and light-winged qualities of a butterfly, and it is of a crawling, insignificant, and verminous nature. The response reflects a very primitive and undeveloped personality. The fact that the bug is identified as a shelled bug, (i.e. a bug with a shell), moreover, suggests that this small personality is enclosed in a protective shell which, it would appear, is actually its main feature. Another feature that characterizes many of these subjects is also found here, in his denial of responsibility for his own perception ("I don't know any bug that looks like that"). This is not, however, an unequivocally psychopathic response but should alert us to possible psychopathy.

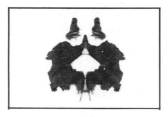

CARD II

1. (∧ ∨ 20″) a butterfly

INQUIRY

1. just the shape, with red tips (W)

Testing the limits: cannot see dancing figures

This is a very vague, generalized, and undifferentiated response whose lack of specificity is typical of children rather than of adults and which, when offered by an adult, is indicative of a limited development of individuality. The same impression is to be derived from the failure to pay any attention to the empty spaces where the body of the butterfly would be—as though he takes for granted his own inner emptiness. All he does with the emotional challenge of the color is to describe the red details arbitrarily as "red tips" on the butterfly, ignoring the incongruity of the black color of the main portion of the blot in relation to the concept of a butterfly. His emotions are decorative rather than intrinsic: mere unintegrated appendages to his being.

CARD III

1. (∧ 8″) could be a drawing by Kubin—can hardly say what (stalling)
   (∧ 90″) could be two people daubed on the card (very uncertain)

INQUIRY

1. Well, it's expressionistic, but very vague—they have arms, legs, high collars. No, I paid no attention to the red spots (W)

Alfred Kubin, an Austrian painter associated with the *Blaue Reiter* group, was known for his choice of grotesque and even repulsive themes. Speer's reference to him is a somewhat pretentious display of his cultural background. But his concept is scarcely sustained by reference to forms on the card and suggests that his intellectual functioning and judgment do not begin to match his mere knowledge. As such, he is an intellectually pretentious and insecure man. More notably, however, the apparent specificity of the remark ("could be a drawing by Kubin") has no real substance or commitment to it, and he takes no responsibility for any resemblance between an actual form and what is on the blot. The evanescence of being indicated by this behavior gives substance to the suspicion expressed in our analysis of Card I that there are psychopathic trends in Speer's personality.

At the same time, the reference to Kubin also indicates some capacity for aesthetic experience in Speer, albeit one which has little if anything to do with the human world, which is devoid of real feeling, and which is associated, in some measure, with the grotesque.

People normally see two live human beings engaged in a live activity in this card. Speer, however, does not indicate what these two people are doing and does not refer to any connection between them. The absence of this common response indicates a strong psychological immobility and the absence of a live, reflecting experiencing of himself as existing in social and historical contexts—indeed, the absence of much experiencing of himself altogether. The psychological immobility of this man is also indicated in other ways. His failure to identify the head and body of the two people points to an incapacity to reach out and move, while the emphasis on high collars suggests a well-developed capacity to separate thinking and feeling. Albeit without the aggressiveness of Goering, for example, he pays no attention to the red spots, which is to say to the emotional aspects of this situation. He responds to emotional stimuli by dismissing them.

CARD IV

Comment: "This is damned hard."
1. (∧ 45″) cross between a bug and a butterfly

INQUIRY

1. Now I would say more like a butterfly: shape of appendages on top; shape of the whole thing (W)

It is somewhat unusual to find a subject in these records responding with an admission of weakness ("This is damned hard.") rather than with a criticism of the situation confronting him. Evidently Speer is on occasion able to acknowledge his own faults; for this group, he shows a notable acceptance of responsibility for himself. Again, however, a long pause results only in a very dull and flat response indicative of low psychic energy. The form here is very poor: there is no such creature as a cross between a bug and a butterfly. On inquiry, he is able to improve this incongruous concept only very slightly, for the butterfly is a poor concept in this card and he makes only the weakest effort to justify or elaborate his response. His intellect seems not to be functioning well, especially when confronted by the darkness and the shading.

CARD V

1. (∨ 20″) a butterfly—a bit clearer

INQUIRY

1. the shape drawn in black and white
Comment: "I understand architecture better."

To call card after card a butterfly or a bug—or a combination of both—approaches a level of perseveration that is often found in young children, in people with central nervous system damage, and in catatonic schizophrenics. He does not quite keep this up here, however, and the perseveration is therefore indicative of the flatness, dullness, and lack of energy within him, of the drab inner world which he inhabits, rather than of damage to the central nervous system.

Speer is under no illusion that he is doing a great job with his responses and, apologetically, says that he can "understand architecture better." The remark is, again, implicitly an acknowledgment of responsibility for his own shortcomings, though it also serves the purpose of reminding the examiner—and himself—that there is at least one area, architecture, wherein Speer can perform more effectively than in the Rorschach.

The flatness of his responses, in fact, explains why he cannot "do better" with the ink blots, for there is evidently so little movement and energy in him that there is not very much for him to say about himself. Given a more defined situation—e.g., architecture—he is, up to a point, capable of coping; but his trouble with the unspecific nature of the Rorschach stimuli makes it clear that in view of the emptiness within him, it is difficult for him to produce very much of any kind of response to a truly challenging life situation.

The failure, in almost all of his responses, to deal with the colors on the cards suggests that his emotional life is practically dead. Instead he concentrates on the forms, but his performance in this respect is also poor, which indicates that although he relies on his control functions, even this part of his personality does not work very well.

Speer's failure to respond to shadings on the cards indicates a notable absence of response to subtlety in human relationships. His scant perceptions of people reflect a very constricted sense of himself as a thinking, imagining, reflecting human being. His responses indicate an extraordinary emptiness of being—he is a flat, rigid, and constricted person. Even within the narrow confines in which he does function there is little depth.

CARD VI

[promptly rejected]

Testing the limits: rejects suggestion of sex

CARD VII

[rejected]

Testing the limits: cannot see suggested women

The paucity of the record here makes it impossible to declare with any degree of certainty what it was that led Speer to reject these two cards, with their strong evocation of both masculine and feminine sexuality, warmth, and interpersonal relationships. It can be hypothesized, however, that his failure to respond indicates an absence of psychosexual development and identity or, more probably, a withdrawal from sexual identity. In part, perhaps, because of the situation in which he now finds himself, he is deadening himself to all feeling. His comment on Card X ("too torn apart") indeed suggests that he was less able than his fellow Nazi prisoners to cope with defeat and humiliation. However, it is also apparent from his responses in general that while he may be deadening himself in reaction to his present situation, he was never really very alive, emotionally, anyway.

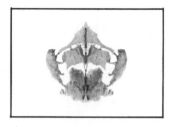

CARD VIII

[blinks in surprise]
1. (∧ > ∧ 30″) coat of arms—two animals on the side, butterfly on bottom and parts on top belong to design

INQUIRY

1. They're shaped like that, but in heraldry the color is independent of the objects it represents (W)

The coat of arms, a symbol of hereditary and status importance, suggests that Speer's sense of importance was obtained through membership in family or other groupings to which he felt he belonged, rather than deriving from his own achievements and personality as an individual. It is also indicative of pretentiousness. But his sense of status and importance rests on the flighty, ephemeral, and flimsy foundation represented by the butterfly underneath the coat of arms, and he is assuredly not secure in it.

By saying that color is independent of the objects which it represents he reveals that his emotions are irrelevant to his being, particularly to that part of his being which connects with other people. His emotional responses to people, then, as well as his social adaptation, are highly artificial. His display of emotion is phony and unrelated to the situation in which it is presented. He is incapable of affective attachment to people or ideas, of empathic response to the former or real involvement in the latter.

CARD IX

[rejected]
[Studies it, gives up after two and a half minutes]

He is trying *very* hard to come up with responses, and examines the card for a long period of time. This card offers a wide range of stimuli and no obvious forms, which is to say that it represents an emotionally and intellectually complicated life situation. Speer makes a strong effort to deal with it, but he is helpless and must withdraw. For there are no inner correlates to that external complexity which the card represents, and he does not have the capacity to respond to the complexity.

CARD X

Comment: "Too torn apart—can't make out a thing."
1. (∧ 80″) could call this a sea horse (green D)

INQUIRY

1. just the shape

Additional: Bottom figure (gray) could be cross section of a flower

Comment: "My fantasies run into musical channels . . . I can entertain myself here in the cell for hours by running over classical musical compositions in my mind. But I can't visualize very well."

Now, instead of merely withdrawing from the complex stimuli confronting him (as he did in Card IX), he makes a direct statement of disintegration. He is too torn apart, and therefore too inadequate, to cope. It is as if he is so empty that emotional challenges pass right through him. Unlike many of his colleagues, he is not even capable of a gushing, sentimental response to this situation. Even by their standards his is a barren being, in which the lack of any feminine elements is notable. The sea horse which, after more than a minute, he discerns in the card happens to be a child-bearing male. If this is of any significance for the interpretation of Speer's response then it is probably as a further indication of his inability to relate to femininity and of the absence of any femininity within him and, by the same token, of any mature male sexuality.

The sea horse, moreover, is not only a primitive and undeveloped animal—pointing to facets of Speer's personality amply manifested in earlier responses—but one which has the superficial appearance of a more developed one. Here, too, therefore, is an expression of the superficiality of Speer's presentation of himself, and of his pretentiousness.

In this highly colored card the only other feature which he can pick out is the single achromatic part of the blot. He sees this as a flower in lifeless and colorless cross section. This is highly suggestive of a flat and empty being and has depressive overtones.

He comments that his "fantasies run into musical channels." There is in this remark some sense of genuine aesthetic experience that is more than merely superficial, but which appears to have little to do with the human world and which, like so many of his other responses, also seems to be associated with a lack of creativity. He then mentions that he cannot visualize very well—a surprising comment from an architect who can "understand architecture" (Card V). What this presumably means is that his concern with architecture is not aesthetic but in line with some of the purely functional approach to modern architecture—with the enclosure of spaces within concrete walls, floors, and ceilings. This enclosure within a hard shell carries some of the connotations of the "shelled bug" of Card I; the adornments on this architecture are presumably as extrinsic to its form as the integration of his emotions with the rest of his being is artificial (Card III).

SUMMARY

"I would have sold my soul like Faust," Albert Speer acknowledges in his memoirs, "for the commission to do a great building" (Speer, p. 37). His comment combines accurate and inaccurate insights into himself. An historian has pointed to Speer as perhaps the outstanding example among the Nazis of the "traditional antisocial indifference of the artist and the technologist, which left him dead to all challenges of political origin" (Fest, p. 199). And he himself wrote, in a memorandum to Hitler, "The task which I have to fulfill is an unpolitical one. I felt comfortable in my work so long as my person and also my work were valued *solely* according to my specialist achievement" (quoted in Fest, p. 199). Speer, it would seem, felt able almost completely to detach his activities from the awesome brutality and degradation of which they were an important part. Even when he opposed violence it was not on humanitarian grounds but because of the waste and inefficiency that it involved. It became clear during his cross-examination at the Nuremberg trial, for instance, that he disapproved of the conditions under which the slave laborers in the factories under his jurisdiction had to live and work for these "practical" reasons (Fest, p. 199).

Speer, then, was not the typical Nazi. It was not a love of violence which led him to join the Nazi party, and he was not a sadist. His Rorschach record, indeed, stands out in this collection for its absence of violent and sadistic indicators. But this, surely, hardly makes him the "morally and intellectually" superior man described by Trevor–Roper and others (Trevor–Roper, p. 240; Fest, p. 200). The fact that he was not a pathological homicide does not make him a decent man or a heroic anti-Nazi any more than does the common-sense practicality he exhibited when he told Hitler that Germany had lost the war, or his disobedience of Hitler's orders to implement a scorched-earth policy as the allied troops entered Germany (Shirer, pp. 1097, 1103, 1118).

But this is not to say, either, that Speer was the complete technocrat interested only in getting the job done. He was, rather, the complete *Nazi* technocrat, interested in getting *Nazi* jobs done. His talents were not at anyone's disposal because it required a particular kind of incentive to mobilize them to their full potential: his Faustian soul was for sale only to the devil. And herein lies the self-deception of Speer's remark that he would have sold his soul for the chance to build a great building. He hardly had a soul to sell—or, for that matter, a soul with which to conceive great buildings. Such soul as he had could imagine nothing grander than the vulgar, power-mad pomposity of the Reich Chancellery in Berlin or the stadium in Nuremberg—and only a devil would wish to buy the services of such a soul.

The dominant impression to be gained from his Rorschach record is of the flatness, drabness, and unevolved, buglike nature of his being. If he was not a Nazi by conviction, it was because there was not enough in him to entertain *any* conviction. He is, to an extent, capable of adaptive emotional response. After first hearing Hitler speak, he reports in his memoir, he retreated to a pine forest, there to glory in the "hope, new ideals, new understandings, new tasks" to which the Fuehrer had exhorted his audience (Speer, p. 19). Yet only a page or two later, he notes that his "feelings probably had nothing to do with political motives" and that his decision, taken the following day, to join the Nazi party was "utterly undramatic. . . . I scarcely felt myself a member of a political party" (Speer, pp. 20–21). Even the vulgar, unintellectual sentimentality of his initial enthusiasm for Hitler's program was an emotion beyond Speer's capacity to sustain for more than a few days. He could not believe in, or be enthusiastic about, anything other than his "great buildings."

Speer's flat, drab evanescence of being surely has its origins in some of the circumstances of his early years, as described in his memoirs. As a boy he had suffered from spells of dizziness and fainting, which were diagnosed as "weakness of the vascular nerve." These episodes, he reports, were "a considerable psychological burden. . . . I suffered all the more because my playmates and my two brothers were more robust that I, so that I felt inferior to them. In their rough-and-tumble way they often made it clear that this was how they thought of me, too" (Speer, p. 5).

"Inadequacy often calls for compensatory forces," Speer then goes on to say. We have seen some indication of the form these took in his personality in our analysis of his Rorschach record. He was a pretentious and snobbish person. In his memoir, the contempt which he expresses for Hitler's petit-bourgeois origins and the loving detail with which he describes the upper-middle-class comforts of his parents' home are expressions of these traits (Speer, pp. 68, 5). So, too, is the bombast with which he declares that at his birth, "the thunder of a spring storm drowned out the bells of nearby Christ Church" (Speer, p. 4).

It is important to note, however, that his attempts to compensate for his feelings of inferiority through this ego inflation and self-aggrandizement rested, as we saw in his Rorschach record, on weak foundations. Significantly, he attributed some of his childhood problems precisely to his family's social status. "My parents," he says, "did their best to provide a happy childhood for us. But wealth and status —social obligations, the large household, the nanny and the servants —stood in the way of their doing as they wished in this respect" (Speer, p. 5).

It was Speer who created the distinctive Nazi style of pageantry and architecture. In the former, "he combined block-line buildings, stairways, pylons, walls of banners and the famous domes of light— circles of searchlights around the arena that created a moving spatial effect as they shone up under the night sky—with arrangements of human masses to create a monumental liturgy" (Fest, p. 201). The crass grandeur, the brutality, the indifference to and even denigration of the individual human being expressed in these pageants as well as in Speer's official architecture were, manifestly, projections of his own emptiness and compensatory pretentiousness.

Speer's spectacles were as phony as his emotional response; his dark, depressive blackness could only briefly and in an essentially meaningless way be penetrated by "the famous domes of light," just as the gaudy and manic architecture he created enclosed within it no activity worthy of man's dignity or decency. It is probable that Speer felt the same ambivalence toward his buildings that he did toward the magnificence of his parents' home: showy as both were, neither could provide more than a superficial compensation for his profound emptiness and inferiority.

It took a very distinctive type of client, then, to make use of Speer's genius, such as it was—a client with Speer's own need to fill a black void with gaudy pomposity.

The inordinate emphasis on structure in Nazi design reflects another aspect of Speer's personality as revealed in the Rorschach analysis. We suggested that he was probably not very effective at functioning under his own volition, or when he had to set his own direction. Of his school days he says that "unconditional faith in the authority of the school was required. . . . it never even occurred to us to doubt the order of things, for as students we were subjected to the dictates of a virtually absolutist system." In retrospect, he finds fault with his school only in its failure to have included the modern social sciences, and modern history, in its curriculum. This, he says, left him "without defenses when exposed to the new techniques for influencing opinion" (Speer, p. 9). Given "a virtually absolutist system" he will function as a wholly socialized being; without such a structure, he makes the terrible mistake, both morally and intellectually, of joining the Nazi movement. If his schoolmasters had taught him that Nazism was wrong, he would never have become a Nazi. Since he was not taught so, and since, moreover, the Nazis provided as rigid a structure as his school had, he joined the Nazi movement—and then helped to make its structure even more apparent than it had been before.

To the end of his public career, at least, Speer retained his ability to function appropriately, or at least adaptively, according to the demands of a structured situation, and to do so with pretentiousness and bombast.

In the prisoners' dock at Nuremberg he acknowledged his guilt in an ostentatiously noble and self-sacrificing manner. The Nazi Party, he declared, had a collective responsibility for all the terrible things that Germany had done under its leadership; the German people, however, he declared to be guiltless. There is, surely, a measure of spuriousness in his identification with a political elite to which he felt, as a technocrat, that he did not really belong; just as there is a measure of pretentiousness in his claim that he, along with a relatively small number of other people, was able to hoodwink the entire German people. Even more strikingly, however, Speer regarded the death sentence he expected to receive in the most noble possible terms. Under his leadership, he declared, scientists and technologists had almost destroyed the world because they had not paid attention to the moral consequences of their work. Such circumstances, he warned, were likely to recur in the future, and would then most assuredly succeed in destroying mankind. He viewed his own execution, therefore, as a deterrent to all scientists and technicians in the world, a warning to them that they should use their skills only for humane purposes and never in the service of power-mad governments. Thus, he declared, his execution would serve the ultimate purpose of redeeming mankind from its otherwise almost certain annihilation (Fishman, pp. 72ff.; Gilbert, 1947, pp. 47ff.).

It is true that Speer's Rorschach record indicates some capacity to acknowledge his own faults. To an extent, then, his guilty plea may have reflected a genuine feeling of guilt. But the record also indicates, and more emphatically, the limited and artificial nature of his emotional responses, along with his capacity to separate thought from feeling. It is truly extraordinary to note, in this context, that his record barely, if at all, provides any indication of depression. During the trial Speer was remarkable for his stable mood, in strikingly marked contrast to his fellow prisoners. After an atrocity film had been shown to the court, "Speer was still cool and collected and quite reconciled to paying the death penalty for the collective guilt. He did not even seem depressed" (Gilbert, 1947, p. 55; cf. p. 74).

Speer's confession of guilt, then, was probably partly authentic but also partly phony, revealing not only his psychopathic propensity for dissimulation and his readiness to adjust to whatever structure surrounded him, but also his ability to pursue his ego-inflating pretentiousness in a new setting.

19

The Mind of the
Nazi Leaders

Readers familiar with the Rorschach method will readily recognize the distinctive nature of the records in this collection. The novice, however, may still be somewhat baffled by—or else skeptical of—the procedures which we have followed in analyzing them. Surely, he will ask, Card I readily suggests a bat or a butterfly, Card II animals or clowns dancing, Card III two people bowing to each other, and so on? Seeing these images in the cards, the reader may conclude either that he shares many of the prominent personality traits of the Nazi leaders, or else that the Nazi mind—to return to the focus of our discussion in Chapter I—is an essentially normal one.

Neither inference would be warranted. In the most general terms, the reader may indeed see many of the same things in the cards that the Nazis saw—a bat, or clowns, or whatever. However, as we indicated in Chapter II, the skilled Rorschach analyst does not look only at the most obvious aspects of the contents of a response but also scrutinizes the particular terminology employed in the response, the features which are emphasized or ignored in it, the contexts in which it is set, the precise ways in which form, color, and texture are used, and so on. And it is frequently in the analysis of such details, which the untrained reader all too easily overlooks, that we find the distinctive characteristics of a response. The bat that the reader sees in Card I, for example, is indeed the same bat that several of our subjects saw. But it is highly unlikely that the reader would then go on to specify that the bat is torn, or dead, these being details of the kind which, as we have seen repeatedly, this group of subjects comes up with in its responses. And even if the reader *did* see the bat in such terms, it is highly unlikely that many of the other attributes, singly and together, which characterize our subjects' responses, would also be present in his.

Appendix B consists of a brief discussion of the Rorschach record of an American businessman, a record selected virtually at random to

	1 depression	2 violence	3 status	4 reject responsibility	5 exotic plants	6 dead, mounted	7 grotesque	8 hard, rough, cold, dry	9 feelers, eyes	10 clarity of obvious concepts	11 marine animals	12 bugs, beetles, insects	13 female figures	14 crabs	15 direct rejection of red	16 explosions, etc.	17 bones	18 devils, gremlins, trolls, etc.	19 torn, ragged	20 chameleons	21 sea horses	22 banners, trophies	23 take responsibility for difficulty	24 number of categories in record
FRANK	16	1	3	—	—	2	4	7	—	3	2	—	2	2	—	1	2	—	—	1	5	—	—	14
FRITZSCHE	4	4	2	—	2	2	1	3	—	3	—	—	1	—	2	2	1	—	4	1	—	—	—	15
FUNK	4	4	1	2	1	—	4	1	—	1	—	—	1	—	1	—	2	2	—	—	—	—	—	12
GOERING	2	2	1	8	—	4	3	—	1	3	1	1	—	1	2	1	—	2	—	—	—	2	2	13
HESS	1	3	2	1	1	3	1	—	—	—	1	2	—	1	—	—	—	—	—	1	—	—	—	13
KALTENBRUNNER	—	1	—	10	1	1	1	—	3	—	4	—	3	3	1	1	—	—	1	—	—	—	—	11
KEITEL	3	3	2	5	2	1	—	—	5	1	2	2	—	—	2	—	—	—	1	1	—	—	—	12
NEURATH	1	1	—	—	1	—	—	—	—	—	—	—	1	—	—	—	—	1	—	—	—	1	1	8
PAPEN	2	2	2	4	—	5	—	—	2	—	—	2	—	—	—	—	—	—	2	—	—	—	—	8
RIBBENTROP	2	1	—	5	2	—	3	—	—	—	1	—	—	1	—	1	—	—	—	—	—	—	—	6
ROSENBERG	3	1	2	1	1	2	—	—	1	—	—	1	1	1	—	—	—	—	1	1	—	—	—	13
SAUCKEL	5	—	5	5	1	—	—	1	—	—	—	—	1	1	—	—	1	1	—	—	—	—	—	10
SCHACHT	5	3	5	3	1	2	1	3	1	—	1	1	2	—	1	2	1	—	—	—	1	—	—	17
SCHIRACH	6	2	4	7	1	—	3	4	—	1	—	1	1	1	—	—	—	1	—	—	2	—	—	12
SEYSS—INQUART	5	1	1	4	2	2	3	3	2	1	—	—	—	—	1	2	2	1	—	1	1	1	—	13
SPEER	1	—	—	3	1	1	—	—	1	1	—	2	—	—	—	—	—	—	1	1	1	2	2	12
Number of subjects	15	14	14	13	12	10	9	8	8	8	8	8	7	7	7	6	6	6	6	5	5	5	3	
Number of responses	60	29	31	57	15	24	21	23	16	14	12	12	9	10	10	8	9	8	10	5	5	10	5	

TABLE ONE: THE OCCURRENCE OF CERTAIN SIGNIFICANT CONCEPTS IN THE 16 RECORDS illustrate for the reader some of the similarities as well as the striking differences between the Rorschach material of psychopathic criminals and that of "ordinary" people. If the reader is unlikely to share many of the significant personality traits of the Nazis studied in this volume, then, it is also true that *these* Nazis, at least, are significantly characterized by a highly distinctive set of traits. A tabulation of these traits appears on page 269. Before we proceed to an analysis of them, however, it seems important to emphasize that our tabulation is a statistical one only in the most superficial sense. Considerable discretion, based, we trust, on clinical experience, has been exercised in devising the categories employed in the tabulation and in assigning responses, or aspects of responses, to each category. The kind of analysis undertaken in this volume, however, means that these categories, and the ways in which they are used here, must necessarily be somewhat arbitrary and cannot be considered exhaustive. Not all responses indicative of violent traits and experiences, for example, appear under the "violence" category, since some are indicators of violence only in the highly specific contexts in which they occur. Nor is the frequency with which a response appears in any one record necessarily an indication of its salience—let alone of the role which it plays —in a subject's personality. Finally, it should also be stressed that the distinctive qualities of this group of subjects cannot be measured against any "normal" or control group since, as we mentioned in Chapter II, statistical norms for the Rorschach have not been established. It is thus primarily on the basis of clinical experience that these sixteen individuals are deemed to constitute, from a psychological standpoint, a highly distinctive group. To a considerably lesser extent, however, the group can also be considered distinctive in terms of several of its responses to what have over the years been established as the intrinsic properties of the cards. Card VII, for instance, has rather strong feminine traits, and the upper two thirds of the blot is frequently seen as the head, trunk, and arms of two women. In our group of sixteen subjects, however, only three—Frank, Schacht, and Schirach—see women in this card. Of these three, Schacht refers to the head alone, while the other two refer to women and do not identify the parts of their bodies used for the concepts. Five of our subjects, moreover, do not see humans at all in this card (Hess, Keitel, Neurath, Papen, Rosenberg); while four reject the card altogether. Thus, ten of the sixteen (if we include Goering's "grotesque . . . half-man, half-animal") are unable to see humans in the card, and only three respond in what might, very generally, be considered a common way.

As a group, then, our subjects share a number of clinically significant reactions which, individually and in the aggregate, can be considered to set them off as a distinct group. A number of these, and the frequency of their occurrence in this group, point up surprising but nonetheless explicable qualities in the Nazi personality.

Depression. Fifteen of the sixteen subjects indicate depressive mood qualities by referring to such concepts as night, darkness, grayness, blackness, and so on. This is, indeed, the single most prevalent quality in the group and, for what the statistic is worth, is found in an average of four responses per subject.

The reader may object that it is hardly surprising that men who have witnessed the collapse of their empire and now face trial for their very lives should be depressed. In our analysis of individual records, however, we noted numerous instances wherein these depressive states appeared to be permanent features of individual personalities, and were exacerbated rather than brought about by the Nazi debacle. From a psychohistorical perspective, there is nothing at all implausible about such a suggestion. The Nazi movement, after all, had its origins in the almost complete collapse of Germany's political, social and economic fortunes after the end of the First World War. These circumstances were surely highly depressing for most Germans and, like the Great Depression (*sic!*) in the United States during the 1930's, frequently left a permanent mark on individual personalities. A number of responses in our group of subjects indirectly reflect or are consistent with a depressive state, and seem to emanate from so integral a part of their personalities that it would be difficult to believe that they were merely a result of recent incarceration. Among the categories of these responses are "dead" (ten subjects); "hard . . . rough . . . cold . . . dry" (eight subjects); and bones, torn, ragged (six subjects each). Seven subjects have the counter-depressive "dance" concept in their responses to Card II, and many of these and other subjects use the "dance" image in other cards.

A further source of depression in our group, unrelated to their imprisonment at Nuremberg, may be found in the fact that well before the end of the war nine of them, in a manner characteristic of the shifting fortunes of the subordinates of a totalitarian ruler, had suffered notable losses of position within the Nazi elite (Frank, Goering, Hess, Neurath, Papen, Ribbentrop, Rosenberg, Schacht, and Schirach).

Violence. The second most frequently occurring category of responses, found in fourteen of sixteen subjects, is one which indicates their experience of violence—as both victim and perpetrator. We have been presented with a veritable chamber of horrors in these records, ranging from Fritzsche's torn heart (Card III) to Funk's scene from the *Walpurgisnacht,* as he would have it (Card X); from Goering's man opened up with the insides in the middle (Card III) to Hess's illustration for a crime novel (Card III); from Kaltenbrunner's cuttlefish (Card IX) to Keitel's bird's head torn below (Card III); from Papen's footprint of a shot animal (Card II) to Schacht's shot rabbit's head (Card IX).

Status. As prevalent as indicators of violence are responses which point to a preoccupation with status, through the use of such concepts as hats, caps, headdresses, and helmets. Of the two men who do not use these images in their records, Keitel appears to have been genuinely unconcerned with status—shunning, for example, such beloved perquisites of ruling classes almost everywhere as large, chauffeur-driven limousines. That Ribbentrop—the man whose efforts to acquire the nobilliary "von" before his name made him the laughingstock of the German aristocracy—should have failed to register any indicators of status concern seems quite anomalous. His record is generally so flat and dead, however, that we can perhaps explain this absence by the fact that he has quite given up his former concern with status along with his concern for, or interest in, almost everything else.

Rejection of Responsibility. Thirteen out of the sixteen men—the fourth largest category in this group—use a variety of terms such as "fantastic," "funny" "not so good," etc., to disclaim responsibility for their concepts: the deficiencies in the concepts are reported by them as being in the blots rather than in what they see in the blots. This characteristic, while not in itself indicative of psychopathy, is found far more often among psychopathic personalities than in any other group of the population. Of the three not tabulated in this category—Frank, Fritzsche, and Neurath—Frank gives responses that indicate psychopathy in Cards I and VI, and Fritzsche in Card VII. Neurath's chameleon response in Card VIII is also suggestive of psychopathy (in the overall context of his record) in its opportunistic implications.

Neurath, Goering, and Speer, are the only three men to take responsibility, on occasion, for the difficulties they encounter in dealing with the stimuli of the blots. It is tempting to speculate that the "Nuremberg defense"—the argument of obedience to superior orders, and hence of nonresponsibility for one's actions—has a certain psychological valence in the psychopathic nature of the defendants' personalities. Of the three individuals who acknowledged responsibility for their deeds during the Nuremberg trial (Frank, Goering—who did not pretend to feel guilty about them—and Speer), two—namely Goering and Speer—can be seen to acknowledge their difficulties in responding to certain cards; of the three individuals who acknowledged their difficulty in responding to certain cards, two acknowledged responsibility for their deeds during the Nuremberg trial (Neurath being the exception).

In any event, the term "psychopathic" generally refers to people who engage in antisocial activity with apparent absence of guilt. We will elaborate the concept more fully further on in this chapter, but for now it will suffice to point out that the rejection of responsibility for one's own concepts in the Rorschach is tantamount to saying, "I am not really the person who is or does those things; therefore it is not my fault that they exist." While Goering and Speer assuredly *were* psychopathic, they did possess a sporadic and for this group highly atypical ability to accept responsibility for at least some aspects of themselves. (It is also possible, however, as we suggested in our analysis of Speer's record, that his avowals of guilt were manifestations of a psychopathic personality's adaptability, as was probably also the case with Frank.)

Exotic Plants. The next most frequent response, found in twelve of the sixteen records in this collection, is that of exotic, fantastic plants, seen in the multicolored cards. These, as we have seen, indicate sloppy, undifferentiated, sentimental emotional responses—the famous Nazi *schmalz*, which was frequently the only form in which the undeveloped "feminine" feeling aspects of these individuals could express themselves.

Dead, Mounted. Ten of the subjects refer to objects which are dead, mounted as specimens, or seen in cross sections. A bat is "opened and mounted," for example (Frank, Card V); Card IX is the enlargement of a cross section of a flower, with its various parts scattered around (Fritzsche); and so on. The response points to states of disintegration and inner deadness and to the infliction of violence (sometimes justified, perhaps, by spurious scientific rationales) on others.

Grotesque, Distorted. The seventh most frequent category of responses, offered by nine of the sixteen subjects, reflects qualities of grotesqueness and distortion in these individuals which, as we have seen, could be evoked even in fairly conventional situations (Goering, Card VII; Ribbentrop, Card II; etc.)

Hard, Rough, Cold, Dry. Half the subjects use these concepts in their responses, indicating the harshness of their experience of the world and of their behavior in it, and their rejection of potential warmth and of feelings for others.

Feelers, Eyes. Half the subjects, too, reveal a suspicious searching out of their environment.

Clarity of Obvious Concepts. Half the subjects also express their gratification at the clarity of a particular concept—in most cases a conventional or obvious one. Such a response indicates the absence of, and hence a need for, a sense of self and of an understandable environment.

Marine Animals. Eight of the sixteen subjects also see marine animals, often of an unknown kind and often ones which are primitive or have highly unattractive qualities. These reflect the undeveloped, low-level, and in many instances defensive and aggressive nature of the subjects' personalities.

Bugs, Beetles, Insects. Half the subjects unwittingly depict themselves, or aspects of themselves, as unevolved, low-level bugs, beetles, or insects.

Female Figures. Only seven of the subjects see female figures in the cards, and the distinctive qualities of most of these concepts deserve to be noted. Frank's ballerina in Card II appears in the context of public display and a deeply depressed retreat into the void; he is incapable of using the qualities of creativity which she represents. His women in Card VII are mocking each other. Fritzsche's dancing girl in Card I appears in a context of counterdepression, exposure, and a sense of loss of control over inner experience; Funk's woman in Card I is being grabbed, protesting, by two men. Neurath's women (Card II) are ambiguous (are they Chinese *men*?) and exotic and remote ("Chinese"), while Sauckel's ballerina in Card II actually appears in a schizoid setting and reveals his lack of connection with any female qualities that he may have had. Only Schacht (Cards VII and IX) and Schirach (Card VII) appear able to see female figures in a relatively straightforward manner.

Crab. The armored, primitive, aggressive crab, dweller in the depths that can move in any direction without turning, appears as an unwitting portrayal of an aspect of the self in seven of the sixteen records in this collection. Even when the crab is the popular one of Card X, these subjects' concepts are unusual because the crabs' aggressive aspects are stressed or because they are the only detail identified in this varied, complex card.

Direct Rejection of Red. Seven of the sixteen directly reject the red color in Cards II and III or, in the case of Seyss-Inquart, in Card X. The response reflects an inability to integrate emotions, which are experienced as uncontrolled (Fritzsche), repulsive (Keitel), or "grotesque, not very good" (Seyss-Inquart). Emotions are experienced as not belonging and are denied or, in the case of Goering, aggressively cut out of the situation.

Explosions, Fire, Smoke, Gas. These appear in six of the records, pointing to states of violent inner disorganization and disintegration and a sense of loss of control to ego-alien forces.

Bones. The bone concepts which appear in six of the records indicate qualities of coldness, hardness, flatness, emptiness, and lifelessness in the subjects, often accompanied by the experience of inner weakness.

Devils, Gremlins, Trolls, etc. These subhuman and inhuman figures of evil and violence appear as unwitting self-portraits in six of the records in our collection.

Torn, Ragged. Six of the subjects also use concepts which indicate an experience of disorganization and disintegration, frequently in a setting of violence: they and their world are torn and ragged.

Chameleons. This highly original response is, remarkably enough, found in the records of five of our subjects. It is quite unusual for subjects to see the side details in Card VIII even as lizards, for example, or as salamanders (whose color more nearly approximates that on the card than does that of a chameleon, which cannot turn red). This distinctive response, then, shows the way in which the otherwise weak instinctual drives of these subjects are devoted to opportunistic goals.

Sea horses. This primitive, undifferentiated marine animal, superficially resembling the far more developed horse—and thus, in the Rorschach, implying qualities of primitivity and compensatory pretentiousness—appears in five of the records in this collection.

Banners, Trophies. These indicators of display, frequently seen as heraldic devices and often in a setting of violence, point up qualities of showiness and ostentatiousness in five of our subjects. As heraldic devices, they indicate a sense of importance that is derived from family connections.

We have already noted the idiosyncratic way in which members of this group of subjects responded to the intrinsic properties of Card VII, revealing their inability, on the whole, to express what in our culture are considered the female aspects of personality—qualities of tenderness, warmth, nurturance, etc. No less striking is the idiosyncratic nature of their animal responses. The records are marked by a paucity of live animal responses in general and mammalian concepts in particular, and by the insipid and unaggressive nature both of the live animals seen and of the movements in which they are depicted. Altogether, there appear to be thirty-four live animals in the sixteen records, of which only eighteen seem to be mammals as opposed to birds, fish, reptiles, or insects. Of these mammals, six are either unspecified—i.e., described only as "animals"—or are described as "mysterious" or "unknown." What is particularly striking about the mammalian responses is their unaggressive nature. In general, the animals seen are not aggressive; where they might be considered such, their vigor is vitiated by qualifying adjectives. Fritzsche's grizzly bears in Card I, for example, become "little grizzly bears," and Goering's dogs (Card X) are "little dogs." The movements of these animals are also unaggressive: two of the three bears are dancing (the third is climbing), and other animals are seen looking up, sitting on their haunches, going away, reclining, etc.

These responses indicate the very considerable extent to which the impulse life of this group of subjects was weak, repressed, and distorted. The distortion is perhaps particularly notable in the number of unanimallike things which several of the animals are shown doing—

holding a bottle (Frank, Card II) or blowing out red smoke (Schirach, Card IX)—and is implicit in the general, and marked, lack of vitality in the animal responses as a whole. Psychopathic personalities, so often regarded as people who are inordinately driven by their instinctive "animal" drives, actually, as in this group, turn out to be people who are cut off from their vital impulses and are unable to be free and spontaneous. Their antisocial attitudes are not expressions of normal impulses, but rather of the repression and distortion of these impulses.

It will be recalled that the deep shading of Cards IV and VI is frequently used for such concepts as the furry hide of an animal. In an unpublished study, Kemple recalls an Irish folk tale, discussed and analyzed as a psychological metaphor by Zimmer:

> A young prince has to go on a dangerous journey to a magic city and bring home certain trophies before he can qualify for the throne of his kingdom. On this journey he rides a shaggy talking horse which guides and advises him so that they manage to reach the gates of the city. At this point the horse gives the prince his final instructions: that he must kill the horse, flay it and put the skin around himself, in order to protect himself from the terrible fires which surround that city. The horse also gives the prince a magic ointment which he is to put on the carcass after he has returned from the city. The prince, of course, is very resistant to performing this last and most difficult task of killing the horse which has been his best friend. The task involves both hurt to himself and cruelty to animals. But finally he is persuaded, carries out the instructions and succeeds in entering the city. He emerges unharmed with his trophies. As instructed, he now puts the magic ointment on the carcass, which is transformed into a young man like himself who becomes his best friend and who assists him in gaining his rightful throne.

Kemple calls attention to the relevance of this myth to the shading responses in the Rorschach. As we mature, aspects of our instinctual, "animal" self are, like the horse in the story above, "killed off." We learn to inhibit and adapt our instincts and to moderate the strong egocentricity of the very young. In return, we acquire the capacity to attain adult goals—the kingdom which the prince seeks to inherit—and to relate in a sensitive, nourishing, and enhancing way to our own feelings and to those of others. "Killing" aspects of our impulse life, learning to adapt and inhibit our instincts, however, is a process that can lead in many different directions. Most of our subjects have succeeded in inhibiting their instincts in a most general sense, but the results of this process were, for them, striking and disturbing.

For the decisive question, once we have, as it were, "killed the animal," is what we are able to do with its skin. Can we transform it into something which will protect us—including from the fires of our inner nature—and can we utilize it in a way that will make us into our own "best friend" and enable us to have rewarding relationships with others—as the prince in the story succeeded in doing?

In six of the responses in this group we find the fur in a setting of display—two quite literally in a show window display (Greenacre, p. 171). Sensitivity to nuances of feeling in human relationships is used by these respondents to manipulate and hoodwink others, rather than for the establishment of real relationships. The show window display quality, in particular, indicates a psychopathic tendency to assume that the form and outward appearance of sensitive emotional response is the same as the substance of such a response.

In five of the responses, moreover, the animal skin is described as stretched, pointing to the considerable strain experienced by the subjects in such response as they are capable of making to human feelings.

In a number of instances, too, elements of violent and predatory qualities appear in the use of shading—as in Keitel's beast of prey (Card IV), Schirach's tiger skin (Card VI), and Seyss-Inquart's beast of prey (Card IV). Several of our subjects, then, experienced what might ordinarily be considered sensitive human feelings as violent ones.

Perhaps most striking of all, however, is the number of instances in which there is no response to the furry qualities of the cards at all, but only a bizarre series of concepts ranging from "funny animal, sea animal, the kind you make smoked fish out of" (Goering, Card IV), to Keitel's "a kind of birdlike insect . . . more a marine animal" (Card IV), to Papen's "dead specimen of insect or crawling animal or insect" (Card IV), and Speer's "cross between a bug and a butterfly" (Card IV). These responses indicate the destruction rather than the transformation of the subjects' instinctual life. Far from being able to change the horse into a living companion, as the prince in the story succeeded in doing, these subjects passed through the fiery city of their early life in a way that led to the vitiation of their impulses.

A noteworthy characteristic of these subjects, then, is the low level of development of their instinctual life in general, and of their responses to nuances of feeling in human relationships in particular. Typically, other peoples' feelings are experienced by members of this group either as virtually nonexistent or as providing opportunities for manipulative exploitation or invitations to violent and brutal rejection. By the same token, the capacity on the part of most members of this group to experience their own feelings in subtle, differentiated, and sensitive ways is minimal. In general, these appear to be individuals who are undeveloped, manipulative, and hostile in their relations with others. From early on in their lives their emotional needs went unfulfilled; as a result, they are unable to respond to the emotional needs of other people.

Instead of real relationships and vital connectedness with their own impulse life and that of others, members of this group relied heavily on qualities of superficiality, display, and performance. We have already noted the frequency of their *sentimental* exotic plant responses. Concepts involving performance, decoration, art collections, museum displays, etc., figure in ten of these records. Indicators of phony bonhommie also abound in their responses to Cards II and III, with the superficial adaptation of the use of the red in the frequently jovial clown, dancer, or similar concept in the former card and the emphasis on formality in the latter. Assuredly, these were people who did not relate in any real way to each other or to their own limited feelings and impulses, but habitually put on an act of doing so instead. The highly unusual red socks which abound in their responses to Card II reveal their lack of solid grounding, as well as their loss of standing; the poor form of this concept indicates a loss of judgment in connection with these experiences.

Our listing of the distinctive characteristics of this group could be extended further. Enough have been identified here, however, to enable us to integrate them into a portrait of the psychological dynamics of these subjects. The central concept around which this is most appropriately done is that of psychopathy.

The term "psychopath" generally refers to people who engage in antisocial activity with apparent absence of guilt, and who seem capable of no real feeling for, or loyalty to, other human beings, and no real commitment to principles or ideals. Actually, it is not that they are totally lacking in feelings or ideals; it is rather that these qualities operate at an extremely primitive level, so that feelings are highly egocentric, loyalties are to idealized hero figures, and ideals are ones like power and the outward appearance of success. While the most extreme and easily identifiable psychopaths are criminals, imposters, confidence men, and such, psychopathy is sometimes a dominant characteristic in people whose outer adaptation bespeaks conformity and social responsibility. These people not only pay lip service to virtue, morality, and altruism, but they convince themselves that their constant deviations from those ideals are not deviations at all; rather, they are in the service of a higher purpose. An "end justifies the means" philosophy becomes the foundation for a complex and subtle system of rationalization by which the person justifies extremely primitive aggressive egocentric behavior.

In an important study of the psychopathic personality, Phyllis Greenacre has specified some of the salient characteristics of the psychopath as follows (Greenacre, p. 167):

1. engages in irresponsible behavior in a singularly unplanned and undeliberated manner;

2. may recognize the consequences of such behavior but totally disregards them in practice;

3. lives only in a series of present moments, without real consideration for past or future except insofar as he pays lip service to them; this same lack of emotional depth is also manifested in

4. an *as if* quality: intentions are accomplished merely by having them as intentions, so that the actual performance (e.g., repaying a debt) becomes unnecessary; the psychopath feels righteously outraged if punished for having failed to behave properly—did he not, after all, *intend* doing so?

5. frequently verbalistic, plausible and charming

Greenacre also notes frequently recurring characteristics of the families of psychopaths she studied, which are, perhaps, of considerable significance for an understanding of our group. In numerous instances, the father or grandfather has been an unusually prominent and respected man, or, if not this, then someone who has been in a position of conspicuous public trust and authority, such as a clergyman, judge, civic leader, or, more modestly, policeman, truant officer, etc.,—someone who was a "father" to his community as well as to his children.

Most frequently, the father of the psychopath is stern, remote, and fear-inspiring to his children, and often obsessional in his conduct. The mother, on the other hand, is often indulgent, pleasure-loving, frivolous and frequently pretty and tacitly contemptuous of her husband's importance. There is generally a marked discrepancy or definite conflict between the parents' ideals on the one hand, and their attitudes toward the child's immediate experience, on the other, and a conspicuous contrast between the brave facade presented to the world and the conflict and misery that lie behind it.

In such families, both parents are generally highly narcissistic in their dependence on the approval or admiration of their contemporaries. The relationship between parents and child is generally poor from the infant's earliest days, with indulgence and solicitude substituting for real love. The parents' overvaluation of external appearances promotes a kind of "show window display" role for the child, with a premium on formally good behavior for the sake of reflecting favorably on the parents (Greenacre, pp. 170–71).

In these situations, the child has a grotesquely exaggerated fear and awe of his parents, a circumstance that has its origins in two factors. One is that the narcissistic attachment of the mother, in particular, to the child inhibits the normal development by which the child overcomes his tendency to project his own anger onto the external world (a development which plays the decisive role in the formation of the child's superego) and begins to internalize it instead. Frequently, moreover, the mother's narcissistic attachment to the child is also negative in the sense that the child is seen by her as evidence of her sexual shame and guilt—an attitude to which the child succumbs even as he rebels against it (Greenacre, p. 183). Secondly, the child's actual experience of the father—distant, awe-inspiring, and superhuman as his behavior often appears to be, and devoid of real love and warmth—tends to confirm in reality the frightening images which the child has raised, as it were, from within himself (out of his own aggression) and projected onto the outside world.

These experiences stunt the development of healthy love impulses in the child—but they do more than this. They make his world feel like a hostile and frightening place, just as they have undermined his development of a healthy superego. The parents' narcissism, and the lessened ability of the child as a result of it to detach himself from them, contributes directly to "the show window display" qualities of which Greenacre speaks:

> Such children are treated as though they must not fail. They are habitually on show, and failures are either denied, concealed or explained away. Thus they are robbed of the full measure of reality testing, and performance even in the earliest years becomes measured largely by its appearance rather than by its intrinsic accomplishment. One sees in miniature the attitudes which later are so characteristic of the psychopath, i.e., what *seems to be* is more valued than *what is*. This characteristic, together with the essential emotional impoverishment, tends to create a very thin stage-property vision of reality in which the facade at any given time is the prime consideration (Greenacre, p. 172).

> The degradation of the sense of reality by the opportunistic need to be pleasing seems in these children to develop early a charm and a tact which gives the semblance of responsiveness and consideration for others, but which generally later is unmasked in all its superficiality, and may be the foundation of a later adroitness in managing people which savors of blackmail (ibid., p. 173).

Perhaps the most remarkable fact about the group of subjects in our collection is that at least fifteen out of the sixteen were, in varying degrees psychopathic—Neurath being perhaps the sole exception. It is probable that these traits are to be found in large numbers of *any* group of "power seekers"—whether in politics, commerce, the arts, or elsewhere—but the proportion here seems extraordinary.

It must be stressed, moreover, that this diagnosis is based not only on the high frequency of rejection of responsibility for concepts in these records. It is based on numerous additional factors, one of which is indeed the infrequency with which our subjects *do* acknowledge their difficulties in responding to the blots. Only three of the subjects make this acknowledgment (and one of them is Neurath), and they do so a total of five times—as compared with fifty-seven instances of rejecting responsibility!

If the psychopath's "stage-property vision of reality" is reflected in the frequent rejection of responsibility for concepts by our subjects, it is also seen in other places in their records—in the superficiality of their adaptive responses, which we have encountered so frequently; in their stress on status, display and decoration; and, in one instance, in a literal "stage designer's fancy" (Sauckel, Card VIII).

Psychopaths, Greenacre also writes, "do not suffer from depersonalization because they have never been really personalized" (p. 184). This surely holds true for the subjects in this collection. We have seen how flat, empty, dried-out, and insubstantial their beings were, aspects of their personalities described in such terms as dead, mounted, hard, rough, cold, dry, bones, torn, ragged, and so on, which recur so frequently in their records, and the same qualities are revealed in the nature of their live animal responses. We have also seen how in many respects these people were undeveloped and primitive, how their unwitting self-portraits included (frequently "unknown") marine animals, bugs, bats, and insects; and we have noted the limited nature of their emotional response: their frequent rejection of the red in Cards II and III; their limited and frequently rather horrifying use of the shading in Cards IV and VI; their equally limited and often grotesque responses to the female qualities of the stimuli of Card VII; and the crude, undifferentiated, and sentimental form in which alone they were able to experience feelings.

We have seen, too, how suspicious they were, both in terms of lacking trust in others, and of being untrustworthy. Their impulse life, restricted as it was, existed largely in the devilish, troll-like form of some of their responses, compounded of the opportunistic ambition of the climbing chameleon, the arbitrariness and meaninglessness of frequent explosions, and the qualities of grotesqueness and violence that recur in these records. These qualities were overlaid by a veneer of superficial adaptation, formality, and spurious plausibility that was as unreal as was their vision of reality.

Much research still needs to be done on the biographies of these men. Their Rorschach records, however, as well as what biographical information is available, strongly suggest that their early years and their family life were characterized by the kinds of dynamics to which Greenacre attributes the formation of the psychopathic personality.

Power has many attractions, on the psychological as well as the practical level. So much of the pain and frustration in all our lives stem from the disparity between what we would like the world to be and what it is, between what the world is and what we perceive it to be, between whom we would like to be and who we are. We suffer from the fact that our desires go unfulfilled and our perceptions of reality are frequently undermined.

Three types of responses to these circumstances are, basically speaking, possible. We can withdraw from the reality of the world into a false but elaborately constructed and impregnable reality of our own. Or we can respond to the dissonances which we experience by adapting our sense of reality in a way which strengthens it and thereby contributes to the maturation of our personality. Or, finally, we can attempt to adapt reality to ourselves, rather than the other way around. Power, it is frequently suggested, is sought in order to compensate for low self-esteem. But this would seem to be only a specific expression of a more general phenomenon. Power, we may say, is sought in order to reshape the world according to our expectations of what it should be—these expectations, in fact, ultimately reflecting our assumptions as to what the world really *is*. The power seeker sets out to reshape the world in his own image. And the dilemma—and much of the tragedy—of mankind is that those who seek to do so frequently have such a tenuous and overcompensated image of who they are.

The Nazis created a world which reflected the distinctive qualities of their personalities. It was a cold, hard, brutal, empty world whose elaborate and detailed structure was a facade for an endlessly shifting evanescence (Arendt, 1958, pp. 400ff.; Friedrich and Brzezinski, p. 19); whose carefully programmed expressions of joy and celebration were a frenetic retreat into nothingness, as vacuous and life-denying as Speer's famous columns of light in the pitch-black night sky; and whose boisterous camaraderie scarcely masked its participants' inordinate capacity for manipulation and treachery—and their *in*capacity to feel human feelings even for one another. Yet, vile and gruesome as this world was, it represented, for the decade or so of its existence, a solution to the problem of existence for the men who created it. A vile and gruesome world, it was the one in which, more than any other, these men could feel at home.

It seems important to stress our recognition of the fact that the Nazi movement was not solely a product of the distinctive psychological characteristics of the men whose records we have been examining here and of their colleagues. Not every psychopath, after all, becomes a Nazi and not every Nazi was a psychopath. Every moment in history is compounded of a vastly complex interaction of personality factors and social forces. We do not "explain" the rise of Nazism when we succeed in attaching a clinical label to the Nazi leaders. "Psycho-pathic personalities," G. M. Gilbert does well to point out,

> undoubtedly play an important part in major manifestations of social pathology, particularly when they achieve positions of leadership in social groups and movements. It is all too clear that they played a decisive role in the revolutionary nucleus of the Nazi movement, and thus determined the complexion of the government of Nazi Germany. But that does not mean that the crux of our problem is the detection and elimination of such personalities from political life. Even if that were possible, it would be an endless palliative process at best. . . . without the support of "normal and respectable" leaders in that society, without a considerable following among the masses of the people, and without the facilitative action of certain cultural trends, it would hardly have been possible for the Nazi leaders to precipitate as great a social catastrophe as they did (Gilbert, 1950, p. 286).

A detailed exploration of the interactions between German society and history and the Nazi leadership lies beyond the scope of this study. Yet it is important to stress that these elements do, indeed, *interact*. That is to say, the personality factors involved give rise to historical events, just as they are reshaped by the historical events which they have called forth. In a very real sense, the distinctive social forces which led to the rise of Nazism were distinctive because the individuals who harnessed and reacted to them were the particular kinds of individuals whom we have seen them to be. Equally, these individuals were who they were in large part because of the social forces surrounding their lives, individually and collectively. The question thus is not one of whether the Rorschach material in this book and the interpretations of it *explain* the rise of Nazism and its distinctive nature; rather, they must be seen as an indispensable *part* of any explanation.

Apart from typologies identifying their political and administrative roles and a number of rather sensationalistic biographies, little work has been done on Hitler's immediate subordinates (Friedrich and Brzezinsky, pp. 19–21; F. Neumann, pp. 365–99, S. Neumann, pp. 77ff.). Indeed, one attempt to study this group concludes that it possessed few if any distinctive features of its own: "The composition of the inner circle," Gerth declares, "does not seem to be subject to any rule other than to the changing personality preferences of the leader and to the power which the individual may secure through 'friends.'" (Gerth, p. 521).

There are at least two reasons for supposing that an understanding of the common attributes of Hitler's henchmen may further our knowledge of Nazism. For one, it seems reasonable to assume that our knowledge of Hitler's personality can be deepened, or at least confirmed, by an analysis of the individuals with whom he surrounded himself and on whom he relied most closely. While it is true that a number of Hitler's closest associates—Bormann, Goebbels, Himmler—do not appear in this collection and that some of our subjects—Fritzsche and Funk, for example—did not belong to Hitler's inner circle, we nevertheless suspect that the analyses in this volume will be of use to students of Hitler's personality. Highly suggestive in this context is Speer's observation of Hitler during the closing days of the war. "There was actually something insubstantial about him," he writes, "but this was perhaps a permanent quality he had. In retrospect, I sometimes ask myself whether this intangibility, this insubstantiality, had not characterized him from early youth up to the moment of his suicide. It sometimes seems to me that his seizures of violence could come upon him all the more strongly because there were no human emotions in him to oppose them. He simply could not let anyone approach his inner being because that core was lifeless, empty" (Speer, p. 471). We hardly need to elaborate here on the extent to which Speer's reflection about Hitler mirrored the personalities of the group to which Speer himself belonged.

The task of analyzing Hitler's personality falls beyond the scope of this study. The men who appear in this study, however, administered the Nazi government far more directly than did Hitler himself. To be sure, it was usually Hitler who determined the major policy objectives, but these men provided the information he used in doing so, debated with him, to an extent, as to what the best policy for any given situation was, devised the steps which had to be taken in securing the policy objectives, and supervised their implementation. Many of the early triumphs of the Nazi regime and many of the circumstances which led to its ultimate collapse are thus surely attributable in part or in whole to these people, to their executive capacities and political skills. To the very considerable extent that those capacities and skills were shaped by and reflected in their personalities, an understanding of their personalities contributes to an understanding of the rise and fall of the Third Reich.

The men in this collection constituted an important part of the leadership of Nazi Germany, even if none of them was the Fuehrer himself. More than the mere fact of leadership binds leaders and followers together. While this question, again, falls beyond the scope of this study, it will not be out of place here to speculate briefly on what it is that our data tell us about the bonds that united the German masses with their Nazi leaders.

A number of studies have examined the psychological foundations for the acceptance of the Nazi ideology among the general population. The most famous study is that conducted by Adorno and associates and published under the title of *The Authoritarian Personality*. Important aspects of the methodology of this study have been questioned (cf. the discussion in Greenstein, pp. 99ff.), but some of its findings that are relevant to us here would seem to be unaffected by these methodological criticisms.

In Adorno's study, the "F-Scale" identifies personality correlates of the so-called Fascist personality. These are discussed in detail in *The Authoritarian Personality* (pp. 392–448), and only a brief indication of their nature can be given here. This should suffice, however, to establish the striking similarity between high scorers on the F-Scale and many important aspects, at least, of the personalities of the subjects studied in this volume:

Attitudes toward sex: sex is isolated and depersonalized, peripheral to rather than integrated with the ego (p. 393); little fusion of sex and affect (p. 395); "an ambivalent underlying disrespect for, and resentment against, the opposite sex, often hidden behind an externalized and excessive pseudoadmiration" (p. 399); an exploitative and manipulative type of power orientation in relations with the opposite sex as indeed in all interpersonal relationships (p. 400)

Attitudes toward other people: "extrapunitiveness" (i.e., blaming others rather than oneself) (p. 409); distrust and suspicion (p. 411); hierarchical rather than egalitarian concept of human relationships (p. 413); "diffuse, ego-alien dependence, which is not really love-seeking" as opposed to "a focal, love-seeking succorance" from other people (p. 414); exploitative, manipulative, opportunistic (p. 415); stress on social and economic status of friends and acquaintances rather than on their intrinsic worth as friends (p. 418)

Attitudes toward self: self-glorification as opposed to self-appraisal (p. 423); pseudo-masculinity—e.g., boastfulness and less admission of passivity (p. 428); think of themselves as highly moral and controlled, and regard any conduct which contradicts this norm as a breakthrough of tendencies which cannot be explained or influenced (p. 429); conformity of self and ideal —i.e., the ideal person has the same traits as the ones which they ascribe to themselves (p. 430); the overlibidinization of property, which is regarded as an extension of self (p. 433)

Remarkably similar in important respects to the high scorers on the F-Scale were the "F1" types—fanatical, wholehearted Nazis—identified in a series of studies of German prisoners of war conducted by a British psychiatrist, H. V. Dicks, Adorno and Dicks, it should be said, had not known of each other's work and devised their scales independently (Dicks, 1972, pp. 69–70). Dicks' F1 types are characterized by an "essential shallowness of being" and "affectionless character" (Dicks; 1950, pp. 149–50). Intolerant of tenderness, lacking "deep positive relations to maternal figures and attitudes," sadistic, and with a disposition to compensate for feelings of inferiority through grandiosity, they bear a notable similarity not only to high scorers on Adorno's F-Scale but to the subjects whose records we have examined in this volume.[1]

This is, we believe, an important finding. It shows that leaders share not only a common ideology with their most devoted followers but, in important respects, a similar personality structure as well, of which the ideology is a rationalized outgrowth (both the Adorno and Dicks studies found a strong tendency toward projection in their high-scoring subjects). A striking anticipation of this finding, couched in general, theoretical terms, may be found in Freud's *Group Psychology and the Analysis of the Ego*:

> in many individuals the separation between the ego and the ego ideal is not very far advanced; the two still coincide readily; the ego has often preserved its earlier narcissistic self-complacency. The selection of the leader is very much facilitated by this circumstance. He need often possess only the typical qualities of the individuals concerned in a particularly clearly marked and pure form, and need only give an impression of greater force and of more freedom of libido; and in that case the need for a strong chief will often meet him half-way and invest him with a predominance to which he would otherwise perhaps have no claim. (Freud, p. 61)

---

[1] The reader will find, in Appendix A, a rather poorly administered Rorschach record of Adolf Eichmann, given while he was awaiting trial in Jerusalem, along with a brief analysis identifying the number of his responses which fall into the categories used in our tabulation of the sixteen records examined in this book. Eichmann's personality resembles those in our study and those in the Adorno and Dicks studies. The finding is of some interest in bridging the gap between the Nazi rank-and-file studied by Adorno and Dicks and the elite group in our own study, since Eichmann can surely not be considered more than a middle-level official.

Dicks (1972, p. 19) appears to discredit the diagnosis of psychopathy in the Nazi personality and speaks instead (p. 25) of individuals whose personality development has remained "stuck" at the "schizoid–paranoid" level. In fact, however, the prolongation of the introjection–projection stage which results in schizophrenia also underlies the development of psychopathy, as we have seen (cf. Greenacre, p. 169); and it has been suggested that psychopathy may in fact be a "mask" for schizophrenia (Cleckley, 1964).

The psychological significance of the leader-follower nexus certainly extends far beyond the actual *formation* of the group which is the principal focus of Freud's discussion. In particular, we may speculate that where the narcissistic component underlying the group's cohesion and identity is also reflected in an ideology that defies the objective realities of the world as boldly as the Nazi ideology did, leaders and followers require each other to authenticate and sustain their highly distorted version of reality. But this, and related questions fall beyond the scope of our present study and will have to be pursued elsewhere.

Given the weight of evidence contained in this study it seems almost ungallant to return to the question which we asked in the first chapter; yet for the sake of completeness we must do so. The answer can be stated briefly and decisively. The Nazis were not psychologically normal or healthy individuals.

APPENDIX A
*The Rorschach Record of Adolf Eichmann**

Examiner: Dr. I. M. Kulcsar (no date) (1960?)

(no timing)

CARD I

∧ 1. Bat, from a collector or a museum,
with spread-out wings   (no inquiry)   (W)

CARD II

∧ 1. Two brown bears pressing against
a glass, hats on their heads which
are blown away as in dueling.
Even the snout is drawn on the left
one, and the ear on the right one.
Very clear bear ears. Quickly
drawn with sketching ink   (W)

CARD III

("This is also a humorous sketch.")
∧ 1. Two very polite dandies tipping
their hats to each other, greeting
each other very formally; there are
even patent leather shoes there

---

* Reprinted by permission of I. M. Kulcsar, M.D.

2. Two clowns who want to do their best, masked; white collars at the neck.   (W)
3. The red could be an eye-catching stage decoration in the background   (D)

CARD IV

∧ 1. A stretched-out cowhide, stretched for drying, or already treated. It is also trimmed—the forepaws and the rear. The head is very badly drawn; the backbone well drawn; it also goes well toward the side   (W)

CARD V

∧ 1. Bat—much better than the first one   (W)

CARD VI

∧ 1. Also a skin, but the head part doesn't fit—also a skin of a wild animal   (W)
2. The head part like the head decoration of the Aztecs (upper D)   (D)

CARD VII

∧ 1. Outlines of continents, if I cover the lower part   (D)
∨ 2. South America down to Tierra del Fuego; Caribbean Sea with Brazil, Argentina, Chile   (D)
∧ 3. Again a humorous drawing: two dancing elephants, trunks raised, eyes slightly indicated, standing on one foot   (D)

CARD VIII

∧ 1. A leaf chewed up by insects,
pressed for (display in) herbar-
ium; the color shading would look
different in a fall leaf, but there is
a leaf in Argentina whose color is
similar   (W)

CARD IX

∧ 1. A coat of arms (covers half);
above is the helmet, heraldry in
the middle, drawing below—but   It's more
one side must be covered   the color.   (D)

CARD X

∧ 1. A colored drawing from botany,
a flower with pistil and stamens   (W)
> 2. A detailed drawing of stamens,
drawn for a better view for school
use   (W)

SUMMARY

The reader will note the absence of female concepts in Card VII—
or anywhere else—in this record, and the lack of response to the furry
texture of Cards IV and VI. Notable features of the animal skin concepts are the emphasis on the stretched-out hide, the fact that it is or
has been cured and dried as well as trimmed, and the reference to
the backbone, indicative of feelings of weakness. Both responses indicate that the control functions do not go together with the very minimal sensitivity and indeed belong to an exotic, remote, and chronologi-
cally distant past ("Aztecs")—one, moreover, in a context of human
sacrifice.

Of the categories employed in the tabulation of responses in Chapter 19, Eichmann's record includes responses which fall into ten of
the twenty-three categories, among them eight of the twelve to which
at least half of the group responded:

depression
violence
status
reject responsibility
exotic plants
dead, mounted
hard, rough, cold, dry
clarity of obvious concepts
torn, ragged,
banners, trophies

The thirteen categories into which Eichmann's responses do not fall are:

grotesque
feelers, eyes
marine animals
bugs, beetles, insects
female figures
crabs
direct rejection of red
explosions, etc.
bones
devils, gremlins, trolls, etc.
chameleons
sea horses
taking responsibility for difficulty

The sixteen subjects in our collection employed an average of 11.63 of the categories in this tabulation; Eichmann used ten, or somewhat below the average.

APPENDIX B

The Rorschach Record of an American "Pillar of the Community," c. 1945

Examiner: C. Kemple

The Rorschach record of James, age 48, a midwestern American banker and leader in civic affairs, was obtained at about the same time as were the records of the Nuremberg defendants. The authors came upon it as a result of asking colleagues for a record of a person who roughly met these criteria. An acquaintance of the examiner, James took the Rorschach at her request, because of her interest in obtaining "nonclinical" Rorschach material. Because he tended in the inquiry merely to repeat what he had said before, inquiry was done only to clarify a few responses.

CARD I

∧ 1. Looks like the head of a black cat, or tiger, or Halloween mask (WS)

      At first I thought this thing like ears looked like bat's wings, but that was only the ears.

    2. Well, those little things look like lobster claws (top center d).

      As many things as you see?

∨ 3. Well, this looks like the face of a cherub with an eye there and a nose and a dimple in his chin. Have to turn it upside down. [Inq: d on upper left side]

∧ 4. Of course the whole thing might be the map of some coastline, Guess I don't see much else. I don't have a very good—

CARD II

Oh, red yet. What's the red for?

∧ 1. Well, this looks like two pigs, pushing their snouts up against each other.

The red doesn't mean anything.

Two pigs drooping their paws like this [gesture]. I suppose they could be dogs. Are you supposed to see lots of things in these? (W)

2. These red blobs up top here are meaningless to me. They could be two seals facing each other, sticking their noses up in the air. Always I see animals—oh heavens. (D)

CARD III

∧ 1. Well, first thing I saw was men in tuxedos, but—well—I suppose those could be their lapels flying out like that. And they have got sort of basketballs in their hands, or wicker baskets. And they might be doing a dance. (W)

2. Red thing in the middle looks like a butterfly. [Inq: just shape]

3. And the two red things on the outside look like sea urchins upside down, or maybe even a monkey with a long tail. Yes, that thing looks like a monkey's head. [Inq: just describes head and tail again]

4. And this thing [points to bottom center D] looks like a soft shell crab.

CARD IV

∧ 1. Is that right side up? (10″) Well, about all I can see out of— that is, imagine out of it, is a prehistoric monster. These are his ears (upper side projections). These are his tusks (lower side). This is a trunk (lower center) or his snout. (W)

2. Is the whole thing supposed to mean something or can you take a little bit like that and say it reminds you of Cape Cod? (d: tip of "boot")
I suppose if you studied it long enough, you could see lots of things.

3. This looks like Long Island, Long Island Sound, if you want to pick out little things like that. (L.I. is projection toward side from "heel" or "boot"; Sound is S between that and "sole" of "boot": dd, S) Well—

CARD V

∧ 1. This could be a malformed butterfly or a moth or a bat, his feet trailing out behind him. The antenna up ahead (W)

2. Oh, I see a woman's leg sticking out at the side here (laughs). What do you know? At least, I suppose it's a woman's leg. A man's leg wouldn't have a calf like that or an ankle like that. (d) 'Fraid I'm not—

CARD VI

1. This looks like a leopard skin on a floor, to make a rug out of it. It's a queer-looking leopard. [looks at card about 1'] No, I can't get much out of that. [Inq: a leopard or a lion's skin. Queer-looking because of shape of head at top. Shading used for fur. W]

CARD VII

∧ 1. Well, the first thing that occurs to me is that these are a couple of kids, or they might even be puppets . . . dressed up for some kind of stunt or game or party or something. That's that much of it (top ⅔). [Inq: couple of kids . . . could be playing a game]

2. This much of it I don't know (lower D). Looks like a couple of filets from a sword fish or something.

CARD VIII

Oh, color!

∧ 1. Well, the first thing this reminded me of was that picture in *Life* of the Delta of the Mississippi, wasn't it? Looked like a tree, the silhouette of a tree. (W: general form suggests picture of delta fanning out which suggested tree outline)

> 2. This thing looks like a rat or a guinea pig, maybe. I mean musk-rat. More like a muskrat than anything else. All I can see is animals or shellfish or something in any of these.   [Inq: describes shape, no movement]

CARD IX

∧ 1. Well, once again lobster claws—what this business reminds me of (d: center projection in orange)

2. This looks like a dunce's cap, or clown's cap (dd: top of orange)

3. This looks like the part of me below the belt line (laughs—pointing to the "paunch" of usual orange figure)

4. This green thing looks as though it might be an island in a lake or a sea. [Inq: like looking at a map in colors. Has a uniform color. Could represent a sea or a lake and the white the land. DS]

5. These little things look like the toenails or feet on a muskrat or some such animal. (green projections into pink: dd)

6. And this looks like four apples in a row. [Inq: pink D, form and color]

CARD X

Oh, more color. I didn't know these were in color.

1. There are two crabs, soft shell crabs (side blue D).

2. Here are some men from Mars, talking it over. Or else they are lugging something between them. (top center D)

3. That looks as though it might be a cigar they picked up. (D between above)

4. Once again the blue might be a lake on a map and the red might be a mountain range and the white a plain. [Inq: DS, colored map; shading in pink like mountains on a map. Middle blue]

5. These look like caterpillars carrying something home. [Inq: "not *just* the color."] (lower green D)

6. Oh here, a couple of fried eggs, what do you know? (inner yellow D—used color)

   I did pretty well on that one.

7. This looks like the governor on a machine of some kind. (center orange D)

8. Oh here's really a wow. That looks like a trapeze artist in a jump. (side brown D: arms toward side of card. Very good form)

Notable in this record, in marked contrast to those of the Nazi leaders, is the variety of animals, both aggressive and nonaggressive, depicted—many of them mammals, many of them lively. Similarly the people he sees, although like those of the Nazis they do not include women, have considerable variety both in content and in movement. The animal skin in Card VI is furry—and functional.

If we cling to a very strict and literal application of the criteria we used to characterize the records of the Nazis, James's record would appear to contain these seven traits: depression, status, reject responsibility, crabs, grotesque, marine animals, direct rejection of red.

Careful analysis and examination of context, however, reveal that all or nearly all of these instances are distinctly different in quality from the Nazi responses.

The sole "depressive" indicator is the "black cat" in the first response to the first card, and even this is flexibly transformed into a tiger and a playful mask.

Literal application of our criterion puts the dunce or clown cap in Card IX in the "status" category, but far from appearing in a context of display, as do most of the Nazis' headdresses, these, especially as they are followed by the response "part of me below the belt line," are self-depreciating rather than self-aggrandizing.

What at first glance appear to be rejections of responsibility for his own concepts ("malformed butterfly" in Card V and "queer animal skin" in VI) and "grotesque", do not really belong in these categories, because he explains in relation to the blot what is "queer" about the skin, and substitutes "moth or bat" in Card V, both the better to explain the concept and to make the grotesque quality unnecessary.

James's crabs are both "soft shell crabs," surely in the vulnerable rather than the "armored, aggressive" category, and along with his "marine animals" (sea urchins and fish filets) seem to underline his "oral-dependent" rather than "oral-aggressive" tendencies—along with his "fried eggs," "pigs," and "lobster claws" and his "paunch." All this emphasis on oral gratification and dependence imply, of course, deep, largely unexpressed (or only indirectly expressed) needs for self-assertion and aggression. The emphasis on detail, the high proportion of responses using only form, and the high level of form quality suggest that these needs find an outlet in critical use of his intellect and meticulous concern with the details of his work.

In Card II, where he first rejects the red as meaningless, he shortly thereafter takes responsibility ("meaningless *to me*") and proceeds to use the shape of the red blots for a lively animal response with good form.

As we have seen, among the sixteen Nazi records, in only five in-stances and in only three individuals did the person accept responsi-bility for his own difficulty or inadequacy. James's record contains six entries in this category.

Bibliography

Abel, T., *The Nazi Movement: Why Hitler Came to Power* (New York, 1966).

Adorno, T. W.; Frenkel–Brunswick, E.; Levinson, D. J.; and Sanford, R. N., *The Authoritarian Personality* (New York, 1950).

Arendt, H., *The Origins of Totalitarianism* (paper ed., New York, 1958).

Arendt, H., *Eichmann in Jerusalem: A Report on the Banality of Evil* (rev. ed., New York, 1964).

Asch, S. E., "On the use of metaphor in the description of persons," in H. Werner, ed., *On Expressive Language* (Worcester, Mass., 1955).

Bayles, W. D., *Caesars in Goosestep* (New York, 1940).

Bernstein, V., *Final Judgment: The Story of Nuremberg* (New York, 1947).

Bewley, C., *Hermann Goering and the Third Reich* (n.p. 1962).

Bracher, K. D., *The German Dictatorship: The Origins, Structure, and Effects of National Socialism* (New York, 1970).

Brook–Shepard, G., *The Anschluss* (Philadelphia, 1963).

Broszat, M., *German National Socialism: 1919–1945* (Santa Barbara, Ca., 1966).

Burden, H. T., *The Nuremberg Party Rallies, 1923–39* (New York, n.d.).

Cecil, R., *The Myth of the Master Race: Alfred Rosenberg and Nazi Ideology* (New York, 1972).

Chelminski, R., "West Germans Screw up Courage to Show Nazi Art," *Smithsonian* 1975 (11), pp. 70–79.

Cleckley, H., *The Mask of Sanity* (St. Louis, 1964).

Davidson, E., *The Trial of the Germans* (New York, 1966).

Dicks, H. V., "Personality traits and National Socialist Ideology," *Human Relations* 1950 (3), pp. 111–54.

Dicks, H. V., *Licensed Mass Murder: A Socio–Psychological Study of Some SS Killers* (New York, 1972).

Douglas–Hamilton, J., *Motive for a Mission: The Story Behind Hess's Flight to Britain* (London, 1971).

Dutch, O. [pseud. for Otto Deutsch], *Hitler's Twelve Apostles* (Freeport, 1969).

Fest, J., *The Face of the Third Reich: Portraits of the` Nazi Leadership* (New York, 1970).

Fishman, J., *The Seven Men of Spandau* (New York, 1954).

Freud, S., *Group Psychology and the Analysis of the Ego*, (Norton ed., New York, 1959).

Friedrich, C. J., and Brzezinski, Z., *Totalitarian Dictatorship and Autocracy* (Cambridge, Mass., 1956).

Frischauer, W., *The Rise and Fall of Hermann Goering* (Boston, 1951).

Fritzsche, H., *The Sword in the Scales* (London, 1953).

Fromm, E., *Escape from Freedom* (New York, 1941).

Gerth, H., "The Nazi Party: Its Leadership and Composition," *American Journal of Sociology*, 1940 (45), pp. 517–41.

Gilbert, G. M., *Nuremberg Diary* (New York, 1947).

Gilbert, G. M., *The Psychology of Dictatorship* (New York, 1950).

Gilbert, G. M., *Personality Dynamics: A Biosocial Approach* (New York, 1970).

Goebbels, J., *The Goebbels Diaries, 1942–1943*, ed. and trans. L. P. Lochner (New York, 1948).

Greenacre, P., "Conscience in the Psychopath," in Phyllis Greenacre, *Trauma, Growth, and Personality* (New York, 1952), pp. 165–187.

Greenstein, F., *Personality and Politics* (Chicago, 1969).

Grunberger, R., *The Twelve-Year Reich: A Social History of Nazi Germany, 1933–1945* (New York, 1971).

Hall, C. S., *The Meaning of Dreams* (New York, 1952).

Haensel, C., *Das Gericht Vertagt Sich* (Hamburg, 1950).

Hausner G., "Eichmann and His Trial," *Saturday Evening Post*, November 10, 1962.

Hutton, J. B., *Hess, The Man and His Mission* (London, 1970).

International Military Tribunal, *IMT: The Trial of the German Major War Criminals: Proceedings of the International Military Tribunal Sitting at Nuremberg, Germany* (London, 1946).

Jackson, R. H., *The Case Against the Nazi War Criminals* (New York, 1946).

Jung, C. G., *Ueber die Energetik der Seele und andere psychologische Abhandlungen* (Zurich, 1928).

Jung, C. G., *Two Essays on Analytical Psychology* (New York, 1953).

Jung, C. G., *The Practice of Psychotherapy* (New York, 1954).

Keitel, W., *The Memoirs of Field–Marshal Keitel* (New York, 1966).

Kelley, D. M., "Preliminary Studies of the Rorschach Records of the Nazi War Criminals," *Rorschach Research Exchange* 1946 (10), pp. 45–48.

Kelley, D. M., *Twenty-two Cells in Nuremberg: A Psychiatrist Examines the Nazi Criminals* (New York, 1947).

Kemple, C., "Shading: Animal, Animal Skin" (unpublished paper, n.d.).

Kersten, F., *The Memoirs of Doctor Felix Kersten* (Garden City, N.Y., 1947).

Klopfer, B., and Davidson, H., *The Rorschach Technique* (New York, 1962).

Klopfer, W. G., "Interpretive hypotheses deprived from the analysis of content," in Klopfer, B.; Ainsworth, M.; Klopfer, W.; and Holt, R., *Developments in the Rorschach Technique* (Yonkers, 1954), vol. I, pp. 376–402.

Kohlberg, L., "Relations between the Development of Moral Judgment and Moral Conduct." Paper presented at Symposium on Behavioral and Cognitive Concepts in the Study of Internationalization at the Society for Research in Child Development, Minneapolis, Minn., March 26, 1965.

Krausnick, H., et al., *Anatomy of the SS State* (New York, 1965).

Krebs, A., *Tendenzen und Gestalten des NSDAP* (Stuttgart, 1959).

Krueger, K., *I was Hitler's Doctor* (New York, 1943).

Leasor, J., *Rudolph Hess* (London, 1962).

Lenz, F., *Zauber um Dr. Schacht* (Heidelberg, 1954).

Lerner, D., *The Nazi Elite* (Stanford, 1951).

Manchester, W., *The Arms of Krupp, 1587–1964* (Boston, 1968).

Manvell, R., and Fraenkel, H., *Hermann Goering* (London, 1962).

Miale, F. R., *An Approach to Projective Material* (unpublished doctoral dissertation, Graduate Faculty of Political and Social Science, New School for Social Research, 1959).

Miale, F. R., "Symbolic Imagery in Rorschach Material", to be published in M. Rickers–Osiankina, ed., *Rorschach Psychology* (2d ed., 1975 in press).

Milgram, S., *Obedience to Authority* (New York, 1974)

Mindess, H., "Analytic Psychology and the Rorschach Test," *Journal of Projective Techniques* 1955 (19), pp. 243–52.

Murphy, J., *Who Sent Rudolph Hess?* (London, 1941).

Nazi Conspiracy and Aggression [NCA], Office of United States Chief of Counsel for Prosecution of Axis Criminality (Washington, 1946), 8 vols.; supplementary vols. A and B.

Nazi Conspiracy and Aggression: Opinion and Judgement (Washington, 1947).

Neumann, F., *Behemoth* (New York, 1942).

Neumann, S., *Permanent Revolution* (New York, 1942).

Neurath, K., "Der italienisch-griechische Konflikt vom Jarhe 1923 und seine Voelkerrechtliche Bedeutung," *Voelkerrechtsfragen* (Berlin, 1929), vol. 5.

Papen, F., *Memoirs* (New York, 1953).

Peterson, E. *Hjalmar Schacht, for and against Hitler* (Boston, 1954).

Piotrowski, Z., "The Rorschach Inkblot Method in Organic Disturbances of the Central Nervous System", *Journal of Nervous and Mental Diseases*, 1937 (86) pp. 525–37.

Rapaport, D., "Principles underlying Projective Techniques," *Character and Personality* 1942 (10), pp. 213–19.

Rauschning, H., *Men of Chaos* (New York, 1942).

Reck–Malleczewen, F. P., *Diary of a Man in Despair* (New York, 1970).

Rees, R. J., ed., *The Case of Rudolph Hess* (New York, 1948).

Rorschach, H., *Psychodiagnostics* (Bern, 1921).

Rosenberg, A., *Memoirs of Alfred Rosenberg* (Chicago, 1949).

Schacht, H., *My First Seventy-Six Years* (London, 1953).

Schirach, B., *Ich glaubte an Hitler* (Hamburg, 1967).

Schmeller, H., *Hitler and Keitel: An Investigation of the Influence of Party Ideology on the High Command of the Armed Forces in Germany between 1938 and 1945* (Hays, Kansas, 1970).

Schuschnigg, K., *Austrian Requiem* (New York, 1970).

Schwarz, P., *This Man Ribbentrop* (New York, 1943).

Seyss-Inquart, A., *Vier Jahre in den Niederlanden: Gesammelte Reden* (Amsterdam, 1944).

Shirer, W., *The Rise and Fall of the Third Reich* (New York, 1960).

Simpson, A., *Hjalmar Schacht in Perspective* (The Hague, 1964).

Singer, K., *Goering: Germany's Most Dangerous Man* (London, 1940).

Snell, J., ed., *The Nazi Revolution: Germany's Guilt or Germany's Fate?* (Boston, 1959).

Speer, A., *Inside the Third Reich* (New York, 1970).

Steinbauer, G., *Ich war Verteidiger in Nuernberg: Ein Dokumentenbeitrag zum Kampf um Oesterreich* (Klagenfurt, Austria, 1950).

Stevenson, W., *The Bormann Brotherhood* (New York, 1973).

Taylor, T., *The March of Conquest* (New York, 1958).

Trevor–Roper, H., *The Last Days of Hitler* (New York, 1947).

Warmbrunn, W., *The Dutch under German Occupation, 1940–1945* (Stanford, Ca., 1963).

Wheaton, E., *The Nazi Revolution, 1933–1935: Prelude to Calamity* (Garden City, N.Y., 1969).

Wheeler–Bennett, J. W., *The Nemesis of Power* (New York, 1953).

Wighton, C., *Heydrich, Hitler's Most Evil Henchman* (Philadelphia, 1962).

Wrightsman, L. S., "The Most Important Social Psychological Research of This Generation?" *Contemporary Psychology* 1974 (19), pp. 803–805.

Zeman, A., *Nazi Propaganda* (London, 1964).

Zimmer, H., *The King and the Corpse* (Washington, D.C., 1948).

About the Authors

FLORENCE R. MIALE has a Ph.D. in psychology from the New School for Social Research. She has taught courses in projective methods (including the Rorschach) at the New School, at the City College of New York and at a number of other universities and hospitals. She now practices individual, group and marital psychotherapy in New York City and supervises trainees in diagnosis and psychotherapy.

MICHAEL SELZER was educated in England at Bedales School and Balliol College, Oxford, and has his Ph.D. in political science from the Graduate School of the City University of New York. An assistant professor of political science at Brooklyn College, he teaches courses in psychopolitics and is currently working on a psychological biography of Benjamin Disraeli, the nineteenth-century British prime minister.